War, Law, and Labour

To my parents, who, as children,
were there at the time.

War, Law, and Labour

*The Munitions Acts, State Regulation,
and the Unions,*
1915–1921

GERRY R. RUBIN

CLARENDON PRESS · OXFORD
1987

Oxford University Press, Walton Street, Oxford OX2 6DP
Oxford   New York   Toronto
Delhi   Bombay   Calcutta   Madras   Karachi
Petaling Jaya   Singapore   Hong Kong   Tokyo
Nairobi   Dar es Salaam   Cape Town
Melbourne   Auckland
and associated companies in
Beirut   Berlin   Ibadan   Nicosia

Oxford is a trade mark of Oxford University Press

Published in the United States
by Oxford University Press, New York

British Library Cataloguing in Publication Data
Rubin, G. R.
War, law and labour: the Munitions Acts,
state regulation and the unions, 1915–1921.
1. Industrial relations—Great Britain—
History—20th century   2. World War,
1914–1918—Economic aspects—Great Britain
I. Title
331'.0941   HD8390
ISBN 0-19-825538-1
Library of Congress Cataloging in Publication Data
Data available

Typeset by Cotswold Typesetting Ltd, Gloucester
Printed in Great Britain
at the University Printing House, Oxford
by David Stanford
Printer to the University

ACKNOWLEDGEMENTS

I owe a debt of gratitude to many individuals whose advice, encouragement, and assistance have sustained me in the years spent on preparation of this book. Accordingly I wish to express my thanks to Dr Jay Winter, Professor Royden Harrison, and Dr Tony Mason, who supervised the doctoral research on which the book is based; to Dr James Hinton and Dr Iain S. McLean, who examined the thesis; to Professor Hugh Clegg and Dr John Lovell, who read the entire manuscript prior to publication; and to Dr Richard Davenport-Hines and Dr Howard Gospel, who read Chapters 1 and 7 respectively. I am confident that the text has benefited significantly from the constructive comments readily offered to me.

I wish to thank, also, Dr Noel Whiteside for her advice on archives; Rosalie and Monty Chalmers and Léonie and David Sugarman for their generosity; and Angela Blackburn and Richard Hart of Oxford University Press for their support.

For the speed and efficiency with which they accomplished the arduous task of typing a ragged manuscript, I am grateful to Mrs Sue Macdonald and to Helen Bonnett, Babs Brennan, and Jane Humphries.

My greatest debt is to my family. To Rona, I express my appreciation for her encouragement and for her self-sacrifice. To Ilan and Gareth, I am grateful for their tolerance, and, indeed, for their occasional curiosity about the labour aspects of the First World War.

Crown copyright material in the Public Record Office appears by permission of the Controller of HM Stationery Office. The extract from the unpublished diary of Beatrice Webb appears by permission of the Passfield Trustees.

G.R.

Canterbury
August 1986

CONTENTS

LIST OF TABLES

ABBREVIATIONS

ABIS	Associated Blacksmiths and Ironworkers' Society
AIMS	Associated Iron-Moulders of Scotland
ASCJ	Amalgamated Society of Carpenters and Joiners
ASCM	Amalgamated Society of Coremakers
ASE	Amalgamated Society of Engineers
BEV	Beveridge Collection on Munitions
CSA	Clyde Shipbuilders' Association
CWC	Clyde Workers' Committee
DORA	Defence of the Realm Act
EEF	Engineering Employers' Federation
FEST	Federation of Engineering and Shipbuilding Trades
FRD	Fabian Research Department
HC Deb.	House of Commons Debates
ILP	Independent Labour Party
MAR	Munitions Appeal Reports
NWETEA	North-West Engineering Trades Employers' Association
OHMM	Official History of the Ministry of Munitions
PP	Parliamentary Papers
PRO	Public Record Office
SEF	Shipbuilding Employers' Federation
SMAR	Scottish Munitions Appeal Reports
SSA	Shipconstructors' and Shipwrights' Association
TUC	Trades Union Congress
USB	United Society of Boilermakers etc.
WMV	War Munitions Volunteers

'Wha sae base as be a slave'—let him seek employment in a 'Controlled Establishment'.

William Diack, in the *Scottish Review* (1917)

LABOURER. Have we to return and work for this starvation wage?

SHERIFF FYFE. You have; that is the law at the present time. For the time being, you are in a situation which you have never been for generations. You are under discipline.

LABOURER. Coercion, my Lord.

SHERIFF FYFE. Well, coercion, if you like. But it is in the national interest.

(1916)

W. G. SHARP [*trade union official*]. The object of the Ministry seemed to be to secure as many convictions as possible.

LORD DEWAR [*appeal tribunal judge*]. I have no reason to believe that the attempt is to get convictions against men: the object is to try to keep them at work.

(1916)

Wee Deoch and Doris

(Extra verse)

Now our heroes in the trenches
    Need the proper kind o' shell.
If they'd only had them long ago
    They'd have given the Germans Hell.
And all the blame at first was laid
    Upon the working man,
But Lloyd George sees his great mistake
    And tries the proper plan.

Chorus

Jist a wee clever lawyer,
    Jist a wee yin, that's a'—
And although he called us shirkers

Yet we'll help him yin and a'.
For the Boilermakers' members
Still are British workin' men.
At the ship or the bench,
Like the lads in the trench,
Oh, 'We're a'richt, ye ken.'
United Society of Boilermakers' song (1915)

'Is anything being done to place on record the Department's appreciation of the services rendered by these [Munitions] Tribunals?'
Ministry of Labour official (August 1920)

Introduction

This study seeks to examine the working of the code of labour legislation, the Munitions of War Acts 1915–17, during the First World War. The munitions code, fragments of which remained operative until April 1921, appeared to constitute a radical break with the pre-war 'voluntarist' tradition of industrial relations. A system said to be remarkable, even in 1914, for the degree to which collective labour relations were 'so little regulated by law'[1] became, in the wake of war, one pervaded by intrusive legal restrictions.

The broad objective of the 1915 Act, which was the principal measure among the code of three munitions statutes, was to promote industrial discipline in the factories and shipyards, and to minimize interruptions to the production of war *matériel*. For our purposes, its major provisions were five-fold. These were, first, to declare work stoppages illegal and to substitute compulsory arbitration in their place; second, to institute a system of statutory wage regulation; third, to promote a system of factory discipline, the details of which were contained in the Ordering of Work regulations which accompanied the Munitions Act; fourth, to render unlawful any rules, customs, or practices of organized labour which hindered the output of munitions, in particular to forbid the maintenance of the craft unions' restrictive practices and to permit the introduction of female and less-skilled labour on skilled work under the authority of a 'dilution of labour' programme; and, finally, to discourage turnover of labour by requiring workmen to obtain a leaving certificate from their employers before undertaking alternative munitions employment, with a penalty normally of six weeks unemployment imposed on the workman in the event that such a certificate had been lawfully withheld. The enforcement of these provisions was the responsibility of specially constituted munitions tribunals, modelled on the

[1] E. H. Phelps Brown, *The Growth of British Industrial Relations*, London, 1959, p. 355.

panels set up under the national insurance legislation brought forward by Lloyd George before the war. They therefore comprised employers' and workmen's assessors as well as legally qualified chairmen. There were two classes of tribunal, though the distinction is not historically of much significance. To the general munitions tribunal were reserved originally those cases which the Ministry of Munitions, the sponsoring Government department, assumed to be of greater importance, in particular strike prosecutions and prosecutions of employers accused of having poached munitions workers from rival firms. The second class of tribunal, the local munitions tribunal, dealt with the more frequent proceedings, that is, with leaving certificate applications and with prosecutions of workers alleged to have infringed the Ordering of Work rules.[2] In addition, from April 1916, an appeal tribunal was established over which presided a Court of Session judge in Scotland and a High Court judge in England and in Ireland.

A principal objective of this study has been to explore the legal proceedings conducted before these tribunals and to devote particular attention to events surrounding the busiest and most controversial tribunal during the war, that which sat in Glasgow. However, in pursuing this exercise, one obstacle has been the virtual absence of individual case papers. Thus, in terms of tribunal statistics, the proportions of, say, women to men applicants or accused, young persons to older workers, skilled to unskilled, engineers to shipbuilders or other occupational categories cannot be ascertained. Therefore, in order to recover tribunal hearings from day to day or from week to week, reliance was placed principally (though by no means exclusively) on the local press covering Glasgow and the surrounding district. Some individual case papers still survive among the records available in the Public Record Office. However, the vast majority relate to Appeal Tribunal hearings which tended to be published in specialist series of law reports.

As a study of the relationship between war, law, and labour, this work cannot avoid focusing on certain institutional features

---

[2] For a fuller discussion of the structure, organization, and jurisdiction of the munitions tribunal from the perspective of the lawyer, see G. R. Rubin, 'The Origins of Industrial Tribunals: Munitions Tribunals During the First World War', *Industrial Law Journal*, v (1977), 149–64.

of that relationship. Yet the *political* analysis of wartime labour legislation (explored primarily in Chapter 1) offers in addition an indispensable theoretical context within which the empirical dimension to our study can be comprehended. Indeed, it is perhaps of no little significance that the title, *The Politics of Industrial Relations*, has been chosen in recent years by two separate authors whose studies examined the emergence of industrial relations legislation in the 1970s.[3] As Royden Harrison has reminded us, it is, in fact, the political importance of labour laws which helps to explain their unique reversibility when compared to other branches of law, such as commercial law.

Conscious of our own limitations, we have eschewed the attempt to engage the *economic* analysis of the munitions code. The economic analysis of law, involving the application of sophisticated statistical tests of measurement, is currently one of the growth areas of socio-legal studies. Indeed, the approach has even begun to influence our understanding of the impact of specific labour controls on social structure, and might, if capable of application to the working of the Munitions Acts, enrich our understanding of their effects. Yet as a technique for the evaluation of the impact of statutory provisions concerned with the history of employment and of industrial relations, the approach is still in its infancy and, perhaps, not free from controversy.[4]

Finally, we may pose the question whether our study of *wartime* legal controls on industrial relations can shed light on questions pertaining to the regulation of modern, peacetime industrial relations. Since the late 1960s, different Governments have attempted with little success to impose a restrictive legal framework on an essentially voluntarist system of British industrial relations. Some initiatives have proved spectacular failures, such as Barbara Castle's white paper, *In Place of Strife*, in 1969[5] or the Conservative Government's Industrial Relations

[3] Michael Moran, *The Politics of Industrial Relations*, London, 1977; Colin Crouch, *The Politics of Industrial Relations*, London, 1979.

[4] For an example from the field of labour regulation in the nineteenth century, see Howard P. Marvel, 'Factory Regulation: A Reinterpretation of Early English Experience', *Journal of Law and Economics*, xx (1977), 379–402. The 'Chicago' school of economic theory seems to favour such an approach.

[5] See Peter Jenkins, *The Battle of Downing Street*, London, 1970.

Act 1971.[6] More recently, the Employment Acts 1980 and 1982 and the Trade Union Act 1984 have sought to inhibit trade union militancy by limiting drastically the scope for lawful industrial action, including picketing and blacking activities, and by removing from trade unions their historic immunity from liability for damages (and indeed from liability for contempt of court orders to obey labour injunctions). Research published in 1983 seems to suggest that while the 1980 Act may have stiffened management authority in the face of trade union demands (while there still prevailed a powerful culture of 'law avoidance'), the most significant influence on industrial behaviour was probably the economic recession.[7] Such a finding supports the view of the late Professor Otto Kahn-Freund that the pattern of industrial behaviour, like the 'welfare' of workers,

depends in the first place on the productivity of people's labour, which in turn is, to a very large extent, the result of technical developments . . . in the second place on the forces of the labour market on which the law has only a marginal (though not a negligible) influence . . . [and] thirdly on the degree of effective organisation of the workers in trade unions to which the law can again make only a modest contribution.[8]

Indeed, elsewhere Kahn-Freund has opined that,

Many people have something like a magic belief in the efficacy of the law in shaping human conduct and social relations. It is a superstition which is itself a fact of political importance, but a superstition it is all the same. I am not suggesting that the threat of legal sanctions cannot create a marginal motive determining conduct, but where there are strong forces or traditions favouring a pattern of action such as the sudden spontaneous strike, the role which the law can play in improving the situation, though not negligible, can never be decisive.[9]

[6] See Brian Weekes *et al.*, *Industrial Relations and the Limits of Law*, Oxford, 1975. Some industrial relations academics still look back nostalgically on an opportunity lost. See E. H. Phelps Brown, *The Origins of Trade Union Power*, Oxford, 1983, ch. 11, 'The Attempt to Impose Order: the Legal Code of 1971'.

[7] Peggy Kahn, Norman Lewis, Rowland Livock and Paul Wiles, *Picketing: Industrial Disputes, Tactics and the Law*, London, 1983. But cf. W. E. J. McCarthy, J. W. Durcan and G. P. Redman, *Strikes in Post-War Britain*, London, 1983, who argue that political explanations for Britain's strike pattern, such as labour legislation, are more significant than economic ones, such as the level of employment.

[8] Otto Kahn-Freund, *Labour and the Law*, 3rd edn., P. L. Davies and Mark Freedland (eds.), London, 1983, p. 13.

[9] Id., 'Industrial Relations and the Law—Retrospect and Prospect', *British Journal of Industrial Relations*, IX (1969), 301–16, at 311.

The law can, of course, be effective in individual instances, such as in the dispute involving the National Graphical Association at Warrington in the winter of 1983 when the infliction of massive fines amounting to £725,000, plus the freezing of the union's remaining assets, compelled the executive to call off their industrial action against a local printing firm. But it would be a foolish and unsubtle commentator who would seek to infer from single episodes such as this, the validity of a more general positive proposition linking law with the preservation of 'order' and with the elimination of conflict in industrial relations.[10]

Our own study seeks to emphasize the complexities and paradoxes which surrounded Government efforts during the First World War to employ the munitions code to regulate industrial relations in accordance with the exigencies of the war emergency. We will, in fact, argue that 'conflict management' was a key, though not the sole, ingredient characterizing the proceedings of the Glasgow munitions tribunal. Indeed, as those who have researched the impact of the recent Employment Act 1980 on industrial behaviour have observed, 'Short of outlawing trade unions[11] and/or reproducing outright wage slavery, every modern industrial state is in the business of institutionalising conflict. The Employment Act is a minor contribution to that process.'[12] Moreover, the researchers continue, the process of institutionalization will include 'persuasion, bribery, direction and all manner of means more or less subtle'.[13]

The identification of a 'conflict management' approach is undoubtedly an important insight. However, in respect to our own study, the crucial qualification should be added that it was not pursued by its practitioners during the First World War in such an undirected manner that they lost sight of the original,

[10] As one respected journalist wrote of the posture of the Tory leadership during the mining industry dispute of 1984, 'The law which, for political purposes was deemed imperative in 1980 is, for political reasons, deemed an embarrassment in 1984.' See Hugo Young, 'The party of law and order that fears its own legislation', *Guardian*, 21 May 1984.

[11] The combined effect of the 1980, 1982, and 1984 Acts is, on paper at least, to deprive trade unions of most of the strike weapons they have used effectively in the recent past. The 'right to strike' is still preserved, but in a severely attenuated (and possibly in an irrelevant) form.

[12] Kahn *et al.*, *Picketing*, p. 191.

[13] Ibid p. 192.

State-dictated policy of maximizing munitions production. Subject to this caveat, the present study, located within the context of war, militancy, radicalism as well as patriotism, inflation, and full employment, may yet, we hope, offer glimpses of insight to analysts of modern industrial relations, probing the darker corners of 'conflict management'.

CHAPTER 1

From Voluntarism to Wartime Corporatism

THE CREDO OF PRE-WAR VOLUNTARISM

To what extent did the enactment of the Munitions of War Act in 1915, by subjecting industrial relations to a regime of tight legal restrictions imposed by the State, constitute a radical break with the past? Did its appearance on the statute book alter beyond recognition the relationship between the State, capital, and labour? On the one hand, it can be argued that the legislation signalled an abandonment of the voluntarist, non-statist, and non-legally hidebound system of pre-war industrial relations. On the other hand, it might be argued that the measure capitalized on changes already occurring within the pre-war system which were pointing to a more interventionist role by the State in its relations with employers and trade unions. In either case, by mid-1915, an abstentionist State strategy towards industrial relations was both non-existent and inconceivable.

The characterization of the pre-war industrial relations system as voluntarist, by which is meant the preference both for non-legally enforceable collective agreements and also for the autonomous settlement of terms and conditions of employment by the parties themselves, rather than by third parties or by the State, is widely shared. Kahn-Freund observed in 1954 that, 'the whole of British labour law reflects the history of British industrial relations, and the principal feature of that history was that these relations developed in a sphere of industrial autonomy'.[1] Indeed, studies of the growth of collective bargaining (first district, then national, then plant-level bargaining) in the later nineteenth and early twentieth centuries, notably those by the Webbs, Clegg, Fox and Thompson, Rodger Charles,

[1] Otto Kahn-Freund, 'Legal Framework', in Allan Flanders and H. A. Clegg (eds.), *The System of Industrial Relations in Great Britain*, Oxford, 1954, pp. 42–127, at p. 89.

John Lovell, Clegg, and Alan Fox,[2] might be taken to suggest that the growth of collective bargaining in industries such as printing, cotton-spinning, boot and shoe, tailoring, shipbuilding, and building, was achieved in spite of judicial efforts to confine the scope of lawful industrial action following the legislation of the 1870s favourable to trade unions. Thus, in the face of setbacks at the hands of the judiciary in the 1890s, which culminated in the *Taff Vale* decision in 1901,[3] trade unions enthusiastically endorsed their faith in a voluntarist system of industrial relations free from legal restraints.
The tradition of self-regulation was crucial. As Flanders has observed,

Traditions are not accepted simply because the routines in which they are expressed have been sanctified by the passage of time. They derive their strength from the fact that they embody for the group the lessons of its corporate, social experience. The normative and binding character which traditions acquire is due to their having proved their worth as patterns of behaviour which have consistently succeeded in advancing the group's goals and values. Indeed, its traditions may become the sheet anchor of the group's goals and values, which may never be separately articulated.[4]

That 'corporate, social experience' included the recognition that trade union organizational rights were achieved before working-class *political* rights were partially obtained in 1867. Organizational rights did not therefore depend on parliamentary influence. For it was only a hostile legal interpretation of trade union organization and activity, and not the failure to organize collectively, which drove trade unions later to secure

---

[2] S. and B. Webb, *The History of Trade Unionism*, London, 1920; id., *Industrial Democracy*, London, 1920; H. A. Clegg, Alan Fox and A. F. Thompson, *A History of British Trade Unions Since 1889*, vol. I, London, 1964; Roger Charles, *The Development of Industrial Relations in Britain 1911–1939*, London, 1973; John Lovell, *British Trade Unions 1875–1933*, London, 1977; H. A. Clegg, *A History of British Trade Unions*, vol. II, 1910–1933, Oxford, 1985; Alan Fox, *History and Heritage*, London, 1985.

[3] Cf. A. W. J. Thomson, 'The Injunction in Trade Disputes in Britain before 1910', *Industrial and Labor Relations Review*, XIX (1965–6), 213–23; R. Brown, 'The Temperton v. Russell Case (1893): The Beginning of the Legal Offensive against the Unions', *Bulletin of Economic Research*, XXIII (1971), 50–66; John Saville, 'Trade Unions and Free Labour: The Background to the Taff Vale Decision', in A. Briggs and J. Saville (eds.), *Essays in Labour History*, London, 1960, ch. 9.

[4] Allan Flanders, *Management and Unions*, London, 1970, p. 279. Cf. id., 'The Tradition of Voluntarism', *British Journal of Industrial Relations*, XII (1974), 352–70.

legislative immunities. To exist and to negotiate with employers did not, in principle, require trade unions to embrace politics, Parliament, and law. Since 'law' was invariably hostile to trade unions, they chose instead the path of voluntarism and autonomous collective bargaining.[5]

Moreover, voluntarism was favoured by employers as well as by unions. Thus,

Employer associations saw their defence of managerial prerogatives as being not only against unions but also against the state. They were rather different bodies in their approach from their present-day successors, being much more aggressive and self-confident.[6]

They were, in particular, highly suspicious of politicians and of their legislative proposals for reform. As Sir Andrew Noble of the Engineering Employers' Federation (EEF), and vice-chairman of Armstrong Whitworth, told the Royal Commission on Trade Union Legislation in 1903, 'the way to improve industrial relations was not to pass new laws but to extend conciliation on the principles of the [Engineering Industry] Procedure until the desire for legislation on the conduct of trade disputes disappeared'.[7] Ten years later a similar verdict was recorded by the Industrial Council, a joint body of senior trade union officials and employers, which reported in 1913, that

the whole organisation of collective bargaining is based on the principle of consent. We have found that such collective agreements have as a rule been kept, and we are loath to interfere with the internal organisation of the associations on both sides by putting upon them the legal necessity of exercising compulsion on their members.[8]

To this end, 'moral influence', and not legal sanction was recommended as the means to ensure compliance with collective agreements.

---

[5] The oft-quoted words of Lord Wedderburn that 'Most workers want nothing more of the law than that it should leave them alone', seem particularly apposite. See Lord Wedderburn, *The Worker and the Law*, 3rd edn., Harmondsworth, 1986, p. 1.

[6] A. W. J. Thomson and S. R. Engleman, *The Industrial Relations Act: A Review and Analysis*, London, 1975, p. 7.

[7] Quoted ibid., p. 8.

[8] Quoted in Kevin Hawkins, 'The Future of Collective Bargaining', *Industrial Relations Journal*, x (1979–80), 10–21, at 13.

PRE-WAR CRITIQUES OF VOLUNTARISM

However, what appealed to, say, the engineering employers did not necessarily satisfy employers in those trades where the basic procedural norm of recognition[9] had not yet been established. Many employers, most notably in the railway and shipping industries, demanded the vigorous containment of trade unionism by law, and long resisted the attempts by unions to achieve recognition for bargaining purposes. The obverse was that a number of trade unions were prepared to contemplate reliance on legally enforceable collective agreements; that is, they were prepared to favour an interventionist, rather than an abstentionist, legal framework for industrial relations. Pelling has pointed out[10] that such proposals tended to reflect the weakness of the bargaining position of such trade unions, or their difficulties in maintaining internal union discipline (the Amalgamated Society of Railway Servants, which was embroiled in the *Taff Vale* litigation, is a case in point). In this respect, such proposals might be interpreted as opportunistic. However, it was also possible to conceive of them in a more ethical light. Thus George Barnes, general secretary of the Amalgamated Society of Engineers (ASE) saw in such proposals a means to secure, by the unions, a new vision of civic responsibility within the State. As he wrote to Sidney Webb in 1903, 'it seems to me that ante-Taff Vale is after all anti-social and but a glorified individualism, in as much as it seems to get for groups of men anti-social rights'.[11] Many politicians and civil servants were also prepared to argue that the Trade Disputes Act 1906, with its abstentionist trade union immunities, ought to be replaced, not by a return to *Taff Vale*, but by a system of positive legal rights and obligations which would act as a restraint on trade unions' disposition to take industrial action and would accentuate their responsibilities.[12]

---

[9] For the 'norms' of collective bargaining, see Charles, *The Development of Industrial Relations in Britain*, pp. 28–32.

[10] Henry Pelling, 'Trade Unions, Workers and the Law', in Henry Pelling, *Popular Politics and Society in Late Victorian Britain*, London, 1968, ch. 4.

[11] Ibid., p. 81.

[12] Roger Davidson, 'The Board of Trade and Industrial Relations, 1896–1914', *Historical Journal*, XXI (1978), 571–91; José Harris, *William Beveridge: A Biography*, Oxford, 1977, pp. 92–4.

Moreover, apart from reform proposals, albeit ones which might be inspired in the case of politicians solely by electoral considerations without regard to their empirical basis, the pre-First World War period witnessed a sufficient number of initiatives on the part of Government to justify a historical reassessment of the role of the State towards industrial relations. A number of developments in the five years or so before the outbreak of the war, including the enactment of minimum wage legislation, government reactions to the labour unrest of 1910–13, and the wider promotion of conciliation and arbitration, occasionally directly instigated in some disputes by government ministers themselves, seemed to underline the State's departure from a 'hands-off' approach to industrial relations. Ministers were now concluding that the consequences for the State of unions' and employers' failure to reach settlements in particular industries were too important to be ignored by governments.

This public recognition of a wider 'national' interest in the 'private' squabbling of collective bargaining parties did indeed, as Wrigley has argued,[13] make 'Lloyd George's task much easier in setting up a war-time system to control industrial relations'.

But it also cleared the ground for a profound shift towards the creation during the war of a new political and economic strategy for industrial relations, which we describe as 'corporatism'. It is a central thesis of this book that the industrial relations policies and aspirations of the wartime corporatist State were embodied in the Munitions of War Act 1915.

CORPORATISM

Though corporatism cannot be reduced to a monolithic theory, one writer has recently observed that

the common premise was that class harmony and organic unity were essential to society and could be secured if the various functional groups, and especially the organisations of capital and labour, were imbued with a conception of mutual rights and obligations somewhat

[13] C. J. Wrigley, *David Lloyd George and the British Labour Movement*, Hassocks, 1976, p. 77.

similar to that presumed to have united the medieval estates in a stable society. Accordingly, corporatist programmes advocated a universal scheme of vocational, industrial or sectoral organisation, whereby the constituent units would have the right of representation in national decision-making, and a high degree of functional autonomy, but would have the duty of maintaining the functional hierarchy and social discipline consistent with the needs of the nation-state as a whole. A limited organisational pluralism, generally operating under the aegis of the state as the supreme collective community, would guarantee the major value of corporatism—social harmony.[14]

Thus, emphasis is placed on the minimization of class divisions, on disciplined role-playing towards 'national' goals, and, to some extent, on the outflanking of the parliamentary process, with its assumption of legislative supremacy through the mediation of individual Members of Parliament. Parliament thus becomes merely a rubber stamp for executive decisions reached in collaboration with the representative organs, at the highest level, of capital and labour.

Among British businessmen before and during the war, the Midlands industrialist Dudley Docker was a powerful advocate for corporatism. As Davenport-Hines has recently observed, 'Like other productioneers, he felt that British organization was deficient and that traditional British individualism would have to be abandoned for the collectivism and regimentation which had made Germany and the USA such deadly rivals.'[15] The consequence was a preparedness to 'sacrifice personal independence and to risk diminishing individual initiative, in return for more national discipline and unified purpose'.[16] The mood expressed was one which chimed in with Government thinking during the war, though implementation of such a strategy within the munitions industries proved fraught with difficulties, as we shall see.

Within the specific context of industrial relations, Robert Currie has argued that

Pre-war collective bargaining had, in the main, developed as a system of bipartite corporatism that acknowledged the conflict of sectional

---

[14] Leo Panitch, 'The Development of Corporatism in Liberal Democracies', *Comparative Political Studies*, x (1977), 61–90, at 61.
[15] R. P. T. Davenport-Hines, *Dudley Docker*, Cambridge, 1984, p. 85.
[16] Ibid.

interests within an industry by allowing either side to take industrial action against the other after the exhaustion of negotiating procedure.[17]

With the advent of the war, however, and the consequential Government reorganization of industry under collectivist principles, the policy to be adopted, argues Currie, was 'unitary corporatism'. This would entail the denial of conflicts of interest and would confirm that 'overall industrial control' would reside with employers. Though this last observation, as we shall see throughout this work, is an over-simplification of Government intentions, Currie's conceptual emphasis in respect to wartime strategy is persuasive.[18]

Perhaps the best-known corporatist analysis of this period is that advanced by Middlemas[19] who identifies the existence of 'corporate bias' within the system. Crisis avoidance and the State's arrangement of 'a continuous series of compromises between oligarchic interest groups' resulted in the elevation of trade unions and employers' associations 'to a new sort of status: from interest groups they became "governing institutions"', sharing political power with an accommodating Government desperate for military victory. Yet in our view, Middlemas underestimates the directive role of the State, with its propensity to monopolize the planning and implementation of policy. It tended only to 'bargain' when confronted with massive displays of rank-and-file militancy after mid-1915. Moreover, it is open to question whether the phrase 'governing institutions' does not tend to exaggerate the power of representative bodies of employers and unions which often, indeed, faced difficulty 'governing' their own component elements. Nonetheless, 'corporate bias' does capture the sense in which both the pursuit of sectional or atomistic competition was abrogated for the duration of the war and in which 'bargaining' took place at an institutional level between Government and the highest eche-

---

[17] Robert Currie, *Industrial Politics*, Oxford, 1979, p. 92.

[18] For the pre-war period, we prefer Kahn-Freund's familiar term, 'collective laissez-faire', to 'bipartite corporatism', especially as Currie himself acknowledges that bipartite corporatism entailed a *sectional* bargaining strategy. See ibid., p. 50. For Kahn-Freund's term, see Otto Kahn-Freund, 'Labour Law', in Morris Ginsberg (ed.), *Law and Opinion in England in the 20th Century*, London, 1959, pp. 215–63 at p. 224.

[19] Keith Middlemas, *Politics in Industrial Society*, London, 1979, pp. 13, 22.

lons of the trade union movement, albeit, for the most part, only during moments of crisis.

In the light of the above analysis, we would therefore argue that the legislative campaign to regiment labour towards maximizing munitions production was far from being an exercise of a wholly undoctrinaire and empirical war collectivism. It is, in fact, better understood as one of the products of a Government policy which advanced, sometimes haphazardly, sometimes ruthlessly, a wartime brand of corporatist strategy. Informed by the corporate values of 'order' and 'unity' (which, together with 'nationalism' and 'success', have recently been said to mark the onset of the 'Coming Corporatism' of the mid-1970s),[20] State direction towards bureaucratically determined goals was the object of the Government's wartime munitions programme. Yet it constantly found that, despite consensus on national aims, the progress of its strategy became littered with complaints from both capital and labour on matters of implementation. As a result, the State's dependence on the continued co-operation of both labour and capital required it to compromise its claim to absolute decision-making on numerous matters affecting munitions production. It therefore found itself compelled to cede to representative bodies of employers and unions a voice in the smoothing-out of policies which could not be carried without bipartite involvement. Indeed, the negotiating process at the higher levels of Government and union organization occasionally resulted in the

---

[20] R. E. Pahl and J. T. Winkler, 'The Coming Corporatism', *New Society,* 10 Oct. 1974, 72. The pursuit of 'success' does, of course, seem to be a self-evident aim of virtually *any* social, economic, military, or political strategy. Indeed, according to Westergaard, the four corporate goals enumerated above are present to some extent in any social system; but he denies that within modern society, they are indicative of a distinctive corporatist order. See John Westergaard, 'Class, Inequality and "Corporatism"', in Alan Hunt (ed.), *Class and Class Structure,* London, 1977, p. 169. Yet given the wartime abandonment of market principles in the munitions trades after mid-1915, especially in respect of the labour market, we argue, for the purposes of this study, for the analytical usefulness of—at least—'unity', 'order', and 'nationalism'. We develop our theoretical argument in detail in Gerry R. Rubin, 'Law, War and Economy: The Munitions Acts 1915–17 and Corporatism in Context', *Journal of Law and Society,* XI (1984), 317–33. Of course, it need hardly be said that the march of corporatism as conceptualized by Pahl and Winkler was abruptly halted in 1979 with the election of a Thatcher Government in Britain.

withdrawal of Government plans for the munitions sector. 'Bargained corporatism'[21] could evidently cut both ways.

THE MUNITIONS ACT

A corporatist analysis does challenge existing interpretations of wartime Government labour policy. For example, one significant debate on the question centred on Hinton's argument that wartime labour controls should be conceived as a component of the 'Servile State', and that the statutory measures constituted 'new and formidable weapons in the arsenal of the ruling class', which were then unleashed in an offensive launched against the shop stewards' movement.[22] It was a view disputed by Roger Davidson who denied that the Act was 'designed to implement [a leading industrialist's] proposals for repressive labour controls and to reinforce the employers' control over their workers against the pressures of wartime full employment'.[23] Instead, he argued that the Act was a 'desperate expedient to facilitate labour supply', having emerged as the 'logical outcome' of a departmental review, conducted by the Ministry of Munitions, into the extent to which the bottleneck in the supply of munitions workers and the failure to obtain maximum output from existing labour was generating a munitions supply crisis for the military. As the 'last and not the first resort of wartime labour administrators' confronted with a manpower crisis, the statutory measures, according to Davidson, lacked 'repressive intent'. For the principal objective of the Ministry of Munitions in 1915, Davidson concluded, 'was to harness both labour *and* capital more effectively to the war effort and to the security of society as a whole'.

[21] A term employed by Colin Crouch, who distinguishes it from 'statist corporatism' where the state (self-evidently) refuses to engage in such horse-trading. See Colin Crouch, *Class Conflict and the Industrial Relations Crisis*, London, 1977.

[22] James Hinton, *The First Shop Stewards' Movement*, London, 1973.

[23] Roger Davidson, 'The Myth of the "Servile State"', *Bulletin of the Society for the Study of Labour History*, No. 29, Autumn 1974, 65. He developed his critique of Hinton's argument in more detail in his paper, 'Government Labour Policy, 1914–16: A Reappraisal', *Scottish Labour History Society Journal*, No. 8, June 1974, 3–20. See also Iain McLean, 'The Clyde Workers' Committee, the Ministry of Munitions and the Suppression of the "Forward": An Alternative View', *Scottish Labour History Society Journal*, No. 6, Dec. 1972, 3–25.

It may be observed that there is no inconsistency in viewing the Munitions Act both as a 'desperate expedient' designed to 'harness labour . . . more effectively to the war effort' *and* as a measure containing 'repressive legal controls'. Yet the approach of the present chapter is to argue that while both interpretations possess a considerable degree of merit, neither succeeds in doing full justice to the complexity of the question of wartime control of munitions labour.[24] We argue that there did indeed occur during the war a 'ruling-class' offensive mediated through legal controls, the object of which was, in crucial respects, to strengthen the power of employers over their work-forces. However, this 'offensive' was not confined to overcoming the potential revolutionary challenges of the shop stewards' movement in engineering, nor directed solely to sweeping away the hostility of craft trade union officials to the dilution of labour skills brought about by the introduction of women and semi-skilled men into the factories. For the Munitions Act constituted a comprehensive code of employment controls extending beyond the authorization of dilution (for which purpose it was not, in fact, felicitously phrased) and beyond the prohibition of strikes (which, in most instances, it proved unable to prevent). Restrictions on labour mobility, the control of wages, and the attempt to eliminate manifestations of industrial indiscipline, especially bad timekeeping, were as central to Government labour policy in the munitions trade as were the more

---

[24] The intentions of the wartime authorities and of the employers in respect to post-war industrial developments remain a matter for controversy among historians. There is circumstantial evidence to the effect that employers viewed the wartime changes as an opportunity to advance deskilling in the post-war era. But the evidence is far from conclusive. It is also improbable that government officials, at the time of the enactment of the Munitions Act, were seriously considering the post-war reorganization of an engineering industry bereft of trade union restrictive practices. They were, after all, devoting part of their energies to persuading trade unions that restrictive practices were to be *restored* at the conclusion of hostilities. The view that employers were intent on 'regaining the ground lost' before the war is expressed in Middlemas, *Politics in Industrial Society*, p. 72. Moreover, the *Official History of the Ministry of Munitions* observed that 'more serious was the workman's suspicion that under cover of the Munitions of War Act, the employer was seeking to introduce changes which had long been matters of prejudice and controversy.' See *Official History of the Ministry of Munitions* (henceforth *OHMM*), vol. IV, pt. II, p. 30. According to the *New Statesman*, 'Some of the great captains of industry have openly avowed their intention of taking the opportunity to secure permanently that autocracy in the management of their own concerns which has been temporarily given them under the Munitions Act.' See *New Statesman*, 2 Sept. 1916, 509. The problem of separating genuine intention from rhetoric still, however, remains.

controversial matters of strike prevention and dilution. Indeed the Act's labour controls were not limited to engineering but also encompassed a wide range of trades in building, mining and quarrying, chemicals, textiles, clothing, paper, wood, leather, transport, and public utilities, as well as the metals trades, including shipbuilding and iron and steel manufacture.[25] As Susan Lawrence, a member of the Labour Party executive and leading trade union official, wrote in 1915,

Tents are munitions; boots are munitions; biscuits and jam are munitions; sacks and ropes are munitions; drugs and bandages are munitions; socks and shirts and uniforms are munitions; all the miscellaneous list of contracts which fill up three or four pages of the *Board of Trade Gazette*, all, all are munitions.[26]

Thus, in one rather obvious sense, the restrictions of the Munitions Act, though associated in the public mind with the metals sector, entailed State controls over a much larger proportion of the working population. Indeed, by July 1918, almost five million persons were engaged on Government work, of whom less than half were employed in engineering, shipbuilding, and iron and steel manufacture.[27]

Yet to conceive of the Munitions Act as a weapon against recalcitrant workers (which it undoubtedly was) is to risk ignoring a further dimension to the Government's strategy, which was to bring employers within the sphere of Government regulation of the factors of production. Admittedly, the upholding of managerial authority in respect of their labour forces tended to attract the approval of Government spokesmen and munitions tribunal chairmen. Moreover, workers rather than employers were likely to incur the disciplinary wrath of the Munitions Act, while, unlike some shop stewards, no employer was deported for allegedly having hindered munitions output. None the less, though playing second fiddle (at least on paper) to a battery of Defence of the Realm Act (DORA) regulations, the Munitions Act did possess a limited potential, as we shall see, to

---

[25] *OHMM*, vol. VI, pt. IV, p. 47, Table XIII(c); ibid., pp. 52–3, Tables XVI and XVII.
[26] *Labour Woman*, III (August 1915), 315.
[27] *OHMM*, vol. VI, pt. IV, p. 47, Table XIII(c). The term 'government work' was broader in scope than 'munitions work' as popularly understood. The *legal* definition of munitions work appeared to include 'every kind of work indirectly essential to the needs of war'. See ibid., p. 48.

curb the managerial and entrepreneurial freedom of employers, where that freedom was considered by the authorities to pose a threat to the 'national interest'.

Thus, as conceptualized in the present study, wartime corporatism in Britain proceeded upon the footing both of a tightly controlled and disciplined (or better still, self-disciplined) labour force *and* a regulated network of employers. For the latter as well as the former were to be subject to centralized direction emanating from bureaucratic élites in order that increased munitions output might be achieved. If this meant the imposition on employers of minimum standards of conduct in industrial relations, then Government agencies were prepared to ruffle a few employers' feathers.

RULING CLASS REPRESSION?

In the light of the foregoing, a number of points require elaboration. The first matter concerns Davidson's allegation that the Munitions Act lacked repressive intent, and that the resulting injustice to labour was unintentional. Though the point is scarcely conclusive, it is enlightening, perhaps amusing, to cite first the opinion of A. J. Jenkinson, who, in drafting one of the crucial sections of the *Official History of the Ministry of Munitions* after the war, informed his general editor, G. I. H. Lloyd, that 'I have substituted "the principles of the Munitions of War Act" for "their policy of repressive action"—an innocuous phrase which means the same thing! You will remember that we looked at the file.'[28]

But perhaps more substantively from the point of view of evidence, the Government's creation of the institution of the 'controlled establishment' under the Act, that is, a munitions factory whose owner was subject to profits limitation, was designed in part to further this disciplinary aim. For it enabled employers to check bad timekeeping without diminishing

---

[28] PRO, MUN 5/328/160/R.2, 'Ministry of Munitions Officials to G. I. H. Lloyd re Constitution of Official History of Ministry of Munitions: re IV, Part II'. It is perhaps, worthwhile to recall that Davidson's exact words were 'the Act was the logical outcome of a series of memoranda on the problems of munitions labour supply submitted by Llewellyn Smith and Beveridge . . . Moreover, these memoranda do not betray any repressive intent.' See Davidson, 'The Myth of the "Servile State"', pp. 65–6.

output by dismissals or suspensions, and allowed them (at least on paper) to insist on the removal of restrictive workshop practices without having to resort to protracted (and possibly fruitless) discussions with full-time trade union officials.[29] A leading official at the Ministry of Munitions, W. J. Larke, summarized (if inelegantly) one of the Government's motives in introducing the institution. The controlled establishment, he pointed out, offered the opportunity

to prosecute labour for maintaining restrictive practices or any other action calculated to reduce output, such as abstention from work without reasonable cause, etc., before a munitions tribunal, thus ensuring better discipline of labour at a time before war conditions had permeated the whole community, and labour was still acting in accordance with the traditions that had obtained in peacetime.[30]

Thus from August 1915, the ministry postbag began to be swelled by requests from numerous employers, hitherto antagonistic to the prospect of 'external' control of their private businesses, that their firms be scheduled as controlled establishments under the Act. For these employers, the windfall opportunity of compelling trade unions to abandon their restrictive practices, and the licence granted to impose tighter factory discipline consequent on the issuance of a control order, now outweighed the assumed disadvantage of the modest profits limitation provision included in the Munitions Act as a symbol of equality of sacrifice.

Within this context, therefore, individual firms appealed to the ministry to resolve their labour difficulties by scheduling them as controlled establishments. Small firms such as Clarke's Crank and Forge Co. Ltd. of Lincoln argued that deliveries would be improved if the management could 'deal with their labour under the conditions of control',[31] while the Great Central Cooperative Engineering and Shipbuilding Company of Grimsby was advised by the ministry's labour officer to apply

[29] MUN 5/353/360/3, 'History of Controlled Establishments, March 1915 to April 1917: Principles of Control, prepared by Captain F. M. Cornford, August 2, 1917.' It may be noted that the restrictive practices in question were not exclusively, perhaps not even predominantly, concerned with dilution.

[30] MUN 5/353/360/4, 'Notes on Controlled Establishments, by W. J. Larke, August 25, 1917'.

[31] This and the following examples are taken from MUN 5/353/360/3.

for a control order to enable it 'to avoid friction over the employment of non-union labour' (here, indeed, is one of the many paradoxes thrown up by the operation of the Munitions Act, with the Government, as we shall note, seeking the stamp of official union approval for a statutory measure indirectly sanctioning non-unionism). In the case of the large public utility, the South Staffordshire Mond Gas (Power and Heating) Company, control was sought in the wake of serious labour troubles, in order that the management might 'secure more power over their men',[32] a justification for control advanced also by other utilities after 1916. Similarly, in September 1915 the ministry's labour officers in South Wales advised that a number of local steel companies 'where the men were restive' ought to be controlled. The optical firms, likewise, were also considered by the ministry as ripe for control in order 'to secure better control over the men generally'.

In the light of this evidence, therefore, there can surely be little doubt as to one of the motives informing the ministry's labour policy. For the creation of a custom-built institution, the controlled establishment, was, in part, primed to advance that repressive policy. Far from being the unintended consequence of a 'last resort' decision to legislate, the legal regimentation of labour was consciously and expressly designed to underpin employers' control over the workforce. In this respect, Hinton's interpretation is more convincing than Davidson's.

But there is a further point, crucial to the theoretical perspective of this study. This is that, however imperfectly in practice, the Munitions Act purported to embody restrictions on *employers* as well as on labour. The idea of 'control', for example, though exerted principally against labour, was originally associated, not with the suspension of trade union customs, but with the extinction of private work in engineering and shipbuilding. In consequence, the ministry frequently had to fend off accusations from companies that the incidence of control orders was discriminatory and unfair either between competitors within a given trade group or between one trade and another. The number of firms controlled was constantly

---

[32] Cf. the idyllic picture painted in Wilfred Beswick, *Industrialist's Journey*, Harrogate, 1961, ch. 8. Dealings with the ministry over technical contracts generated acute difficulties.

widened to repel these criticisms, even where there lacked any other industrial merit in controlling certain firms. Intra-class conflict was thus exposed as a focus for containment by the Munitions Act as well as inter-class conflict, though it did, of course, remain a less emotive issue than, say, a strike prosecution. None the less, as early as 22 July 1915 the Manchester Armaments Output Committee emphasized that controlled establishments would be under a disadvantage if they sacrificed the goodwill of private customers to turn to munitions work, while uncontrolled rivals were left free to pick up their private business. Complaints of labour-stealing, to which the Manchester committee had already drawn attention[33]—and, indeed, labour-stealing prosecutions themselves—are further symptoms of intra-class differences illuminated by the operation of the Act.

As a munitions tribunal chairman in Glasgow, Sheriff Fyfe, sought to persuade his listeners during a prosecution of a firm of brassfounders, the Munitions Act 'applied quite as drastically to employers as it did to workmen'.[34] Even the larger controlled establishments in the city were not immune from Fyfe's verbal lashes. The industrial giant, Beardmore, for example, was fined £20 as a result of its foremen's attempts to lure workers away from other workshops, conduct which Sheriff Fyfe described, in moderate tones, as 'bad cases of carelessness, if not of utter disregard of the Munitions Act'.[35] Of course, fines varying from £2 to £25 for labour-poaching might not constitute a powerful deterrent against firms desperate for labour. But deterrence, though one object, was not the sole aim. The ideological objective of promoting a 'national', and not a self-centred purpose, could thus be mediated through this additional tactic.[36]

---

[33] *OHMM*, vol. I, pt. IV, p. 39 n.

[34] *Glasgow Herald*, 28 Oct. 1915.

[35] Ibid. 29 June 1916.

[36] For other case examples from Glasgow, see, ibid., 1, 12 Dec. 1915; ibid., 16 Mar. 1916; ibid., 6, 20 Apr. 1916; ibid., 18, 29, 31 May 1916; ibid., 16 Aug. 1916; ibid., 5, 6, 18 Oct. 1916. For elsewhere, see ibid., 11 Sept. 1915 (Greenock); ibid., 5 Jan. 1917 (Edinburgh); ibid., 2 Aug. 1917 (Edinburgh); ibid., 4 Oct. 1915 (Hull); *Engineer*, 3 Sept. 1915 (Metropolitan tribunal). In one case from the West Midlands, a firm unsuccessfully sought the remission of a fine of £15 imposed for labour-stealing, arguing that through a 'misunderstanding' it failed to attend the tribunal. See MUN 5/97/349/10, 'Treasury correspondence re Fines imposed by the Munitions Tribunals, December 8, 1915 and February 11, 1916'.

Perhaps this point receives emphasis from the fact that even trade unions sought the scheduling of firms as controlled establishments in order to protect the *unions* against the encroachment of employers, with the result that employers found themselves controlled contrary to their own wishes. Thus the unions organizing in the railway workshops thought it worthwhile to incur the disabilities which control entailed for labour, in order to ensure that the companies were bound by the employers' guarantees of working conditions and of post-war restoration of customary working practices, as provided for in Schedule II to the Act. By way of further example, in one small firm of coppersmiths in Burton-on-Trent, the union agreed to the admission of women into the shop only if it became a controlled establishment subject to profit limitation and to the employer's guarantee of post-war restoration. In other respects, employers felt aggrieved at their treatment at the hands of Government labour administration.

They consistently complained of lack of consultation over all sorts of matters, such as the decision to award a major timeworkers' $12\frac{1}{2}$ per cent bonus in 1917 or the communication of the date of repeal of the leaving certificate scheme.[37] According to one employer,

At the present time, the payer of wages has hardly any voice in the fixing of them. This is done, for the most part, without any reference to employers by a [Government] Committee on Production which issues its decrees from time to time with a contemptuous disregard of the employers' interests or convenience, and evidently without knowledge of the details of factory administration.[38]

It was, perhaps, an understandable outburst of frustration, given the relative freedom with which employers had been accustomed to conduct their affairs before the war. Yet no one who reads the secondary accounts of the control of business during the war, commencing with the take-over of the railways in 1914, through to the virtual nationalization of the mines in 1918; the bulk purchases of essential supplies; restrictions on dealing, especially in imports and exports; the directing, for

---

[37] *Glasgow Herald*, 14 Nov. 1917. Cf. the complaint of 'repeated exactions' from employers, in ibid., 8 Oct. 1917.
[38] Ibid., 25 Sept. 1917.

example, of extra shipping tonnage into particular routes solely in order to keep down freights; and, finally, the scrutiny by the Ministry of Munitions, through auditing and accounting methods, of companies' actual costs,[39] can conceive (despite the indecent haste with which the wartime business controls were dismantled after the Armistice),[40] of the deliberate undermining or 'repression' of labour solely for the aggrandisement of industrial capitalism.

Indeed, thoughtful labour 'spokesmen' were inclined to accept such an analysis. Thus, according to G. D. H. Cole, speaking in November 1916,

A significant fact was that Government departments, e.g. the Ministry of Munitions, were now exercising greater control than formerly over raw materials, and so reducing the power of the capitalist manufacturer to exploit the community. The capitalist was being robbed by the State of his useful function as merchant and was becoming a mere supervisor of manufacture.[41]

Another spokesman expressing similar views, but whose constancy to the labour movement was less permanent, was William Mosses. Among the trade union posts held by him, Mosses had been secretary to the unions' side at the negotiations in March 1915 with the then Chancellor of the Exchequer, Lloyd George, which had resulted in the short-lived Treasury Agreement, committing the trade unions voluntarily to securing the acceleration of munitions output and the removal of restrictive practices. No doubt a 'super-patriot'[42] (he later left

---

[39] Though the effectiveness of such scrutiny should not be exaggerated. See Chris Wrigley, 'The Ministry of Munitions: An Innovatory Department', in Kathleen Burk (ed.), *War and the State*, London, 1982, ch. 2, p. 49. Cf. Sidney Pollard, *The Development of the British Economy, 1914–1967*, 2nd edn., London 1969, ch. 11, pts. (1) and (2).

[40] R. H. Tawney, 'The Abolition of Economic Controls, 1918–1921', *Economic History Review*, 1st ser., XIII (1943), 1–30. Cf. Peter K. Cline, 'Reopening the Case of the Lloyd George Coalition and the Post-War Economic Transition, 1918–1919', *Journal of British Studies*, x (1970–1), 162–75; id., 'Winding Down the War Economy: British Plans for Peacetime Recovery, 1916–19', in Burk (ed.), *War and the State*, ch. 7.

[41] *Fabian News*, XXVIII (Dec. 1916), 2. Contrast this with the views of Cole cited in J. M. Winter, *Socialism and the Challenge of War*, London, 1974, ch. 5.

[42] Cf. Royden Harrison, 'The War Emergency Workers' National Committee', in A. Briggs and J. Saville (eds.), *Essays in Labour History*, vol. II, 1886–1923, London, 1971, p. 220. For hints of the importance of working-class patriotism, see J. O. Stubbs, 'Lord Milner and Patriotic Labour, 1914–1918', *English Historical Review*, LXXXVII (1972), 717–54; Fox, *History and Heritage*, pp. 289–90.

the Labour Party and joined the Ministry of Munitions as a section director in the Labour Supply Department), his view was not an isolated one, even for trade unionists. Thus he insisted in 1917 that

Employers are cribbed, cabined and confined to a much greater extent than are their workmen, especially as the abolition of clearance certificates [in late 1917] will restore comparative freedom of movement to the workman. No one can now urge that the employer is master of his own house. The restrictions to which controlled establishments are subject are not known to the bulk of the workmen. Employers no longer have a free market for either buying or selling . . . and altogether they are in the position of a manager to a concern under the absolute control of a State Department which knows little or nothing of the technicalities or difficulties of the industry it dominates.[43]

Of course the fact that, as Mosses himself admitted, the employers were doing 'remarkably well from a financial point of view'[44] could not easily be hidden. Similarly, Robert Young, general secretary of the Amalgamated Society of Engineers, although claiming that, 'there is an uneasy feeling that the demands of the employers are more readily considered and assented to than are the grievances of the workers',[45] none the less admitted that[46] 'In the main industries of the country, the employers of labour are under control.' This verdict did not extend to financial matters where fiscal efforts to restrict profiteering were always unconvincing to labour,[47] which

---

[43] *Glasgow Herald,* 1 Oct. 1917. The severity of restrictions on controlled establishments is well captured in the correspondence between Messrs R. Anderson & Co., a firm of metal manufacturers in Leith, and their lead suppliers, Walkers, Parker & Co. Ltd. of Newcastle. Replying to Anderson's order for a small quantity of lead, their suppliers had to report back that 'under the New Lead Control Order of the 1st September [1917] it is only permissible to supply these small lots of 1 cwt. for the purpose of necessary repairs or renewals requiring immediate execution and for which no other metal can be substituted and that the purchaser shall give a declaration in writing, specifying the nature of the work for which same is required, and the place where same is to be carried out at, and that the Lead purchased is for the purpose mentioned and for no other purpose. If you will kindly favour us with these particulars we will at once put the matter in hand.' See Scottish Record Office, GD327/299, C. Norman Kemp Collection, Walkers, Parker & Co. Ltd., Newcastle, to D. M. Kemp, Messrs R. Anderson & Co., Leith, 19 Oct. 1917.
[44] *Glasgow Herald,* 1 Oct. 1917.
[45] Ibid., 24 Sept. 1917.
[46] Ibid.
[47] Indeed unconvincing to business, according to the *New Statesman,* 7 Apr. 1917, 6–7.

thoroughly distrusted the strength of the Government's commitment to equality of sacrifice. Yet even if the Government's motives, let alone its competence, were suspect, the view remains, in some quarters at least, that 'The war also taught the country to look at its national equipment in a new light, not as private property alone, but as the capital helping to provide the national income.'[48] Of course, the reification implied in this analysis disguises the corporatist lurch which undoubtedly occurred. But a paradigmatic shift none the less did take place, even if confined to a shift in management rather than in mode of production.[49] Thus it is important to appreciate the restrictions which the Munitions Act (and, of course, numerous other legal measures) entailed for employers. The Munitions Act undoubtedly offered the latter substantial advantages in disciplining their employees. Such was the intention of the ministry. The Act, however, also sought to subordinate employers' freedom of business activity to the attainment of a 'national interest' determined by bureaucrats. That, also, was the intention of the ministry. As Lowe has recently observed,

On the trade union side it was often forgotten that even during the war, the Board [of Trade conciliation and arbitration section] antagonised employers as much as the unions and secured for labour important gains which would not necessarily have been won by the exercise of naked economic power. The Board strove to be 'impartial', defending the 'national interest' in industrial disputes (according to Askwith) and preventing the exploitation of whichever side of industry was temporarily at an economic disadvantage (according to Beveridge).[50]

It was a view with which many patriotic trade union leaders readily agreed. Alexander Wilkie, general secretary of the

---

[48] Pollard, *The Development of the British Economy*, p. 62. As the *New Statesman* remarked, 'Some people have said in their haste that no self-respecting manufacturer would submit to such a regulation of "his own" business. But ought it any longer to be regarded as his own business?' See *New Statesman*, 17 Nov. 1917, 152.

[49] According to Wrigley, '*The Ministry of Munitions*', pp. 50–1, the managerial policies of the Ministry of Munitions 'generally smack of tough efficient capitalism'. In respect to labour policy, however, we clearly take a view which diverges from this characterization.

[50] Rodney Lowe, 'The Ministry of Labour, 1916–19: A Still, Small Voice?' in Burk (ed.), *War and the State*, ch. 5, pp. 122–3. Sir George Askwith was the government's Chief Industrial Commissioner during the war, in effect the 'top' conciliation officer. William Beveridge was assistant general secretary at the Ministry of Munitions at the time.

Shipwrights' Association and Member of Parliament for Dundee, insisted that 'The Act, it should not be forgotten, was an Act of consent of both the employers and the workmen,[51] and as such was designed to operate impartially as between the employers and employees.'[52]

Indeed, the elevation of the 'national interest' above sectional interests was perceived by such trade union leaders as an advance on the previous political and economic order. John Hill, general secretary of the Boilermakers' Society, remarked that the enactment of the Munitions Act represented 'our latest national confession that uncontrolled private enterprise and production for profit has hopelessly failed us, as it always has done when our need was greatest'.[53] Though collaboration was now to be installed in place of competition, so that both class conflict and market conflict were to be abandoned as features of the discredited past, none the less, added Hill, 'All our usual machinery for dealing with grievances and questions in dispute will be continued, i.e. reporting to the foreman, calling the district delegate, meeting employers in conference, etc.'[54] In the event of failure to agree, however, resort to trial of strength was

[51] This was technically incorrect since, as Hinton has pointed out, the rank and file were not balloted on the Bill, though they had been in respect to the Treasury Agreement. See Hinton, *The First Shop Stewards' Movement*, p. 33 n.

[52] Shipconstructors' and Shipwrights' Association (SSA), *Quarterly Reports*, July–Sept. 1915, 5. The *Forward*, reflecting Independent Labour Party (ILP) opinion locally, adopted a nice line in sarcasm at Wilkie's expense, whom it described as 'a doughty, if somewhat incoherent champion of the Munitions Act'. It continued, 'when he lets loose his eloquence upon a paralysed Senate, Sandy is said to have a great advantage over all the other members, in that he is never called to order by the Speaker. The reason why he enjoys this exceptional privilege and is allowed to meander on at his own sweet will is that a bewildered Speaker (like any member who happens to be present) does not understand a single word of what Sandy is saying . . . But Sandy loved the Munitions Act, pressed it to his breast and made it his own peculiar care. So much was quite clear, even if his reasoning and arguments were as drumlie as a burn in spate.' See *Forward*, 18 Sept. 1915.

[53] United Society of Boilermakers (USB), *Monthy Report*, July 1915, 10–11. The same item was repeated in ibid., Nov. 1915, 13–14 on the ground that, 'A good many who have never read the Act have condemned it because of some harsh and stupid interpretations and unreasonable penalties which have been inflicted.' This was an obvious reference to the mass prosecution of Boilermakers' Society members at Messrs John I. Thorneycroft, Southampton, who struck over the recruitment by the firm of non-union, unskilled riveters (n. 66), and reveals Hill's commitment to 'responsible' behaviour whether on the part of employers, or of unionists, or even of munitions tribunal chairmen. Class consensus and disciplined role playing are indeed characteristic of corporatism.

[54] USB, *Monthly Report*, July 1915, 11.

forbidden. Instead, the 'inexpensive experts' of the Government's wartime Committee on Production or the Board of Trade's arbitrators were ultimately to impose an award. As the Webbs had earlier remarked, 'Two professional men seldom find any difficulty in agreeing upon an identical award.'[55]

For such trade union leaders, the commitment to the restoration of trade practices after the war would have been irreconcilable with an analysis pointing to the use of the Munitions Act as an instrument with which employers might launch a capitalist offensive (with or without the active participation of the State) in order to annihilate trade unions. In short, the above labour spokesmen took pains to stress the bilateral nature of the sacrifices involved, thereby underscoring the unity so central to a corporatist strategy. Indeed some trade union leaders were even prepared to express mild ecstasy at certain of the statutory proposals. John Hill, for example, had no reservations about describing Schedule II to the Act, which contained the provisions for restoration of trade practices after the war, as a 'trade union charter'.[56] The *Seaman*, the organ of the National Seamen's and Firemen's Union, for its part, saw the Act as the means by which 'labour difficulties will be overcome';[57] while John Beard, president of the Workers' Union, also wrote a glowing account of the measure.[58] In his case, a spot of 'war profiteering' of his own, in the form of potentially dramatic growth of membership in his union as a result of the dilution proposals to employ female and less-skilled labour in engineering workshops, may have been an added attraction.[59] Yet whether such optimistic views were genuinely held, whether it was a case of whistling in the dark, or whether such trade union leaders actually believed in the potency of their patriotic appeals to doubting members, they none the less

---

[55] S. and B. Webb, *Industrial Democracy*, cited in Tom Keenoy, 'Industrial Relations and the Law: From the Webbs to Corporatism', in Z. Bankowski and G. Mungham (eds.), *Essays in Law and Society*, London, 1980, pp. 180–203, at p. 188.

[56] USB, *Monthly Report*, July 1915, 11.

[57] *Seaman*, 2 July 1915.

[58] Richard Hyman, *The Workers' Union*, Oxford, 1971, pp. 82–3.

[59] Davenport-Hines has noted that, 'Beard and [Dudley] Docker collaborated on munitions committees in 1915, and agreed on the need for higher production and corporatist social structures to unify the material interests of employers and employed.' See Davenport-Hines, *Dudley Docker*, p. 73.

expressed the belief that where the lifting of trade practices was, 'shown to be unquestionably necessary, there will be nothing but cheerful acquiescence'.[60]

While trade union officials were prepared to tolerate the imposition of drastic restrictions on their members' freedom of movement and freedom of action, the State also took steps designed to integrate *employers* into the national endeavour, indicating to *them* the diffused sense of commitment and sacrifice which had excited the trade union leaders. To some extent, the idea of bilateral sacrifices was reflected in the requirement of the Munitions Act that employers were to make compensatory payments in prescribed circumstances to munitions workers laid off work or dismissed with inadequate notice. But such provisions insufficiently emphasize that which has recently been described as the 'conformative' role of the State, a role which seeks to 'contain, incorporate and moderate the conflicts within capitalist society'.[61] For it is apparent that conflicts of interest might also arise between individual capitalists on the one hand, and the State as controller of more extreme abuses of power on the other, a struggle which might even threaten national consensus and stability. For example, it was the employment practices of one major shipbuilding firm in Glasgow, Fairfield, which, as we shall see in subsequent chapters, triggered a major explosion of militancy in the Clyde district in late 1915, and which were, as a consequence, heavily criticized by government officials and tribunal chairmen as well as by outraged trade unionists.

With a view to preventing such fractious occurrences, State institutions—in this case, the munitions tribunal—sought to inhibit *employers* from pursuing what might be thought to be provocative courses of action against trade unions, and imposed on firms direct obligations designed to compel them to conform to State directives. Such conformative devices did not simply

---

[60] *Cotton Factory Times*, 2 July 1915. Although the newspaper claimed that, 'There is no unkindness to the workmen in this Bill', the cotton unions insisted on exclusion from the scope of the Act. If they abandoned their right to strike, they pleaded, then every local dispute, especially over bad workmanship, would be settled on the employer's terms. Such special pleading, accompanying the call for 'cheerful acquiescence', could justifiably invite accusations of hypocrisy.

[61] Michael Barratt Brown, 'The Welfare State in Britain', in R. Miliband and J. Saville (eds.), *The Socialist Register 1971*.

attempt to offer palliatives to the working class to ensure the latter's integration within the given structure of ownership and control, they also sought to focus attention on *employers* and on *their* conduct and attitudes.

Take, for example, the case of the Glasgow apprentice pattern-maker who complained in 1916 that he had been suspended by his employer.[62] The firm stated that he had refused to work overtime on urgent Government work, and that it was company practice to suspend apprentices for the sake of discipline. Yet, as the Glasgow tribunal chairman, Sheriff Fyfe, insisted, 'all such practices had gone by the board for the war period. Firms could not work under the Munitions Act unless they adhered to it.'[63] Thus a firm might prosecute, but it could not suspend when employees went absent without leave. In this respect, therefore, the Munitions Act actually *removed* certain disciplinary powers from employers.

Another wartime illustration concerned the asserted rights of workers to join trade unions despite the opposition of their employers. It is certainly true that State institutions remained unmoved by the claim of trade unionists to refuse to work alongside non-unionists, as Lloyd George, the Minister of Munitions, made clear to the ASE at a meeting with them on 31 December 1915 to discuss amendments to the 1915 Act.[64] Thus employers who upheld the wishes of non-unionists or who refused to consult with trade unions before introducing non-union labour were not prevented by the State from doing so. Indeed Section 15 of the 1916 Amendment Act plainly approved the introduction of non-union labour into a controlled establishment where a closed shop had existed prior to the war. For the Section expressly provided for the restoration of the pre-war closed shop at the end of hostilities. None the less, it is significant that the necessity for giving notice to the workmen and for providing, where possible, the opportunity for local

---

[62] *Glasgow Herald,* 4 Oct. 1916.

[63] Ibid. The tribunal awarded the apprentice one day's pay in consequence of the illegal suspension.

[64] Beveridge Collection on Munitions (at the British Library of Economic and Political Science; henceforth BEV) III, 9, fos. 43–61. On the campaign to amend the 1915 Act, see G. R. Rubin, 'The Enforcement of the Munitions of War Acts 1915–1917, with Particular Reference to Proceedings before the Munitions Tribunal in Glasgow, 1915–1921', Warwick Univ. Ph.D. thesis (1984), ch. 2.

consultation (conditions applicable, on paper at least, to every other type of workshop change) was omitted from this highly contentious alteration. Ironically, though the intention was to advance the output of munitions by allowing the employer to bring in whoever could perform the tasks, irrespective of membership or non-membership of a trade union, such a stance occasionally had the opposite effect. For it was just the sort of issue which could lead to prolonged and bitter conflict involving trade unions. In Glasgow, twenty-two sheet-iron workers at Messrs John Broadfoot and Sons Ltd., Whiteinch, were fined £1 each for having imposed an overtime ban in response to the company's 'deliberate attempt to introduce non-union labour into the Clyde yards'.[65] The best documented illustration is, however, a major dispute involving the boiler-makers at Thorneycroft's shipyard at Southampton in September 1915, which eventually resulted in the prosecution of fifty of the 1700 strikers.[66]

Unwilling to go as far as enforcing a closed shop,[67] for this was

[65] *Glasgow Herald*, 11 Nov. 1915. Interestingly, the tribunal chairman, Cmdr. Gibson, remarked that if the union had referred the matter to the Board of Trade for arbitration, instead of imposing its overtime ban, it would probably have received a favourable decision. Here, already, is an early indication that tribunal chairmen might not consistently follow the ministry line in their *obiter* utterances.

[66] For this strike, see Lord Askwith, *Industrial Problems and Disputes*, London, 1920, pp. 396–8; John Mahon, *Harry Pollitt: A Biography*, London, 1976, pp. 49–51; *Woman's Dreadnought*, 9 Oct. 1915; *Glasgow Herald*, 4 Oct. 1915; USB, *Monthly Report*, Oct. 1915, 11; *Labour Gazette*, Nov. 1915, 422.

[67] In 1917, one of the regional committees set up by the Government to enquire into the causes of widespread industrial action that year, the Welsh Commissioners on Industrial Unrest, did, however, recommend compulsory unionism as conducive to greater industrial stability. See *Glasgow Herald*, 2 Aug. 1917. The Scottish Commissioners pointed to the not unconnected problem of arrears of union membership which had arisen as a result of the prohibition on industrial action contained in the Munitions Act. Unions were now more hesitant to take retaliatory action against a member who deliberately allowed his subscription to lapse or against an employer who tolerated such 'rebellious' conduct among his employees. The institution of the closed shop would prevent such union dissatisfaction from arising, a point of which the Ministry of Munitions was itself cognizant. It suggested that unions should indicate to their members that where membership of the union terminated as a result of subscriptions being overdue, such ex-members would, under Section 15, be liable to discharge from employment on the termination of the war, where a pre-war closed shop had existed. For the ministry's correspondence, see USB, *Monthly Report*, Dec. 1916, 35–6; Associated Blacksmiths' and Ironworkers' Society (ABIS), *4th Quarterly Report*, Oct.–Dec. 1916, 2159–60. For the Scottish Commissioners' observations, see ibid., *2nd Quarterly Report*, Apr.–June 1917, 2343. For other aspects of the arrears question, see ibid., *1st Quarterly Report*, Jan.–Mar. 1918, 2573; SSA, *Quarterly Reports*, July–Sept. 1915, 7; ibid.,

to be left to negotiations between employers and trade unions,[68] the ministry none the less determined to support the right of workers, as against their employer, to *join* a trade union. Thus, on the extremely rare occasions when workers complained to the munitions tribunal that their membership rights had been denied by employers, the ministry was prepared to back up the complaints or even to institute proceedings against the employers themselves. For example, the ministry supported the appeal of an iron moulder, Alfred Guillet, sacked by his employer, E. H. Bentall & Co. Ltd., engineers, for having joined a union, even though the company, a controlled establishment in Essex, had compelled its workforce to sign a statement renouncing trade union membership. Imaginatively exploiting to his own advantage the statutory prohibition on restrictive practices which impeded munitions output, Guillet obtained a ruling from the English Munitions Appeal Tribunal, supported by counsel for the ministry who also spoke at the hearing, that the employer's anti-union policy was an unacceptable restraint, and therefore unlawful under the Munitions Act.[69] Similarly, the ministry decided to prosecute the manager of a controlled establishment in Loughborough, who was alleged both to have locked out his staff contrary to the

---

Jan.–Mar. 1916, 20; ibid., Apr.–June 1916, 34; USB, *Monthly Report*, Mar. 1917, 35. We may also note at this point the 'double-edged' quality of Section 15; primarily a measure to permit the dismantling of the closed shop for the duration of the war, it could yet be employed *by* unions in order to threaten members to toe the line as far as subscriptions (and possibly also other questions) were concerned. This contradictory feature is merely one of the many paradoxical dimensions, as we shall see, to the enforcement of a code of restrictive legislation principally designed to regulate labour.

[68] For one example, see ABIS, *1st Quarterly Report*, Jan.–Mar. 1918, 2575.

[69] For discussion of the case, see *Guillet* v. *E. H. Bentall & Co. Ltd.*, reported in the Munitions Appeal Reports, 1 (1916), 86–98, 19 May 1916; *Scottish Law Review*, xxxii (July 1916), 152; USB, *Monthly Report*, June 1916, 53; SSA, *Quarterly Reports*, Apr.–June 1916, 40; Associated Iron-Moulders of Scotland (AIMS), *Monthly Report*, May 1916; *Trade Union Worker*, Mar. 1916, 8; ibid., Apr. 1916, 8. A postscript to the case was the offence taken by the Workers' Union to the claim of the Brassworkers' Union to have fought the case on behalf of Guillet. The Brassworkers' action was condemned for its 'barefaced impertinence'. See ibid., July 1916, 8. That the Workers' Union was the stronger body is probably to be inferred from its ability in the winter of 1917–18 to force Bentalls to arbitration over a wage claim. See LAB 2/118/IC 707, 25 Jan. 1918. The Munitions Appeal Reports and the Scottish Munitions Appeal Reports will henceforth be cited as (1916) 1 MAR 1–10; 1916 SMAR 1–10 etc., with the dates of judgment, if appropriate.

prohibition on industrial action in Part I of the Act, and to have prevented them from joining the Workers' Union. This latter step, the ministry believed, was a breach of Section 4(3), the measure requiring the lifting of those restrictive practices[70] which interfered with the maximization of munitions production.

From a broader perspective, ministry support for the trade unionists in these cases was a clear signal to employers that the State was prepared to discredit manifestations of discrimination which posed even a minor threat to the delicate consensus which it sought to foster. Thus pragmatic considerations undoubtedly lay behind its support for the principle, even where it intruded directly on the competing principle of managerial property rights. Indeed, a provision was inserted in the Munitions Act of August 1917 which declared it an offence for an employer to discharge a munitions worker on the ground that he was a trade unionist or that he had taken part in a trade dispute.[71] Though the initiative seems to have sprung from the trade unions during a period of hard bargaining over ultimately abortive proposals to extend dilution to private, and not just to munitions work, the Government clearly was not unhappy about legislating against the interests of employers, in the belief that the national interest demanded the promulgation of 'conformativist' measures.

Such a concept of conformativism does represent an important stride towards corporatism, and offers further support to the thesis that wartime Government policy must be understood as entailing temporary, if relatively mild, restraints on employers, as well as severe restrictions upon munitions workers.

---

[70] LAB 2/57/CE 102/6, 'Yorkshire and East Midlands General Munitions Tribunal, Constitution File'. The hearing was conducted in the Nottingham Guildhall on 7 Sept. 1917.

[71] Under Section 9 of the 1917 Act, a fine of not more than £10 might be imposed on an employer, and the whole or part of the fine could be paid to the worker as compensation. It is tempting, but perhaps not wholly convincing, to believe that the Government's influence on employers was such that very few tribunal complaints under this provision were received. For the only Glasgow case discovered, see *Glasgow Herald*, 26 Apr. 1918, where Sheriff Fyfe found no evidence to support the charge. He remarked that the provision was 'very impracticable . . . as any enactment must always be which tried to create an offence based upon motives, not upon actions'.

THE ROLE OF THE MUNITIONS TRIBUNAL

It is, of course, possible to identify the existence of corporatist influences on the decision-making of munitions tribunal chairmen. Naturally, it goes without saying that they frequently commended the patriotism ('nationalism') of those accused munitions workers appearing before them, and correspondingly imposed lenient sentences in such cases. For example, though twenty-three shipwrights employed by Elderslie Graving Dock had admitted refusing to continue to dock and undock vessels on the Clyde after 10 p.m. one night in pursuance of a wage grievance, the tribunal chairman Cmdr. Gibson none the less

> congratulated the respondents all the same on the patriotic attitude they had taken up in undertaking to do Government work night or day in all sorts of weather, and he believed that a little tact on the part of the management would have solved the whole situation.[72]

He consequently imposed a modified fine of 5*s.* on each accused. Indeed, the patriotic posture by munitions and shipyard workers, inasmuch as it was not contrived for the particular audience of the munitions tribunal members, even informed the nature of some of the outbursts and protests heard at tribunal hearings on a number of occasions throughout the war. During a major prosecution of Fairfield shipyard coppersmiths in Glasgow in August 1915 (ch. 3), the tribunal chairman Professor Gloag reproved the actions of those accused who were standing up and interrupting the proceedings. 'Remember this country is at war. Does that never occur to you?' he demanded,[73] whereupon one of the accused, Owen Rodgers, stood up and replied, 'I am as much a patriot as any man in this room. We have been looked upon as unpatriotic in this matter. I have seven relations both in the trenches and on the sea. No man dare tell me that I am sacrificing their lives by remaining out.'[74] Similarly, at Liverpool, where a large number of shipyard workers employed by Cammell Laird at Birkenhead had been

---

[72] *Glasgow Herald*, 29 Mar. 1916. The incident arose in the midst of strikes over the deportation of a leading Glasgow shop steward, David Kirkwood (ch. 3), but was wholly unconnected with that dispute. Gibson's choice of words may, however, have been conditioned by such events.

[73] Ibid., 3 Aug. 1915; *OHMM*, vol. IV, pt. II, p. 50.

[74] Ibid.

fined, the *Glasgow Herald* vividly described the ensuing event. There was, it declared,

a scene of indescribable uproar at the close. Men leapt to their feet, shouting denunciation of the firm, and of some of their officials, one man declaring that the court was causing a revolution in the country by its finding, another shouting, "It is time the Germans were here if this is how British working men are to be treated. We are here, not as slaves, but as workmen, and we can do our work.'[75]

Clearly, not every munitions tribunal chairman was sensitive enough to appreciate the predictable responses of large numbers of predominantly patriotic munitions workers who, frequently critical of the managerial shortcomings and litigious zeal of their employers, found themselves fined by the tribunal and reproved for *their* want of patriotism.

Some tribunal chairmen were, however, conscious that the impression of unity and consensus which it was corporatist policy to promote necessitated, from time to time, certain expressions of condemnation of managerial practices which threatened the shaky edifice. Thus not only might chairmen such as Cmdr. Gibson in Glasgow mildly reprove those employers whose tactlessness, as in the Elderslie dock case (above), contributed to the dispute; but fierce condemnation might be uttered against employers, such as on the occasion when Gibson pilloried Fairfield shipyard for its 'reprehensible conduct' in refusing for three weeks to grant a leaving certificate to a worker whose services they no longer required.[76] What is significant is the desire on the part of the tribunal chairman to publicize criticisms of employers. 'He thought it right to make the public intimation now, that that court in particular looked askance on such conduct on the part of employers.'[77] In another hearing at Bradford munitions tribunal, the chairman strongly attacked the conduct of a foreman who had instituted a prosecution for bad timekeeping against an employee. The accused argued that the charge had been brought vindictively by the foreman because the former had complained at the latter's bad language. Indeed, when a sample of the language

[75] *Glasgow Herald*, 20 Sept. 1915.
[76] Ibid., 5 Oct. 1915. See also ch. 8.
[77] AIMS, *Monthly Report*, Jan. 1916, 250.

was repeated to the tribunal chairman, he indignantly declared, 'I don't think working men ought to be subject to such language, and I ask the firm if they should not consider whether you are a suitable man for the position. You are the foreman, and ought to set a good example and, instead, you have set a filthy example.'[78] Yet what clearly perturbed the tribunal chairman was not bad manners or the gratuitous expression of obscenities, but the threat to 'order' and 'unity' in the establishment posed by the foreman's actions.

Certainly, the tribunals imagined themselves as reliable allies of a policy which, on paper, eschewed class partisanship. As Sheriff Fyfe of Glasgow, the most outstanding tribunal chairman during the war, sought to convince the readers of his textbook on the Munitions Acts,

The purpose of the Munitions Code is to protect all interests, and to remove causes of friction whether between employers and workmen, or between classes of workers. It is perhaps hardly to be expected that either employers or workers should regard very cordially legislation which calls upon employers to forgo the enhanced profits which the exceptional economic situation might confer upon them, and which suspends for the time being certain long-cherished privileges by which workmen set great store. But, however difficult it may be for the industrial world to grasp legislation which temporarily upsets long-accepted notions of freedom of contract, some form of sacrifice is the lot of all classes in the present exceptional times, and the temporary abandonment of cherished ideals is the form of sacrifice which, in the national interest, the Munitions Act requires of the industrial community. If the Act curtails individual liberty of action as it does, it at any rate treats employers and workmen alike in that respect . . .[79]

None the less, while chairmen of munitions tribunals frequently invoked the 'national interest' as the criterion by which their decisions might be adjudged; while they often commended the patriotism ('nationalism') of those defendants appearing before them; while they chided, in the name of 'unity', those employers and foremen who coercively and insensitively wielded the Munitions Act against aggrieved workmen; and while in general they sought to discourage 'disorder' in the labour

[78] Ibid., Dec. 1915, 243.
[79] T. A. Fyfe, *Employers and Workmen under the Munitions Acts*, 3rd edn., London and Glasgow, 1918, pp. 22–3.

market by refusing to grant leaving certificates to those who simply wanted to better themselves; yet, in the final analysis, as we shall see in Chapter 4, a number of tribunal chairmen in Glasgow (though not elsewhere) proved too unreliable for the bureaucratic élite who inhabited the offices of the Ministry of Munitions. For, leaving aside the history of disorder which accompanied so many of the major hearings at the Glasgow tribunal (ch. 3), it was evident that not every tribunal chairman chose blind loyalty to the executive will in place of devotion to the 'rule of law'.[80] In one case in Glasgow, a number of men had been prosecuted for refusing to work overtime as a protest against the employment of a non-unionist. The prosecuting labour officer had intimated to the chairman, Cmdr. Gibson, that the ministry 'were rather anxious that it should be tried before the other court [i.e. the *general* munitions tribunal], as it was really a partial strike.'[81] However, this remark drew an astonishing, indeed suicidal, attack by Gibson on the ministry for daring to encroach on the independence of the judiciary. 'It does not matter one jot or tittle to me', he declaimed indignantly,[82] 'what are the views held by the Ministry of Munitions in London. I am here as chairman of this Court to weigh up the facts submitted to us, and I will not be influenced one way or another. I am here to act as judge and I will do so.' It was a brave but foolish outburst, no doubt inspired by the lofty (though in this case, naïve) tradition of judicial neutrality which insisted that the law was no respecter of persons, even if that person were none other than Lloyd George, the Minister of Munitions, himself. It was, indeed, a display of dissidence among the ranks of the officer corps, and was unlikely to be tolerated for long.[83]

Moreover, what further unnerved the Ministry of Munitions in London was that the local tribunal chairmen were the repositories of discretion in decision-making, a licence which, in

---

[80] For theoretical discussion of tensions between corporatism and the rule of law, see Rubin, 'Law, War and Economy'.

[81] *Glasgow Herald*, 11 Nov. 1915.

[82] Ibid.

[83] Indeed, Gibson's display of petulance possibly hastened his involuntary departure from office as tribunal chairman. See ch. 4.

the event, created too much uncertainty for the peace of mind of a ministry dedicated to centralized direction of labour policy. That discretion (as distinct from flexibility in imposing sentences) could, from the perspective of the ministry authorities, be exercised wisely or foolishly. In the case of certain of the Glasgow chairmen, that discretion was, in the ministry's view, undoubtedly exercised foolishly by legal officials fatally beguiled into over-asserting their judicial independence. As we shall see, it was one thing for Government devotees of centralized administration to confer on tribunal chairmen a limited right to exercise their judgment when faced with the hard case of, say, an individual seeking a leaving certificate on medical grounds, where the loss was confined to the employer in question. Where, however, the tribunal chairmen allowed their discretion to lead them beyond the narrow decision-making contours mapped out for them by the ministry, so that in one episode (ch. 4) they appeared to be formulating a wages policy by their decision-making, they trenched on the directive activities of Government élites. This was viewed by the relevant civil servants as unforgivable, for, it was claimed, it would threaten the collapse of a delicate industrial status quo arranged through centralized direction. It was illegitimate for petty legal administrators remote from a central planning department displaying corporatist tendencies to exceed their allotted, minimal roles by raising false hopes of financial amelioration among rank-and-file workers. Judicial autonomy was therefore inconsistent with corporatist autocracy. Thus, where it seemed to the ministry that the *chairmen's* weaknesses, incompetence or indiscipline were subverting this autocracy, they were dealt with (as will be seen in Chapter 4) as swiftly and as decisively as the perceived enemies of the state, the militant Clydeside shop stewards, who were deported from the district in 1916.

Therefore, against a background which included the regular delivery of policy-oriented decisions by tribunal chairmen, punctuated by occasional, though spectacular, divergences from the executives' desired path, the history of the Glasgow munitions tribunal can be seen in part as the history of how the personnel of one tribunal sought alternately to advance and to repel the embraces of corporatist law.

CONCLUSION

The term 'corporatism' was unknown to British society during the war, having been coined in the inter-war years; but the phrase 'corporate spirit' was in wide circulation. None the less, when tribunal chairmen, Government ministers, and civil servants made their appeals for social peace, and when they formulated industrial schemes with the ultimate aim of achieving military victory, they unconsciously did so in the name of a policy which had absorbed corporatist values. This meant that, for the duration of the war, they set out to subordinate the munitions industries *and* their labour forces to the directives of a State department which sought to impose, in some respects dictatorially, a sense of 'order' and 'unity' on a previously 'free' market for labour and goods essential to the war effort. But they did not *absolutely* elevate the claims of capital above those of labour. They requisitioned both; perhaps not in equal proportions (indeed, one is scarcely comparing like with like) and perhaps without reflecting on the possibilities thereby made available to employers to exploit the law for their own domestic ends. Corporatist officials were undoubtedly naïve, perhaps recklessly so, in this respect; it may even be claimed (though with some difficulty) that they were disingenuous in affecting to trust in the 'good faith' of employers not to take advantage of the Munitions Act for objectives other than the furtherance of munitions output. They were not, however, conspiratorial in the sense of waging, in conjunction with employers, a wartime offensive against the working class, the purpose of which was to destroy trade unionism and to leave private employers undisputed masters in their own establishments. Employers' disciplinary excesses, and especially their abuses of the leaving certificate scheme,[84] were, in fact, the subject of further legislative adjustments deemed necessary to restore the corporatist spirit of 'unity' and 'order'. In pursuit of a moral crusade, it was in keeping with corporatist impulses that the centralized bureaucratic élites were prepared to contemplate and to frame legislative proposals to curb the freedom of workers *or* of those employers whose non-'conformativism' was perceived to be inimical to the 'national interest'.

---

[84] For details, see ch. 8 and Rubin, 'Enforcement of the Munitions of War Acts', ch. 2.

Corporatism thus reflects an extreme form of functionalism, which in turn is reliant upon disciplined role-playing. In the case of the tribunal chairmen in Glasgow, they fought hard to varying degrees to further government policy without, as they saw it, compromising their own judicial autonomy and their guardianship of a rule of law by then severely attenuated. Thus, where their actions tilted too much towards autonomy and too far from the narrowly defined policy of which they were agents, they failed to exercise their discretion wisely and failed to measure up to the ruthless requirements demanded by a corporatist ministry. Perhaps for some of these chairmen, the tradition of judicial independence proved a more powerful and hypnotic, but unfortunately more hazardous, beacon by which to attempt to navigate the rocks of industrial unrest, than were the insensitive dictates of autocratic law. In this respect, such noble sentiments were worthless to a corporatist-inspired élite, whose demands for discipline, commitment, and predictability embraced their own local administrators as well as the munitions workers themselves. For Hinton,[85] the shop stewards' movement represented a revolt against the 'servile state'. But perhaps there were other, more ambiguous, revolts directed against an autocratic department of State conceived in comparable, if in conceptually distinct, terms. The 'maverick' activities of the unfortunate Glasgow tribunal chairmen, which ultimately led to *their* 'deportation' (ch. 4), is clearly one protest, albeit one which the executive determinedly suppressed. But the spectacle of tumultuous and rowdy tribunal proceedings (ch. 3), where trade unionists employed intimidatory and blustering tactics at one moment and went on the legal offensive at another, is evidence, as we shall argue, both for working-class resistance to authoritarian state discipline where the boundaries of 'fairness' were thought to have been breached, *and* for their determination to exploit a legal code informed by corporate values. For the paradox of the Munitions Act was that it possessed two faces, on the one hand a blunt restrictiveness designed to curb trade union freedoms, and on the other, a limited flexibility and opportunistic scope which trade unionists resourcefully sought to exploit to the full. It is this phenomenon, the two faces of the Munitions Act, which constitutes the theme of this study.

[85] Hinton, *The First Shop Stewards' Movement*, p. 78.

CHAPTER 2

The Glasgow Munitions Tribunal

INTRODUCTION

The munitions tribunal in Glasgow, though not the first to conduct hearings under the Munitions Act,[1] was destined to become both the busiest[2] and the most controversial among the fifty-five local, and ten general, tribunals. Given that Clydeside was the premier munitions centre in the country, it would have been surprising had this fact not been reflected in the tribunal case load. Thus the statistics reveal (Table 2.1) that in the three-month period, January to March 1916, the Glasgow local tribunal heard more cases than any other tribunal in the British Isles.

THE MUNITIONS TRIBUNAL CHAIRMEN

At the outset some importance was attached by the Ministry of Munitions, in theory at least, to a more informal atmosphere in the tribunals than that which obtained in the courts of law, especially in the criminal courts. In particular, the experience of the unemployment insurance panels set up under the National Insurance Act 1911 was considered a favourable portent, in contrast to the tortuous, legalistic hearings on workmen's compensation in the courts of law. Yet, as the *New Statesman* never tired of stressing, the Munitions Act *was* a criminal law measure.[3] Perhaps this confusion of objectives—an 'informal'

---

[1] That 'honour' was bestowed on the North-West Coast general munitions tribunal sitting in Barrow on 21 July 1915. See MUN 5/353/349/1, 'History of Labour Regulation to February 1916, by Miss C. V. Butler, 22 August 1917'.

[2] Incomplete figures for individual tribunals are available in LAB 2/65/G129/2 (general munitions tribunals) and in LAB 2/66/G129/3 (local munitions tribunals). For further discussion, see G. R. Rubin, 'The Composition of the Munitions Tribunal in Glasgow during the First World War', *Scottish Economic and Social History*, VI (1986), 47–64.

[3] *New Statesman*, 13 Nov. 1915, 124.

Table 2.1 *Local Munitions Tribunals: Total Number of Cases, 1 January–31 March 1916 (tribunals with 50 or more hearings)*

Tribunal	Number	Tribunal	Number
Glasgow	1279	Huddersfield & Halifax	110
Metropolitan	825	Blackburn	105
Birmingham	698	North Staffs	86
Manchester	477	Liverpool	83
Newcastle	432	Southampton	83
Coventry	335	Derby	76
Leeds	253	Nottingham	75
Tees & Darlington	234	Edinburgh	70
Wolverhampton	216	Sheffield	64
Greenock	139	Dundee	50
Belfast	138		

Source: MUN 5/97/349/8

criminal law—was mirrored in the choice of chairmen for the tribunal in Glasgow. For both a professional judge and part-time chairmen of unemployment insurance panels were initially appointed to the posts, though ministry dissatisfaction with the performance of the latter group, as we shall see in Chapter 4, resulted in their replacement in 1916 by another professional judge, seconded from the Sheriff Court. The initial appointees as chairmen to the Glasgow local munitions tribunal in July 1915 were Professor W. M. Gloag, Commander Robert Gibson, and James Andrew, while those appointed as chairmen of the Scotland division of the general munitions tribunal which sat most frequently in Glasgow were Gloag and Sheriff T. A. Fyfe. On the change-over in personnel in April 1916, Sheriff Craigie replaced Gloag, Gibson, and Andrew.

William Murray Gloag (1865–1934)[4] was Professor of Scots Law at Glasgow University, the son of the Court of Session judge, Lord Kincairney.[5] An outstanding scholar, he unfortunately did not cut an imposing figure on the munitions tribunal bench, despite the claim that he was possessed of a 'resolute,

---

[4] For Gloag's biographical details, see the *Bailie*, LXXXVI, No. 2236 (25 Aug. 1915), 3–4; *Who Was Who, 1929–1940;* (Glasgow University) *College Courant*, Whitsun 1955, 83–6; and D. M. Walker, *The Scottish Jurists*, Edinburgh, 1985, ch. 27.

[5] For Kincairney (1828–1909), see *Who Was Who, 1897–1915.*

slightly choleric, slightly pugnacious, Churchillian mien'.[6] He suffered from a minor physical deformity and an associated defect of speech, though not such as to render him a constant object of ridicule at the tribunal. A man of quiet and retiring disposition, never excessively pompous or remote, he was probably not unsuited to the relatively peaceful waters of the unemployment insurance court of referees, where, if occasion demanded, he could exercise his marked intellectual gifts. Yet, as was soon to become obvious, the Glasgow munitions tribunal was no place for a chairman whose only quality was a superb intellect.

Lieutenant-Commander Robert Gibson, RNVR (1871–1955),[7] a solicitor in Glasgow, had been active in municipal affairs as member of the defunct Partick Town Council, where he was appointed Dean of Guild presiding over the court responsible for approving building plans and for enforcing building regulations. A recognized authority on national insurance law, having published a treatise on the subject in 1912, he was, like Gloag, a chairman of the court of referees, and was therefore a logical choice as munitions tribunal chairman. No doubt his experience as a magistrate also counted in his favour, as did his sporting background, which included a spell playing for Queen's Park FC. Yet despite his 'wide experience of workmen and their ways; intimate knowledge of local industrial conditions, and the keenest perspicacity on every phase of these matters'[8], he, also, did not remain long at his post. Described in a local periodical, the *Bailie*, as being 'Tactful yet not afraid to speak his mind when occasion demands', he also displayed other traits of independence. His keen support for local autonomy no doubt rendered him ill-suited to the centralizing activities of a wartime Government department. So the respect in which he was held by members of the local bar proved of no consequence.

---

[6] *College Courant*, 83.

[7] *Bailie*, LXXXVII, No. 2266 (22 Mar. 1916), 3–4; *Scottish Biographies, 1938*, London and Glasgow, 1938, p. 276. Wrote, with T. S. Haran, *Scottish National Insurance. Treatise on the National Insurance Act 1911* (1912). He is not to be confused with Robert Gibson, KC (died 1965) who later became Labour MP for Greenock (1936–41) and subsequently Lord Gibson, a judge of the Court of Session. The author is grateful to Mrs Ruth Ludlam, formerly librarian of the Royal Faculty of Procurators, Glasgow, for having traced Gibson's later career.

[8] *Bailie*, LXXXVII, 4, for this and subsequent quotations.

To have 'realised the popular ideal of a just judge' was perhaps a suitable epitaph to his juridical qualities, but from the ministry's perspective scarcely fitted him for the specialized task of handling obstructive and aggressive munitions workers indignant at the statutory infringements of their traditional freedoms. The third local tribunal chairman appointed was James Andrew (1855–1932), another Glasgow solicitor.[9] Unlike the case with Gibson, there seems little evidence from Andrew's background that he had had much direct contact with working-class experience. Born near Ayr and educated at Ayr Academy and Glasgow University, he built up a large court and commercial practice. For more than twelve years he was a member of the Glasgow Chamber of Commerce, serving a term as a director; he was also a trustee of Glasgow Savings Bank, director of Glasgow Mental Hospital, and governor of the Royal Technical College. Involved in the activities of the Trades House and director of the Merchants' House, he was appointed Dean of the Incorporation of Weavers in 1923. The previous year, he had received an honorary LL D from Glasgow University in part recognition of his duties as solicitor to the university. He was also Dean of the Faculty of Procurators (the local law society) from 1920 to 1923. Apparently very much of a 'lawyer's lawyer', his activities, as we can see, were confined to the business, professional, and academic élite of Glasgow.

When we turn to the final name among those Glasgow chairmen appointed in 1915, we move, in the Ministry of Munitions' evaluation, from the inept to the incomparable. Thomas Alexander Fyfe (1852–1928) was born in Dundee, the son of Thomas Fyfe, secretary of the Perth and Dunkeld Railway, and spent his early years in legal practice in Edinburgh.[10] Eventually moving to Glasgow, he built up an extensive mercantile practice, acting for some of the leading ship-owning firms and members of the Scottish Shipmasters' Association called before Board of Trade enquiries. It is not,

---

[9] Ibid., cii, No. 2659 (26 Sept. 1923), 4; *Glasgow Herald*, 23 June 1922; ibid., 7 Mar. 1932; ibid., 3 June 1932; *Bulletin*, 7 Mar. 1932; *Glasgow Chamber of Commerce Journal*, xv (Apr. 1932), 65; *Evening Times*, 7 Mar. 1932; *Scots Law Times (News)*, 1932, 54–5.

[10] For biographical details, see the *Bailie*, xlvi, No. 1198 (2 Oct. 1895), 1–2; ibid., No. 1449a (25 July, 1901); *Glasgow Herald*, 12 June 1917; *The Times*, 16 Mar. 1928; *Scottish Country Life*, xv (Apr. 1928), 166; *Who Was Who, 1916–1928*.

however, clear whether this involvement brought him into close contact with the Clyde shipbuilders who were to feature prominently at the munitions tribunals.

It is apparent that Fyfe was an outstanding member of the local bar, for it was uncommon to appoint solicitors to the bench of sheriffs, whose ranks were normally filled by Edinburgh-based advocates. Yet Fyfe attained this honour in 1895, filling a vacancy as sheriff-substitute in Lanark. Six years later he was transferred to Glasgow, which was in reality, if not in form, a promotion. He was instrumental in the drafting of the important Sheriff Courts Act 1907 and gave evidence to several royal and departmental commissions. He published works on Scottish bankruptcy law, on the law and practice of the sheriff court, and, also, on the Munitions Acts in a volume which ran to three editions between 1916 and 1918.

Fyfe was active politically before his elevation to the bench. For a number of years, he was secretary of the Glasgow Conservative Association, developing and improving its organization, and securing a favourable interpretation of the lodger franchise legislation. This enabled his party locally to improve on its previous electoral performances, and in particular, to triumph in 1900.

The quality which he sought to bring to the munitions tribunal was sternness tinged with a touch of humour; and he manifested a contradictory urge both to speak *down* to munitions workers appearing before him and also to establish a *rapport* with them, which may, indeed, have been modelled on Lloyd George's populist appeals.[11] What he stressed consistently was the prevailing spirit of sacrifice (as he construed it) and the bounden duty of workers not to steal a march on the rest of their comrades at home and in the trenches. Strikes and industrial indiscipline were morally reprehensible because they were the actions of selfish individuals at a time when all were expected to limit, if not forgo, advancement in the 'national interest'.

Thus, when a group of strikers of military age appeared before him on one occasion, his condemnation was unequivocal.

---

[11] On one occasion, an apprentice brass-finisher applied for a leaving certificate on the ground that he did not like his job and desired to go into engineering. Sheriff Fyfe observed that he 'didn't like his job either but that he'd have to keep it till the war was over'. See *Glasgow Herald*, 4 May 1916.

Any man who took part in a strike in his country's day of stress showed himself unable to grasp the national situation, and his own feeling had been for some time that the best way, perhaps the most effective way of making them realise the situation would be to send them out to the hottest part of the front. There, he thought, they would probably realise. Of course he had no power to do that. He sometimes regretted he had not. It was disgraceful that young men of military age should deliberately and defiantly ignore the Munitions Act.[12]

One must, however, recognize that he could on occasion be forthright in his condemnation of employers. For the promotion of the 'corporate spirit'[13] also required some minimal conformity among *private*, capitalist interests to the bureaucratically defined national interest. One minor but notable instance occurred in December 1916 when six charge-hand carpenters sought leaving certificates in response to their employer's refusal to award them overtime rates.[14] The employer, a firm of Partick shipbuilders (probably the Meadowside Shipyard), explained that the men had not processed their claim 'through the proper channel'. Sheriff Fyfe, however, wasted no time in putting his message across. 'I wish some employers', he said, 'would get away from domineering methods. There would be less friction if employers would adopt less of the attitude, "It is for us to say". At the present time, it was not for employers to say.'[15] And with a flourish he sent them all packing to hold a conference. The maintenance of social peace, in accordance with the dictates of the Ministry of Munitions, was his principal remit. He did not always get the chemistry right; for experimentation was unavoidable, with the result that industrial unrest was sometimes stimulated rather than suppressed by his judgments, as in the case of the imprisoned Fairfield shipwrights. But his sternness and intimidatory techniques achieved a level of success which clearly satisfied the ministry, in *spite* of the highly explosive atmosphere. For Fyfe was a shrewd operator in a difficult and sensitive situation where his 'no-nonsense'

---

[12] Ibid., 12 Nov. 1917.
[13] A term used by Fyfe in the report of the Scottish section of the Commission of Enquiry into Industrial Unrest which he chaired in 1917. See PP 1917–18 Cd. 8669, xv, 133, para. 6.
[14] *Glasgow Herald*, 25 Dec. 1916.
[15] Ibid.

approach, though liable on occasion to court disaster, contrasted sharply with that of his weaker colleagues on the tribunal bench. Testimony to his prowess in this respect is that the turbulent scenes of the first nine months of the tribunal (ch. 3) receded immediately after the imposition by Fyfe of relatively hefty fines, in some cases amounting to £20 and £25, levied on prominent activists and shop stewards after the 'deportation strikes' in March 1916. Though the dangerous expedient of imprisonment had been removed from the range of punishments available in January 1916, Sheriff Fyfe's harsh and disciplinarian tactics ultimately succeeded in restoring order to the tribunal. His judicial stance, however, enjoyed less success in quelling unrest in the factories outside. Indeed, his experience as chairman of the Scottish division of the Commission on Industrial Unrest perhaps served merely to confirm the unpalatable truth that working-class grievances received prompt attention only when a strike was threatened.[16] His power was therefore limited to altering behaviour *within* the tribunal. He could not influence workshop conduct for the better (as the Ministry of Munitions defined it) by a succession of convictions. What he *did* attempt by his conduct as chairman, though not always successfully, was to seek not to exacerbate the situation in the factories, a task which his fellow chairmen were unable to accomplish.

Yet it is important to recognize the qualities demanded of such a chairman. He was required to acknowledge that the law was coercive, that it had on occasion to be applied uncompromisingly, that it embodied executive policy, and that as a judge (or, perhaps, despite being a judge) he was required to enforce a policy as much as a law. Therefore, it was not his juridical qualities which mattered, but his own commitment to a bureaucratically determined code of discipline. His role was that of policeman, and not judge, nor politician, nor lobbyist; he was to be a policy-enforcer and not a policy-maker gratuitously offering suggestions and venturing opinions from behind the shield of judicial independence. 'You have to remember that for some years past there has been considerable nibbling at the

[16] Cf. M. B. Hammond, *British Labor Conditions and Legislation During the War*, New York, 1919, p. 254.

individuality of the worker. During all his working hours he is merely a cipher—known by a check number.'[17] For 'worker', read 'munitions tribunal chairman'. It was Fyfe's achievement in imbibing this lesson and evidently approving it which made him the Ministry of Munitions' favourite son among tribunal chairman, and which no doubt earned him the CBE as his reward after the war.

As well as presiding at munitions tribunals, Fyfe was also called upon by the Board of Trade to act as arbiter in settling wage disputes, and in this capacity he often voiced sentiments similar to those expressed at the munitions tribunal. For example, in settling a claim between Glasgow Corporation and the Municipal Employees' Association, he observed that it was

frequently erroneously assumed that the object of such awards was to bring present-day remuneration up to the full equivalent, in purchasing power, of pre-war wages; but this he did not think was their purpose. These awards did not contemplate that operatives, any more than any other class of the community, were to be entirely relieved of their quota of the war sacrifice, which was common to all classes. . . .[18]

Indeed, Fyfe himself was to suffer the tragic loss of his two sons, killed in battle, in addition to which he lost his wife in the traumatic year of 1915. For him, 'sacrifice' clearly had an added poignancy. It is possible, of course, that the experience of domestic bereavements among both munitions and military tribunal chairmen conduced to hardened attitudes towards those individuals appearing before such bodies,[19] though in Fyfe's case his strength of purpose had never been in doubt.

From 1 April 1916, Fyfe was joined as tribunal chairman by his fellow sheriff, John Craigie (1857–1919), who replaced the dismissed trio of Gloag, Gibson, and Andrew. Craigie[20] had been appointed to the bench of the Glasgow Sheriff Court in

[17] Clyde Workers' Committee statement to Lloyd George, published in the *Worker*, 15 Jan. 1916, cited in Hinton, *The First Shop Stewards' Movement*, London, 1973, p. 45.

[18] *Glasgow Herald*, 5 Oct. 1917; LAB 2/144/IC4060/2 (24 Sept. 1917). For his award in the dispute between the Amalgamated Society of Woodcutting Machinists and Glasgow Corporation Tramways Department, see LAB 2/149/IC3939 (30 May 1917).

[19] The present author is grateful to Douglas Gourlay of Robert Gordon's Institute of Technology, Aberdeen, for making this suggestion.

[20] Born Blairgowrie, educated Perth Academy and Edinburgh University. Bar 1884; KC 1905. See *Glasgow Herald*, 20 Oct. 1919.

1910, prior to which he had built up a large workmen's compensation practice and had argued the Liberal cause at public meetings. During the war, he also became chairman of the Clyde District Maritime Board, which had been instituted by the Shipping Controller to secure close co-operation between employers and workers, and, in particular, to prevent disputes between employers and seamen. His munitions tribunal work remained modest and unspectacular, and during his tenure of office he was permanently overshadowed by Fyfe's looming presence.

There was one other lawyer on the staff of the Glasgow tribunal who merits consideration. This was the tribunal clerk, Thomas F. Wilson, who worked closely with Fyfe throughout the war. His role was not confined solely to organizing the day-to-day activities of the tribunal, arranging for the order of proceeding, or even offering legal advice when the occasion demanded. His opinions in matters of policy were also sought, though not always followed. Whether he identified closely with Fyfe's general approach is unclear, since the necessary evidence is lacking; he was probably more cautious, but his position clearly allowed him to be so.

Born in 1862, the son of a Glasgow builder and contractor, he became a solicitor, practising in his native city. A Liberal member of Lanarkshire County Council, he was selected as Liberal candidate for the Lanarkshire North-East by-election in 1909, when he successfully held the seat for his party, an achievement he repeated at the two general elections of 1910.[21]

He did not remain long in Parliament, however. Instead, he accepted the appointment of Clerk of the Peace for Glasgow where his work brought him into contact with Fyfe. His experience of the busiest sheriff court in Scotland with a huge criminal division made him an appropriate choice of the Ministry of Munitions for the clerkship of the munitions tribunals in the city, a position which proved enormously lucrative. Indeed, in the first nine months of the tribunal, Wilson received £1,326 11s. 6d. despite a ministry limit of £1,000 for comparable salaried posts. The problem for the

[21] *Bailie*, XC, No. 2332 (27 June 1917), 3–4; *Stother's Glasgow, Lanarkshire and Renfrewshire Xmas and New Year Annual, 1911–12*, p. 151.

ministry apparently was that he was not a salaried official, nor
drawing a pension, so the maximum limit was difficult to
enforce.[22]
Deeply involved in the cluster of committees which mush-
roomed during the war, Wilson became chairman of committees
for recruiting, Belgian refugees, naval and military pensions,
and war savings, as well as acting as secretary to the Scottish
division of the Commission on Industrial Unrest in 1917, the
chairman of which was Sheriff Fyfe. On a number of occasions,
he was also appointed to act as an arbiter to resolve differences
between employers and unions.[23] Certainly, his interventions
during munitions tribunal hearings were rare and unspectacular, amounting to no more than the odd observation or two on
the evidence being presented or asking a particular question
arising therefrom.[24]
But it was his influence in the selection of personnel for the
Glasgow munitions tribunal which we may note. His judgment
of the abilities of assessors and potential assessors was clearly
welcomed by the Ministry of Munitions. For example, apart
from frequent suggestions as to possible candidates, his favourable opinion of individual assessors who subsequently resigned
their positions could persuade the ministry to write to such
individuals requesting that they reconsider their resignation.
One such case in 1917 was that of John Thomson, the general
secretary of the Associated Blacksmiths,[25] who none the less

[22] LAB 2/173/MW167737/7 (Mar. 1916). The scale of fees for clerks was originally 1
guinea per day of sitting, plus 1 guinea per complaint processed. Subsequent alterations
to the amounts took place at various intervals. See MUN 5/353/349/1. For the
complaint of the tribunal chairman, Sir William Clegg, the 'Tsar of Sheffield', that he
was underpaid for his patriotic service at the tribunal, see MUN 5/97/349/8 (13 May
1916).
[23] For example, a wage dispute between the Smiths and Strikers' Union and the
National Projectile Factory at Cardonald. See *Labour Gazette*, June 1918, 244; LAB
2/425/IC432/2 (14 May 1918). For other hearings involving Wilson as arbiter, see LAB
2/486/IC7334/2–3 (Amalgamated Society of Farriers, Manchester, Oct. 1918); LAB
2/498/IC7562/2 (National Union of Corporation Workers and Edinburgh and Leith
Corporations, Gas Commissioners and Water Trust, Oct. 1918); and LAB
2/188/IC/4775/4 (British Aluminium Company, Kinlochleven and Workers Union, 8
Nov. 1918).
[24] Cf. the leaving certificate cases reported in the *Glasgow Herald*, 24 Aug. 1915 and
ibid., 23 Dec. 1915; also a case involving apprentices, in ibid., 6 June 1917.
[25] For Thomson, generally, see Angela Tuckett, *The Blacksmiths' History*, London,
1975.

replied that he had 'done my little share, often at great personal inconvenience'. Inasmuch as Wilson considered Thomson's assistance 'most valuable',[26] we may be sure that the 'national interest' was well served by Thomson's presence.

In the controversy surrounding the removal of the three local tribunal chairmen, Gibson, Gloag, and Andrew (ch. 4), Wilson tended to offer cautious advice to the Ministry of Munitions. He foresaw political and industrial dangers were there to be any changes among the chairmen. Outside observers, he suggested, would conclude that the Act's administration on the Clyde was unsatisfactory *or* that chairmen would be seen to be under threat of removal if not sufficiently suppliant to the ministry's wishes; and in writing to the Ministry of Munitions in London in these terms, he enclosed a recent copy of *Forward* to support his points.[27] The fact is that his arguments were unanswerable. The chairmen were under threat precisely for these reasons.

Clearly lacking the ruthlessness of the officials at the Ministry of Munitions, and more circumspect than Fyfe, his contribution to the administration of the war effort sufficiently impressed Government circles to earn him a knighthood in 1918.

WORKMEN'S ASSESSORS

One of the noteworthy features relating to the tribunal personnel concerns the ambiguous role assumed by those appointed as workmen's assessors to the tribunals. Nominally expected on the one hand to represent the employee's viewpoint in the final adjudication, they were, on the other hand, simultaneously a central element in the enforcement machinery of a measure explicitly framed by the Government to inhibit trade unionism. Thus, in exchange for influence on the tribunal (for power resided with the chairmen); and in exchange for official recognition as an integral feature of the apparatus of the wartime state, the workmen's assessors were expected to subordinate the interest of their class to that of the 'national

---

[26] LAB 2/47/MT107/1, 'GMT, No. 8 Division, Scotland: Constitution File'. R. H. H. Keenlyside to Thomson, and reply, 20, 30 Nov. 1917. Keenlyside was head of the munitions tribunal section of the Ministry of Munitions.

[27] Ibid., Wilson to Wolff, 19 Feb. 1916.

interest' wherever the two were in conflict. It is hardly surprising that this conflict of roles was widely exposed in the shape of trade union criticism throughout the country of the quality of workmen's representatives. Yet given that their appointment as assessors rendered them almost as strait-jacketed as munitions workers themselves, it is difficult not to appreciate their dilemma. For the collaboration of the national trade union leaders had left them with little choice but to seek to exert their modest influence on the tribunal proceedings. There was, in truth, no prospect of any heroic boycott on the part of labour. The contradictory poses of an 'oppositional culture'[28] and the subordination of class differences in order to further the national interest, came face to face in the tribunal. The latter impulse, of course, invariably prevailed; but ironically, it did so on terms which occasionally *favoured* that oppositional culture and inhibited the employing class.

For the most part, however, the tribunal operated as, and was perceived as, a fetter on traditional trade union freedoms; and workmen's assessors were, of course, part of this restrictive mechanism. Yet, despite this, hostility to workmen's assessors in Glasgow, though occasionally heard within the Clyde Workers' Committee, was scarcely noticeable. Partly, they tended to adopt a low profile during hearings, interjecting during the proceedings only on rare occasions. This itself might have been a cause for complaint, but the fact is that a more visible and controversial target, particularly in the shapes of Professor Gloag and Sheriff Fyfe, could be identified. Additionally, the alleged split between the rank and file and local trade union officials (a number of the latter were appointed as assessors) proved in practice to be less pronounced than previous accounts of the Clydeside shop stewards' movement imply.[29] The schism undoubtedly existed. It is manifested in several munitions tribunal hearings where the officials were by-passed. Yet the local full-time officers, as well as doubling as assessors, frequently appeared on the 'other' side of the fence, representing

[28] For this term, see James Hinton, *Labour and Socialism: A History of the British Labour Movement*, Brighton, 1983.

[29] This absence of a split seems to have been particularly true in the case of the shipbuilding trades examined by Alastair Reid in his thesis, 'The Division of Labour in the British Shipbuilding Industry, 1880–1920', Cambridge Univ. Ph.D. thesis (1980).

their members (with aggressive determination) before the tribunals. It is in this sense that the relationship between the rank and file and trade union leaders was often subtle and complex, reflecting the tensions which wartime Government policies were imposing on the structures of trade unions. This feature will, perhaps, become apparent in the course of an examination of those trade union officials who sat on the Glasgow munitions tribunal as workmen's assessors.

The first batch were appointed from the courts of referees established under the national insurance legislation. Yet, as G. D. H. Cole indicated, 'the part played by the labour assessors has been so far negligible.'[30] Indeed, he insisted that appointments from the national insurance panels were 'unlikely to secure the right men for the quite different functions which munitions assessors have to perform'. As a result, claimed Cole, 'all sections of workers joined in the demand . . . for the revisions of the panels of assessors if the system was retained.'[31] This eventually led the Ministry of Munitions to invite nominations directly from the trade unions.[32] In fact, many of the original worker-nominees to the Glasgow tribunal (or to the Scotland tribunal sitting in Glasgow) were trade unionists whose services were retained in spite of the adoption of new criteria for appointment.

Among those trade union officials selected to the panels were John Thomson, general secretary of the Associated Blacksmiths; William Lorimer, his assistant general secretary; Robert Climie, district organizer of the Workers' Union; William Brodie and William Kerr, organizing district delegates of the ASE; Sam Bunton, the ASE district secretary; Harry Hopkins of Govan Trades Council, who replaced Bunton as district secretary when the latter joined the Ministry of Labour in 1917; James Fulton, president of the Associated Iron-moulders of Scotland; Owen Coyle, county councillor and district organizer, then general secretary, pro tem, of the Amalgamated Society of Steel and Iron Workers of Great Britain; W. G. Sharp and James Conley, respectively district secretary and district delegate (until 1916) of the Boilermakers' Society; R. Mitchell, district secretary of

---

[30] *Nation*, 27 Nov. 1915, 325.
[31] G. D. H. Cole, *Trade Unionism and Munitions*, Oxford, 1923, p.116.
[32] Cf. E. Sylvia Pankhurst, *The Home Front*, London 1932, p.188.

the Amalgamated Society of Woodcutting Machinists; Alexander Richmond of the Sheet Iron Workers' Union; Alexander Turnbull, district secretary of the National Society of Coppersmiths; Councillor George Kerr, Scottish divisional organizer of the Workers' Union; J. F. Armour of the Masons; William Lawson, district organizer of the Carpenters and Joiners, and T. Barron, its trade secretary; Councillor William Westwood JP, of the Shipwrights' Association (later its general secretary, 1929–45) and of the Glasgow Labour Party; and Robert Reid, district secretary of the Electrical Trades Union. Among the female assessors appointed in Glasgow after the passing of the Munitions Amendment Act in 1916 were Agnes Adam and Lois Young of the National Federation of Women Workers, and Agnes Dollan of the Women's Peace Crusade.[33]

Many other names of worker-assessors appear either in the Ministry of Munitions papers or in the newspaper reports of hearings, and it may well be the case that a number will have been 'unrepresentative' legacies from the unemployment insurance panels. Among those listed above, Lorimer, Climie, Hopkins, Coyle, Mitchell, Richmond, and Turnbull were in fact recruited as assessors long after the original appointees, though it does not follow that the new appointments in Glasgow were specifically selected to replace assessors considered unsatisfactory by fellow trade unionists. For the tribunal clerk T. F. Wilson constantly faced difficulties trying to recruit an adequate number of assessors, in view of the resignations which occurred and of the difficulties which those working at their trade experienced in trying to obtain time off work to attend hearings.[34] Even without the impetus of criticisms of existing workmen's assessors, the fact that panellists might move out of the area, might die unexpectedly, have too much work, or be recruited into the Army would all contribute to the change in the composition of the workmen's panel.

None the less, the striking feature of the most prominent of the

---

[33] The names are taken either from a small proportion of newspaper reports of hearings or from lists in LAB 2/47/MT107/1. For the sad circumstances surrounding Conley's retirement as a full-time union official, see J. E. Mortimer, *History of the Boilermakers' Society*, vol. II 1906–1939, London, 1982, pp. 86–7. For other assessors, see below.

[34] LAB 2/47/MT107/1, Wilson to Llewellyn Smith, 1 Mar. 1918. This proved to be a problem for tribunal sittings throughout Scotland.

worker-nominees to the Glasgow tribunal was their capacity to indulge in the exercise of role-reversal. From a role as tribunal assessors sitting in judgment on members of their own class (though not on members of their own union), they experienced no difficulty in slipping into a diametrically opposed role the following day when they might be found aggressively attacking the tribunal justice, which was perceived as callously dragging their constituents before a crass and abominable prosecution. It is the recognition of this duality in respect to the wartime activities of the union officials in Glasgow which serves as a warning to historians not to present the internal divisions within the local unions as permanent and irreversible schisms.

EMPLOYERS' ASSESSORS

Those selected to the employers' panel included a number of prominent representatives of the leading engineering and shipbuilding companies in the district. Yet they were only infrequently called upon to adjudicate, given the policy of the Ministry of Munitions of seeking to appoint assessors for particular cases from trades other than those directly involved in hearings. Thus individuals such as Robert Baird of the Coalowners' Association and James Dalrymple, general manager of Glasgow Corporation Tramways Department;[35] Andrew S. Biggart (1857–1917), chairman of the civil engineering firm of Sir William Arrol & Co. Ltd.;[36] Thomas Lyon, another building employer; and representatives of the iron and steel trades such as John King of the National Light Castings Association,[37] James Steven, president of the Scottish Brassfounders, R. M. McDougall, president of the Scottish

---

[35] For Dalrymple, see ch. 3, n. 14.

[36] See his obituary in the *Glasgow Herald*, 27 Apr. 1917. While it is nowhere expressly stated, it seems clear that he was the brother of Thomas Biggart, secretary of the Clyde Shipbuilders' Association and of the local engineering employers' association and who was closely involved in a number of controversial tribunal prosecutions.

[37] King was a former Glasgow bailie (councillor-magistrate) who had solicited the appointment as assessor by writing to Beveridge. He had the backing of Sir Archibald Denny of Denny's Shipyard, Dumbarton, who had resigned as assessor in Sept. 1915. See LAB 2/47/MT107/1.

coppersmiths,[38] and J. Fleming, of the Motherwell steel firm of Marshall, Fleming & Co., were all appointed to the panels alongside the large number of representatives of the engineering and shipbuilding sectors. Among this group were to be found W. Rowan Thomson, president of the local engineering employers' association;[39] George Brown, Coventry Ordnance; N. O. Fulton, Albion Motors; James Lang, Lang of Johnstone; W. MacFarlane, Armstrong Whitworth, Airdrie; Sam Mavor, Mavor & Coulson Ltd.; Hugh Reid, N. B. Loco; Archibald Campbell, Beardmore; J. Fullerton, Messrs John Fullerton, Paisley, shipbuilders; Hugh MacMillan and George Strachan, Fairfield; J. R. Richmond, Weir's of Cathcart;[40] A. Anderson of Queen's Park Loco; and Sam Crush of Yarrow's Shipyard.[41] Many of these firms were, of course, the venues of radical shop steward activity; while in different contexts they were involved as employers in legal proceedings before the tribunals, either defending claims that they had implemented unauthorized wage changes, prosecuting strikers or bad time-keepers, or refusing to grant leaving certificates. The composition of the tribunals often, indeed, took on the character of an incestuous, if not always cosy, relationship among its personnel, especially where, as sometimes occurred, the same three panellists (chairman and two assessors) were reappointed for subsequent hearings.

The surge of criticism directed nationally against workmen's assessors did not find its counterpart in the case of employers' panellists. Employers did, from time to time, express dissatisfaction at the conduct of proceedings, but criticisms from this source were, over all, muted. For example, Matthew Paul, a shipbuilder, reported to the Clyde Shipbuilders' Association on his unsatisfactory experience as assessor at the prosecution of

---

[38] Both Steven and McDougall were signatories to a memorial, *Acceleration of Output on Government Work*, which the Scottish munitions employers' federations sent to Asquith and to Lloyd George in June 1915 and which no doubt increased the pressure on the government to pass the Munitions Act.

[39] He was the inventor of the Rowan premium bonus system. See Hinton, *The First Shop Stewards' Movement*, p. 89.

[40] On Richmond, see W. J. Reader, *The Weir Group: A Centenary History*, London, 1971, and Eric Wigham, *The Power to Manage: A History of the Engineering Employers' Federation*, London, 1973.

[41] For Crush, see below.

strikers from the Robb Caledon shipyard in Dundee in the autumn of 1915, while W. Rowan Thomson echoed these sentiments in respect of his own experiences. When the Ministry of Munitions wrote to the employers' federations in January 1916 inviting suggestions, alterations, or additions to the employers' panels, the executives of the local shipbuilders and engineers expressed their conviction that assessors with practical knowledge of working conditions be appointed. In particular, they felt that such appointees ought to be principals of firms, or managers or assistant managers in charge of workmen,[42] perhaps seeking to eliminate those not from the munitions trades. To a limited extent, therefore, the local engineering and shipbuilding employers were displaying impatience with what they suspected was the subordination of their class interests on the altar of the Government's strategy of wartime 'collectivism'.

In only one instance, however, did this issue assume significance for the Glasgow tribunal when Sam Crush, a director of Yarrow's Shipyard, Scotstoun, decided to register his dissatisfaction with the failure of the tribunal adequately to consider the difficulties of shipbuilding employers.

THE SAM CRUSH AFFAIR

The incident arose in April 1916 following the summary dismissal of three riveters from Yarrow's who had been accused by the management of smoking and idling at work. Under the 1916 Amendment Act which had recently come into force, it was provided under Section 5(3) that a workman dismissed without reasonable cause, and with less than a week's notice or wages in lieu, was entitled to claim compensation from his employer, up to a maximum of £5. It was also stipulated in the Section that an employer was required to report the dismissal and the reason for the action so taken to the Labour Exchange within twenty-four hours. Partly this was to enable a rapid deployment of the workman elsewhere; but it was also laid down in the rules that the manager of the Exchange was to send notice of such report to the workman, enabling him to lodge a

---

[42] Clyde Shipbuilders' Association, *Minute Book* No. 9, 25 Oct. 1915 and 10 Jan. 1916.

complaint with the tribunal if he so desired. In the case of the three Yarrow's riveters, they had accepted their week's money on pay-night (but not the wages in lieu), obtained their leaving certificates, and left the company. However, three weeks later they put forward a claim to the tribunal for statutory compensation, but were turned down by Sheriff Fyfe on the ground that the claim for compensation had not been made within twenty-four hours. As an editorial in the *Glasgow Herald*,[43] noting the requirement on *employers* to report dismissals within twenty-four hours, remarked at the time, 'what is sauce for the goose is sauce for the gander.' The only difficulty, however, was that the statute could not be read in such a way. The limitation applied expressly to the employer's notice to the Labour Exchange and did not impose any limitation on workmen in pursuing compensation claims. The probability is that Fyfe concluded that the riveters had been encouraged by their union to submit claims as a test case; for the possibility of their remaining unemployed for any length of time, given the leaving certificates in their pockets, was remote. Indeed, it seems that Fyfe smelled a rat. The Ministry's local reports officer, J. Turner MacFarlane, wrote to his superior, Walter Payne, in London, pointing out that the brief report of the case in the *Glasgow Herald* (above), together with its leader, 'does not give in full some very emphatic remarks the Chairman made' concerning the scope and intention of the compensation provision.[44] MacFarlane added that the riveters (whose names were James Maclean, J. F. Harper, and John Mullancy) had stated that they could not find employment for two weeks, but they only offered vague explanations. Nor could they deny the common knowledge that there was a great demand for men of their skill and that those with leaving certificates could obtain employment anywhere. The sheriff, 'as he is always doing', hammered out the ministry's policy of constancy and discipline at work, thus justifying the tribunal's decision as being intended to 'discourage any man who can get work, staying off work a single hour'. He therefore warned the workmen that no man would be allowed to 'lie off work' relying on the compensation provision,

43 *Glasgow Herald*, 10 Apr. 1916.
44 LAB 2/63/MT167/6, 'Glasgow Local Munitions Tribunal, Constitution File', MacFarlane to Payne, 10 Apr. 1916.

'which may make him indifferent for the moment to working for wages'. As to the employers' failure to inform the labour exchange of the dismissals within the regulation twenty-four hours, this was brushed aside as a mere technical breach. The men, however, lodged appeals, no doubt with the encouragement, or even at the instigation of their union. T. F. Wilson, the tribunal clerk, in writing to Wolff in London, actually thought Fyfe's decision doubtful under the legislation and also inexpedient, even though a 'considerable' delay between dismissal and claim could, he thought, be time barred.[45] Indeed, the appeal judge Lord Dewar did set aside Fyfe's ruling,[46] and the upshot was that, with the procedural objection of the employers repelled, the case was now remitted to the Glasgow tribunal for retrial on the merits.

The retrial was heard a fortnight later when Sam Crush appeared on behalf of his firm, and William Mackie,[47] the Clyde district delegate of the Boilermakers' Society, represented the riveters. According to Crush,[48] he had found the men smoking between decks on a warship urgently required by the Admiralty. He had cautioned the chief man of the squad and warned him that serious steps would be taken if the smoking were repeated. Four days later, the assistant manager again found them smoking on board and idling their time, as a result of which they were dismissed on 29 February. Three weeks elapsed before he heard anything more about the matter. When asked by Fyfe to explain the delay, Mackie devastated the employers' case by disclosing that nearly all the time was lost in trying to effect a compromise with Crush. The outcome now turned on the issue whether dismissal without notice was too harsh a punishment for illicit smoking. Since Crush himself had admitted that smoking was permitted during overtime and on Sundays, and since the men insisted that they had never heard of a by-law in any Clyde shipyard against smoking, nor had known of any man instantly dismissed for doing so, the outcome was not

---

[45] Ibid., Wilson to Wolff, 25 Apr. 1916.
[46] *Maclean, Harper and Mullancy* v. *Yarrow & Co., Ltd.*, 1916 SMAR 5–8; Fyfe, *Employers and Workmen under the Munitions Acts*, 3rd edn., London and Glasgow, 1918, pp. 293–4; *Glasgow Herald*, 27, 31 May 1916.
[47] On Mackie, see USB, *Monthly Report*, July 1915, 16–17.
[48] For the facts, see *Glasgow Herald*, 14 June 1916.

in much doubt. Indeed, the assistant manager, Calvert, had acknowledged that the firm had offered the squad jobs since their dismissal. The tribunal therefore awarded the men £3 each.

Perhaps Crush took the decision as a personal humiliation. Or perhaps he felt that the authority of shipyard employers would be gravely harmed as a result. He certainly appeared to have an extremely simple view of the functions of tribunals—that they ought to enforce discipline in his yard in the manner in which he himself would impose a rigorous regime. That this tribunal failed to do so sufficiently alarmed him to write on the matter that same day to Christopher Addison, Lloyd George's deputy at the Ministry of Munitions.[49] His specific complaints were directed against the fact that the assessors[50] in the case were permitted by Fyfe to 'determine the value of the evidence'. He had believed that the assessors' task was limited to matters concerning the *amount* of compensation. Having thus implicitly criticized Fyfe, he also found fault with Lord Dewar's handling of the appeal, arguing that instead of limiting himself to questions of law, the judge, 'went out of his way to touch on matters of fact, and prejudiced the case on its re-trial by his statement that, "It is a very serious matter for a workman to be dismissed for misconduct, as these workmen were."'[51] For Crush, the 'serious matter' was his attempt to expedite munitions output by checking idling and smoking. Instead, he complained, he was 'handed over to the Sheriff to be mulcted for £9 without the local officials of the Ministry of Munitions lifting a little finger in defence'. This, moreover, was in sharp contrast to the attitude of the Boilermaker's Society which 'threw the whole weight of their great influence' into defending men who had been absent from work for 33–5 per cent of their normal working hours in the previous two months. His parting shot was to attack those employers' assessors 'out of touch with modern shipyard practice', by which was meant, of course, those not adhering to his own blueprint for yard discipline.

On receipt of his letter, the ministry officials mounted an

---

[49] LAB 2/63/MT167/1, 'Glasgow Local Munitions Tribunal: Constitution File', Crush to Addison, 14 June 1916.

[50] Their identities have not been discovered.

[51] Cf. 1916 SMAR, at p. 7.

enquiry. The first matter was the criticism of Fyfe. In Payne's judgment, 'Sheriff Fyfe has shown himself to be one of the most competent, if not in fact the most competent, of the Chairmen of Munitions Tribunals, and I should be surprised to find that the charge of inefficiency which is brought against him, would be generally upheld in Scotland.'[52] He noted that Fyfe was capable of dealing 'very severely indeed' with misdemeanants and lecturing them gravely on the necessity for continuous work. As tribunal chairman, he also frequently went to lengths to arrange settlements between employers and their men. It was only in the first hearing of this case, Payne believed, that Fyfe had been a 'little unfair' to the men, when he insisted on the twenty-four-hour deadline for lodging complaints. Without using the word, Payne no doubt thought the criticism of Fyfe ironic in the circumstances, given his resolute track record.

In the light of this review, the Ministry of Munitions wrote back to Crush on 6 July. The criticism of Fyfe was, inevitably, refuted, the attention of Crush being drawn to the distinction between what constituted evidence (a question of law solely for the legal chairman) and the value of the evidence, on which the chairman was entitled to consult the assessors. As to Dewar's general observation on the seriousness of dismissals for misconduct, Addison, it was conveyed, personally considered that the comment was *not*[53] calculated to prejudice a retrial. Additionally, Crush was informed that the Glasgow local tribunal had recently been reinforced by a considerable number of nominees of the local engineering and shipbuilding federations,[54] so that no further action was necessary in this regard.

The probability is that the Ministry of Munitions thought that Crush had brought about his own difficulties. For it was pointed out that if employers wished to enforce discipline, they could prosecute under the Ordering of Work regulations or could dismiss men with a week's notice. Yarrow's mistake was in failing to prosecute, or in dismissing these men *without* a week's

---

[52] LAB 2/62/MT167/1, Payne to Keenlyside, 27 June 1916, Section III of memorandum.

[53] The word 'not' was omitted before 'calculated'. The context clearly shows that this was accidental, however.

[54] There were in fact forty-six new names from the engineers and twelve from the shipbuilders. See ibid.

notice or wages in lieu. Relentless to the end, Crush wrote back.[55] First he pointed out that Sheriff Craigie, newly appointed to the tribunal bench, had just issued a decision contrary to that of Fyfe. Since it arose in an identical case, Crush predicted that such inconsistency was 'not conducive to discipline in Clyde Shipyards'. Turning next to the matter of assessors, he believed that in spite of the recent additions, the panels were still 'indifferently reformed'. During a recent hearing,[56] he had sat with a fellow assessor who was, he said, a house plasterer. 'He was perfectly honest, but hopelessly devoid of cognate knowlege', opined the worthy shipbuilder. Indeed, referring to the Yarrow's riveters' case itself, he was clearly outraged that the employers' assessor was from the cashiers' office of a fellow shipbuilding firm.[57] 'In no Shipyard on the Clyde or elsewhere, is it usual in the settlement of disputes with the Black Squad to call in the aid of the Cashiers' Office, or to attach the slightest importance to any views they may hold,' he claimed. His demand for the appointment only of 'technical men' and for the sheriff to call, on occasion, for the advice of the Admiralty Superintendent of Contract Work in deciding such cases certainly harked back to a purer era of the men of 'push-and-go'.[58] But just as wars were too important to be left to the generals, so the Ministry of Munitions no doubt concluded that wartime industrial relations were too important to be left to the suggestions of eccentric, autocratic, and self-opinionated employers,[59] insensitive to the maintenance, so far as possible, of

[55] Ibid., Crush to Addison, 10 July 1916. The ministry had contemplated the possibility of an assessor from the Admiralty sitting in cases in which the Admiralty had an interest, but doubted its practicality. See ibid., Payne to Keenlyside, Section IV. Moreover the Admiralty themselves declined to be represented on the tribunals, according to Keenlyside.

[56] For other hearings involving Crush, see *Glasgow Herald*, 9 Feb., 14 Apr. 1916.

[57] Perhaps this was David Cameron, accountant at the Dalmuir works of the large Glasgow munitions and shipbuilding firm of Beardmore. Cameron featured prominently in the 'gun-mounting' department dispute in Dec. 1915. See ch. 3, for this incident.

[58] This referred to Lloyd George's experiment of introducing businessmen into the newly-established Ministry of Munitions in mid-1915. See D. Lloyd George, *War Memoirs*, vol. I, London, 1933, pp. 246–51.

[59] But in the case of Crush, evidently not without influence in high places. For H. A. Watt, Liberal MP for Glasgow College, raised the matter in Parliament in such a way as to imply that the riveters had been awarded compensation by the tribunal, 'in respect of dismissal due to smoking and idling during working hours'. For Mackie's condemnation of this character assassination, see his letter in the *Glasgow Herald*, 18 July 1916.

harmonious relations between trade unions and employers. Three months later, the Clyde Shipbuilders' Association submitted a further list of names of possible panellists to the general tribunal. Crush's name was on the list. He was not appointed.[60]

CONCLUSION

In truth, it mattered little *who* were the employers' or workers' representatives on the munitions tribunals. They performed a very minor and singularly inept role in the proceedings. Where the tribunal chairmen were weak, the best that workers might expect from the employee assessors was that any punishment fixed might be less than the chairman would otherwise be inclined to impose; while employers' assessors consoled themselves with the knowledge that, at least till the Amendment Act of 1916, the role of assessors was advisory only, with the final decision, whether on fact or law, resting with the chairman. The 1916 Act did declare that the chairman was to be guided by the assessors if they were agreed upon the facts in issue. This, however, amounted to no more than a cosmetic adjustment, for matters were usually never that simple.

Where the chairman was a strong personality, such as Fyfe, he frankly had no need of assessors. Assessors, in short, merely symbolized the appeal to corporate unity which underpinned the Government's strategy for the munitions sector of the war economy. The concept of an assessor both representing the 'interests' of employees or employers and advancing the national interest was always dangerously flawed and contradictory. It is because the assessors in general mutely suppressed their role as representatives of interest groups that conflict between tribunal chairmen and assessors was so rare an occurrence. Class conflict involving worker assessors *within* the confines of the tribunal was thus left to those who, wearing a different hat for a different occasion, also performed the role of

---

[60] Lab 2/47/MT/107/1. This showed a singular lack of gratitude to the informant who had sent the ministry a copy of a pamphlet, 'To All Clyde Workers', issued by the Clyde Workers Committee (CWC), the rank-and-file shop stewards' committee whose leaders were later deported by the Government. See BEV III, 13, fos. 79–85, and ch. 3.

advocates for the defence. To this extent, trade union officials such as Bunton, Brodie, Sharp, Mackie, and Coyle, as we shall see in subsequent chapters, left their imprint on the tribunal in such a convincing manner that the character of the tribunal was shaped by their initiatives. But even their domination of the proceedings, impressive though it was, fell short of the magisterial sway and aplomb with which Fyfe performed his difficult tasks.

CHAPTER 3

Strike Prosecutions and the Tribunal: Constructive Aggression and the Lawyers' Retreat, 1915–1916

INTRODUCTION

William Gallacher, one of the leading wartime shop stewards on Clydeside and later the long-serving Communist Member of Parliament for West Fife, recalled in his memoirs that

> Munition Courts were set up and workers were continually being brought before them. Our small [Clyde Workers'] committee[1] was meeting twice a week and every Saturday afternoon we had a meeting of between 300 and 400 stewards. We were always able to get sufficient lads to pack the court when any worker was called before it. McGill [a minor local activist] was always there with the *Herald* and a selection of pamphlets, and used to go along the rows of seats selling his wares until the Sheriff came in. We were able to make such a farce of these courts that eventually the authorities had to abandon them and drop the practice of summoning on trivial charges.[2]

It may be inferred from the above account that the object of the disturbances was to prevent the tribunals from functioning. To test this proposition, we undertake in the present chapter an in-depth examination of probably the most significant proceedings before the Glasgow tribunal (these are summarized in Table 3.1). In the first instance we will note that the tumult

---

[1] The Clyde Workers' Committee (CWC), an association of local shop stewards, grew out of an *ad hoc* shop stewards' committee formed during the first major spontaneous strike on Clydeside during the war. This was the 'tuppence an hour' strike of February 1915, which had its origins in a wage claim lodged with the engineering employers but which was triggered off by local factors at the firm of G. & J. Weir (Cathcart). Rank-and-file activism on Clydeside during the war is therefore usually dated from this dispute. See Hinton, *The First Shop Stewards' Movement*, London, 1973, pp. 103–7; Iain McLean, *The Legend of Red Clydeside*, Edinburgh, 1983, p. 12.

[2] William Gallacher, *Last Memoirs*, London, 1966, pp. 71–2. Cf. idem, *Revolt on the Clyde*, London, 1936, p. 58.

Table 3.1 Cases Discussed in Chapter 3, August 1915–April 1916*

Date of action	Date of hearing	Chairman	Firm	Prosecutor	Description of employees	Type of legal case	Issue	Number of employees	Outcome	Punishment
27 July	2 Aug.	Gloag	Fairfield	Employer	Coppersmiths	Strike prosecution	Demarcation dispute	28**	All guilty	2s. 6d.
27 Aug.	3 Sept.	Fyfe	Fairfield	Ministry	Shipwrights	Strike prosecution	Sympathy strike over sacking and leaving certificate endorsement	26***	17 guilty; 9 cases withdrawn	£10
30 July– 2 Aug.	9 Aug.	Gloag	Lobnitz	Employer	Holders-on	Strike prosecution	Wage demand	29	All guilty	5s.
29–31 Dec.	5, 8 Jan.	Fyfe	Beardmore, Dalmuir	Ministry	Gun-mounting shop engineers	Strike prosecution	Dismissal of shop steward	28	All guilty	£5 (never paid)
17 Mar. et seq.	29 Mar.	Fyfe	Beardmore, Dalmuir; Parkhead Forge; N. B. Diesel, Whiteinch	Ministry	Engineers	Strike prosecution	Restriction and/or deportation of shop steward(s)	30	All guilty	£5
17 Mar. et seq	13 Apr.	Fyfe	Beardmore, Dalmuir and Parkhead Forge (and elsewhere?)	Ministry	Engineers	Strike prosecution	Restriction and/or deportation of shop steward(s)	c. 60****	c. 35 guilty, c. 25 discharged	32, £5 2, £25 1, £20

Source: Compiled from information in ch. 3.
Notes: *The cases are not listed in chronological order.
**300 had struck.
***426 had struck.
****At its peak, it was estimated that not more than 4,500 workers were on strike throughout the district. See Hinton, *The First Shop Stewards' Movement*, p. 157.

accompanying the hearings was not confined solely to those workers attending as spectators at the trials. For we will discover that both the accused trade unionists themselves *and* also those representing them before the tribunal contributed to the rowdiness of the proceedings by conducting themselves in an aggressively insubordinate manner. Moreover, it will be suggested that the tactics thus employed were designed, not to prevent the tribunals from operating, but to secure as favourable an outcome as possible in an otherwise legally hopeless situation. Finally, it will be argued that a crucial element in the struggle against an adverse tribunal judgment was for trade union defendants to seek to undermine the method which judges invariably employed to maintain control of the proceedings. That judicial method was, simply, to retain control over the content of court room conversation in order to ensure that debate was conducted in the 'neutral' categories of legal criteria. At the same time, social or moral judgments, which might otherwise have roused hostile sentiments, would thereby be eschewed. The extent to which the 'constructive aggression' of trade unionists and of their representatives was successful in forcing the 'lawyer's retreat' had consequences for the continued occupancy of the chairmanship of the tribunals by certain of the Glasgow chairmen, as we shall see in Chapter 4. But it is undeniable that such tactics informed the conduct of the hearings, much to the chagrin and exasperation of the tribunal chairmen, as we shall also observe. Workmen's representatives, whether lay trade unionists, full-time officers, or even solicitors, conducted a fierce and uncompromising campaign of threats, accusations, and delaying tactics during the conduct of the hearings. In short, they set out to harry and to harass the chairmen, to undermine their authority, and to reduce the credibility and dignity of the proceedings. The only self-imposed limit was that at no stage did their representatives refuse to recognize the legitimacy of the court or of its right to try their members. Indeed, during some of the more tumultuous hearings, the men's representatives insisted that if the law had been broken, then it was the employers who had infringed the Act. There was therefore no express repudiation of bourgeois or capitalist law (though some shop stewards, as we shall see, appeared to adopt this rejectionist view during the 'deportation strike' hearings in April 1916). Moreover, it would be wrong to describe the hearings where uproar was prevalent as chaotic. The disorder of the proceedings generated by the men's representatives seemed in fact to be fairly structured, and directed towards securing what for them would be a tolerable, rather than a punitive, tribunal adjudication. In short, the approach which the workers' representatives appeared to adopt in those cases where passions were already clearly inflamed, as in the Fairfield shipyard cases to be discussed shortly, was to intimidate the chairmen into leniency, perhaps to attempt to force upon them an arbitral rather than a judicial function. The tribunal thus became a forum for the ritual display of aggression rather than for adjudication. Expressions of regret or contrition by guilty workers, which invariably led to light sentences, became the exception rather than the rule. In short, working class attitudes to law were clearly not cowed nor marked by deference.

It is not to be expected that those presiding over juridical fora would accept this treatment with equanimity. For they possessed a subtle weapon with which to 'routinize' conflict, by delimiting the boundaries of courtroom discussion. Yet while the analysis of courtroom conversation may illuminate the processes whereby legal authority normally maintains social order during hearings, this control mechanism spectacularly broke down during the tribunal hearings; order suffered as a result; and the chairmen were forced to vacate their traditional domain as judges.

What happened, it will be argued, was as follows. Confronted by controversial cases where the defendants' representatives embarked upon a sustained attempt to undermine the chairmen's authority, the latter, in their efforts to maintain control and order during the proceedings, strenuously sought to invoke both the authority of official legal procedures and, also, their monopoly positions as chairmen to adjudicate upon what evidence was relevant, legitimate, and competent. A good example from a minor case (not discussed in detail in the following account) involved the prosecution of four men who had refused to work a 'reasonable' amount of overtime. In their defence, the men stated that they were complying with a workshop resolution passed in order to persuade the employer to attend to particular grievances over wages and conditions. The men's spokesmen had told the tribunal that 'They had acted honourably as workers standing one by another, and it was their firm conviction that anything they had done had been in the interests of the whole community.'[3] Yet according to the tribunal chairman, James Andrew, 'The Court could not take into consideration the reasons which had influenced respondents in declining to work overtime, because that was outside the purview of the Munitions Act.'[4] Thus by determining what was legally relevant or irrelevant, the judge could structure the proceedings according to his, and not according to the accused's, criteria. Negotiation, in the overwhelming majority of court hearings, could in this way be foreclosed so that controversy, if it existed at all, would inform legal, not social, categories. The tribunal's task could then be confined to determining whether the accused munitions workers did, indeed, strike contrary to the Act. It need not concern itself, strictly, with whether the strike was, in the circumstances, justified or unjustified. Through the instrumentality of legal criteria of relevance, order in the courtroom was normally maintained on the terms of the legal officials. Unfortunately for the tribunal chairmen, however, these patterns whereby 'official legal reality' was imposed frequently broke down, compelling the chairmen, in the teeth of hostility, to devise new, and ultimately no more successful, tactics.

Theoretically, legal procedures, courtroom verbal exchange, and legal language are designed to produce highly specific and definitive rulings on matters which 'ordinary' conversation is not expected to achieve. Some writers stress that the court officials engage in drama, ceremony, and symbolism with a view, ultimately, to 'intimidate, bewilder, oppress, alienate, label or stigmatise' defendants.[5] This legal reality is sharply contrasted with the 'common-sense' view of the world, which one might call the primary reality of experience. The latter, assailed by legal routines and other formal procedures, succumbs to the former, which, in the courtroom, assumes dominance in one's social experience. Thus in one study, it is

---

[3] *Glasgow Herald*, 25 Nov. 1915.
[4] Ibid.
[5] J. M. Atkinson and Paul Drew, *Order in Court*, London, 1980, p. 4.

stated that 'the staging of magistrates' justice in itself infuses the proceedings with a surrealism which atrophies the defendant's ability to participate in them.'[6]
The objective which the creation of specialized legal procedures and modes of argument and discourse in the courtroom seeks to attain is, therefore, the pursuit of social order on those terms which maintain the integrity and authority of court officials. It will be argued, however, that the noticeable failure of 'legal reality' to impose itself unquestioningly on those appearing before the munitions tribunals—an outcome which contrasts strongly with the success of the modern court system to maintain control—is not simply attributable to the feelings of resentment on the part of skilled workers, aware of their strategic importance to the war effort, and whose sense of sacrifice was repaid by their employers and by the local ministry officials with tribunal prosecutions. This failure of 'legal reality' is also due to the rich experience in bargaining which the trade union representatives and workmen themselves had shared in the regulation of industrial relations. The unpopular munitions tribunals, handling collective issues, were seen as yet another forum within which to engage in familiar, if heightened, negotiating processes. A further reason relates to the perception of the tribunals by some of the accused as a political instrument of repression. The tribunals therefore drew a correspondingly political, albeit non-revolutionary, response.

At a more generalized level, however, one may interpret the pattern of events before the Glasgow tribunal as an illustration of the thesis that the attempt of the Ministry of Munitions to regulate industrial labour through a strategy which smacked of incorporation and which in turn depended upon employers' commitment to common goals as well as upon official union cooperation in disciplining its membership, foundered on the

---

[6] Pat Carlen, 'The Staging of Magistrates' Justice', *British Journal of Criminology*, XVI (1976), 48–55, at 48; cited in Atkinson and Drew, *Order in Court*, p. 12, who argue that this assumes that in the 'outside world' there exist conventional norms and normal interaction which themselves are unproblematic. In fact, they insist, 'normal' interaction will itself be conditioned by specific contexts so that the contrast between courtroom and 'outside' interaction may not simply be that between the 'normal' and the 'alien'. See ibid., pp. 15–16. For the ideas of primary and secondary legal realities, the present author is grateful to his colleague, A. D. O. Thomson.

rock of 'system contradiction'.[7] Even the local trade union élites, otherwise despised by the revolutionary shop stewards, recognized that it would be an abdication of their responsibilities, perhaps even dangerous, were they not to defend their constituents before the Glasgow tribunal. And this, to their credit, is what they proceeded to do with both vigour and resilience. Their surrender to a bureaucratic strategy of incorporation, a strategy which by grave irony also led such officials to the tribunals as assessors sitting in adjudication over working-class offenders, was never complete and abject. They were acutely aware of the contradiction for their union and for themselves which the pursuit of a collaborative policy would pose. Thus their behaviour before the munitions tribunals, though primarily instrumental, also contained elements of a revolt against a State bureaucracy which appeared to them to be lukewarm towards employers' unfair exploitation of the Act. None the less, it was a pale shadow of that revolt embarked upon by the Clyde shop stewards' movement. The former sought to minimize penal damage and to maximize opportunities for material gains within the munitions code, whilst simultaneously striving to divert attention to a different legitimate target, the local employer who was genuinely believed to be abusing his new-found powers under the Act. The shop stewards, by contrast, aimed ambitiously at a more fundamental transformation of society.

We would argue, therefore, that the confrontations witnessed before the Glasgow tribunal can be explained partly in terms of a clash of competing ideologies. On the one hand was a statutorily enshrined philosophy whose broad assumptions were an interventionist State imposing its labour policy by legal measures; the pursuit of a single, unified national interest to which all parties were subordinated, and the removal of market freedom in selecting one's employer and negotiating wages and conditions. From all these matters, the pluralist assumption which had traditionally informed trade union conduct in the pre-war period of collective *laissez-faire* diverged sharply. An abstentionist State, legal autonomy, market mobility, and free

[7] A term used in Dominic Strinati, *Capitalism, the State and Industrial Relations*, London, 1982.

collective bargaining (all of these at least in theory) were the context within which the local union officials had formerly exercised their functions. Perhaps representatives rather than delegates (so that it was the *officials'* image of bargaining strategies—in some instances a more limited and conservative vision than that of the rank and file—which prevailed), they could only assume the mantle of industrial policemen under the Government's labour strategy if the employers also played by consensual rules. If not, then what was at risk was the union officials' very existence as representatives. Indeed, clearly disdainful of the neat legal categories which stressed 'rights' rather than 'interests' in respect to job regulation, they used the tribunals not merely to defend their members, but in an attempt to keep alive elements of the voluntarist bargaining spirit which the war legislation had attenuated.

Within the wider theoretical framework expounded above, the fascinating exchanges between the tribunal chairmen and the accused or their representatives must be seen in the light of the latter's attempts to escape the boundaries of tribunal discourse which legal officialdom wished to impose and to maintain in pursuit of order. The verbal struggles which ensued therefore embodied both the endeavours of munitions workers to 'capture' the tribunals for their own criteria of relevance and also the desperate attempts by the chairmen to prevent them wresting this control from legal officialdom's hands.

The following account will vividly illustrate the distinctive features which informed the principal tribunal hearings in Glasgow in 1915–16, the first two such cases involving one major shipyard on the Clyde.

THE FAIRFIELD COPPERSMITHS

The important Glasgow firm of shipbuilders, Fairfield of Govan, became the focal point of acute conflict between management and unions in the second half of 1915. Major strikes by the company's coppersmiths and shipwrights were followed by prosecutions of the alleged ringleaders. Those found guilty were fined; but three of the shipwrights doggedly refused to pay, whereupon they were imprisoned. Such a move provoked threats of a general strike in the district, prompting the Government to appoint a two-man committee of enquiry into the grievances of Clyde munitions workers (the Balfour–Macassey Commission). The crisis was not, however, averted, as the commissioners had no authority to release the imprisoned shipwrights. Instead, a telegram was sent to the Ministry of Munitions by the 'members of the Executive Councils or District Committees of the twenty-three Trades Unions connected with the engineering and shipbuilding industry, representing 97,500 workmen in the Clyde Valley'. This demanded the release of the men and insisted on a reply within three days. Thoroughly alarmed at the prospect of an all-out strike in the country's leading munitions centre, Government ministers, including Lloyd George and the Secretary for Scotland Thomas McKinnon Wood, met a delegation from the Clyde unions. The officials agreed to pay the fines and the men were released. Another crisis had been ridden.[8]

Though such dramatic and controversial events were important factors in persuading the Government to contemplate amendments to the Munitions Act shortly after its original enactment,[9] it is the tribunal proceedings involving the coppersmiths and shipwrights at Fairfield with which we are principally concerned.

The background to the first of the Fairfield prosecutions, that involving the coppersmiths, was that in early July 1915 the firm found itself short of the necessary skilled labour in the copper shops. It then approached the Glasgow and West of Scotland Armaments Output Committee, a tripartite body seeking to co-ordinate munitions production in the district, with a request that the committee approve the use of plumbers for work usually performed by coppersmiths. The request was granted on

---

[8] For detailed accounts, see *OHMM*, vol. IV, pt. II, pp. 49–65; Wrigley, *David Lloyd George and the British Labour Movement*, Hassocks, 1976, pp. 134–5, 141–8; Hinton, *The First Shop Stewards' Movement*, pp. 114–17; Gallacher, *Revolt on the Clyde*, pp. 63–6; McLean, *Legend of Red Clydeside*, pp. 41–2.

[9] For the Balfour–Macassey commission's recommendations with respect to the leaving certificate scheme, see ch. 8. For the trade unions' campaign against the Munitions Act 1915, see Rubin, 'The Enforcement of the Munitions of War Acts 1915–1917, with Particular Reference to Proceedings before the Munitions Tribunal in Glasgow, 1915–1921', Warwick Univ. Ph.D thesis (1984), ch. 2. For a brief discussion of the industrial relations background at Fairfield itself, see ibid., pp. 169–72.

14 July, so long as the Coppersmiths' district secretary, Alexander Turnbull (later to be appointed a munitions tribunal assessor), was informed of the arrangements. In fact, Turnbull was hesitant to approve, whereupon the management informed him that since the firm was by now a 'controlled establishment' (ch. 1), it was going to introduce the change in working arrangements anyway, thus demonstrating clearly its intention of taking advantage of the Act. The Glasgow Fair holiday had then intervened and nothing developed until 7.20 in the morning of Tuesday 27 July when a deputation of three coppersmiths went to see the works manager and told him that, though they did not object to plumbers doing their work on board ship, they would walk out if plumbers were introduced into the copper shop. The coppersmiths then held a mass meeting and left the yard after breakfast.[10]

Almost immediately, twenty-eight strikers were summoned to appear before the munitions tribunal on 2 August,[11] in what was to prove to be a rowdy but fascinating verbal duel between the men's representatives, insisting on the justice of their cause, and the tribunal chairman, Professor Gloag, desperately pressing on the men the illegality of their actions.

A foretaste of these competing perspectives between legal and social reality is to be found in the exchanges over the selection of the tribunal assessors for the hearing. For not only did one of the accused jump up and announce that 'I am one of the strikers and I make an objection to the empanelling of the Court'. But Robert Turnbull, the Coppersmiths' national President, also inveighed against the presence, as employers' assessor, of James Dalrymple, general manager of Glasgow Corporation Tramways Department. For Dalrymple was notorious as the best recruiting sergeant in the district who apparently spared little effort in intimidating his staff into enlisting.[12] Thus, to defiant

[10] *OHMM*, vol. IV, pt. II, p. 49.

[11] *Glasgow Herald*, 3 Aug. 1915.

[12] Dalrymple was later to insist on extending the Munitions Act to his own employees, ostensibly to prevent other employers from poaching his staff, though it was an explanation peremptorily dismissed by the local socialist publisher, John Wheatley, who detected baser motives. See *Glasgow Herald*, 3 Feb. 1916. A historian has recently described Dalrymple as 'autocratic'. See Christopher Harvie, *No Gods and Precious Few Heroes: Scotland 1914–1980*, London, 1981, p. 11. Perhaps it was not for nothing that the Army's recruiting office in Glasgow was at the Tramways Department's head office in

cries from the accused that they were being tried under protest, it was already clear that here was no ordinary criminal trial, marked by pomp and solemnity. Instead, there was a determined pursuit of obstructive (if not quite destructive) tactics which sought to undermine the legitimacy of the hearing. At last the trial itself got under way, with Alexander Cleghorn, director and engineering manager of Fairfield, entering the witness box. For the chairman, Professor Gloag, the issue to be put to Cleghorn was simple: 'whether these men, as a matter of fact, came out on strike'. Turnbull, however, was determined to ensure that the coppersmiths' grievances were fully ventilated and not discarded on the grounds that they were irrelevant to the lawyer's neat conception of the world. He interrupted Gloag's questioning of Cleghorn to announce that the men struck, 'Because of great provocation and due solely to the management of Fairfield.' But, retorted Gloag, 'We want to know if they struck.'

TURNBULL. Yes they struck because of the Fairfield management violating the Act.
GLOAG. It does not matter for what cause. Did they strike?
TURNBULL. But we are trying to place the facts that led up to the cause of the strike.
GLOAG. But the men pleaded not guilty.
TURNBULL. Well, even a murderer is tried.

Turnbull's tactics, therefore, were to harangue Gloag in the hope of weakening the latter's resolve to impose a punitive penalty at the end of the proceedings. But it also entailed a spot of plea bargaining—acknowledging that the men had struck—which, in turn, implied an acceptance of the tribunal's legitimacy to try breaches of the Act. Indeed, Turnbull alleged, the firm itself had infringed the Act by giving the men no

Bath Street, where John Maclean, the socialist school teacher, conducted his anti-war meetings. *Forward* accused Dalrymple of constituting himself the local Lord Derby. 'At one time', it noted, 'he had enlisted so many of his men that there was a danger of the Tramway service coming to a sudden stop for lack of motormen.' He also sacked 5 married men who refused to attest, claiming that work was slack. In so doing, he blatantly ignored the 'last in, first out' principle normally operative in cases of slackness of work. One worker was offered his job back but only if he agreed to attest. See *Forward*, 11 Dec. 1915; ibid., 11 Mar. 1916. Derby organized the Government's recruitment campaign. Those who 'attested' registered with the Army and awaited call-up in due course.

opportunity for consultation before imposing the 'promiscuous' employment of plumbers alongside coppersmiths. His hectoring approach did, in fact, seem to be working. For Gloag, apparently chastened by Turnbull's verbal onslaught, suggested that if the men returned to work and referred the problem to the Board of Trade the amount of the fine might be modified. Turnbull clearly scented the outlines of victory. It was not, he replied, a matter simply for the strikers, but for the whole trade, and 'threats of penalties and such as that [sic] would not deter the trade in the slightest.' Indeed, the mood of a mass meeting to be held that night would turn on the outcome of the tribunal hearing, he hinted darkly. Again, of course, this should be understood as another card played in the negotiating game, not to compel the tribunal to acquit the strikers (for they had scarcely denied their actions, and legal rationality would forbid such absolution), nor to ensure a satisfactory 'arbitral' settlement, but to force down the tariff of punishment to its lowest point. For sentencing was a matter within the tribunal's discretion, and Gloag, it was by now realized, was susceptible to pressure exerted on him to impose a lenient sentence. Yet the men's agreement during lunch to return to work pending a Board of Trade settlement came unstuck when Fairfield told the resumed tribunal hearing that it insisted on employing plumbers on copper work aboard ship, even if not in the coppershops themselves. The announcement, however, brought pandemonium to the proceedings. Several strikers stood up to address the court, including Owen Rodgers who, as we saw in Chapter 1, had protested his loyalty to the war effort. First, he attacked the firm's managerial incompetence which led to much sub-contracting while Fairfield's own employees were standing idle. Then the unfortunate Dalrymple was again singled out for attention. 'I want to know if Mr. Dalrymple, the tramways manager,' asked Rodgers, 'has the authority of the ratepayers of Glasgow, to leave off his own work in order to try other men for being off their work.'

Finally, amid the commotion, Alexander Turnbull, the district secretary, announced that since the union regarded the men's action as 'quite legal', it was going to pay their fine.

In the end, in fact, Gloag imposed penalties of just 2*s*. 6*d*. on each accused, 'in view,' he announced, 'of the men's efforts to return to work'.[13] Yet this manifestly derisory amount can probably be better explained in terms of the success of the union officials' strategy to intimidate the tribunal and to cast Fairfield shipyard as responsible for their own misfortunes. As a deterrent to other potential strikers, Gloag's tribunal was a paper tiger. As the *Glasgow Herald* pointed out, 'The effect of these proceedings, especially when we take into consideration the almost truculently self-righteous and jauntily disrespectful attitude of the men and their leaders towards the Court, is to bring the Munitions Act into open contempt.'[14] What was the point of fining the men a mere 2s. 6d.? Either one should rely on persuasion, as Lloyd George had told the House some days earlier, *or* apply the 'full penalty', a step which ought to include the blacklist, 'until such time as they, and their Union, showed their conviction of sin'.

There was certainly little point in negotiating with such people as Owen Rodgers, the remonstrating and slighted striker. 'This is the type of man', moralized the editorial, 'upon whom argument or persuasion is wholly wasted.' Therefore, it concluded, if Lloyd George were not prepared 'to make his authority respected', then martial law was the only answer. For 'it is brought appreciably nearer by this sorry farce.'[15]

As to the cause of the coppersmiths' strike, the *Official History of the Ministry of Munitions*[16] at first observed that the men's motive in striking was obscure, given that the company, contrary to the men's allegation, had offered consultation before implementing the change. Moreover, some limited lifting of demarcation lines between plumbers and coppersmiths aboard ship had already been conceded. 'Yet,' continued the ministry historians, 'the strike cannot be regarded simply as an act of

[13] *The Times*, 3 Aug. 1915.
[14] *Glasgow Herald*, 3 Aug. 1915. Cf. *Woman's Dreadnought*, 14 Aug. 1915, which referred to the 'futility' of the Munitions Act. The coppersmiths' outcome followed hard on the heels of the failure of the Munitions Act to deter 200,000 South Wales miners, to whose industry the Act had been expressly extended by Royal Proclamation, from taking industrial action over a long-standing wage grievance. Notices pointing out the illegality of strikes in the district and the setting up of a general munitions tribunal had no effect on the miners. Faced with the prospect of prosecuting large numbers of strikers, the government opted to put pressure on the coal-owners to settle, which, eventually, they did. On this episode, see Wrigley, *David Lloyd George*, ch. 7.
[15] *Glasgow Herald*, 3 Aug. 1915.
[16] *OHMM*, vol. IV, pt. II, pp. 45–7.

unreason. The cause is probably to be found in the men's resentment at the firm's declaration of their intention to enforce the change by means of the Munitions Act, and the manner in which the declaration was made.'[17] Thus, the threatened use of the Act was the trip-wire which set off an instantaneous reaction, and a measure designed to restrain strikes was in fact seen to be provoking them.

The coppersmiths' strike and subsequent tribunal hearing is therefore an instructive episode for the sociologist and historian of law, as well as for labour historians. Hardly a 'trivial' dispute (as McLean asserts),[18] it reflected a prime concern by skilled men with the maintenance of craft barriers. For, 'The coppersmiths'', recognized the *Glasgow Herald*,[19] 'desire to keep all the work available to their trade just as do doctors, ministers and lawyers.' But the manner in which the tribunal hearing was conducted reveals not an outright rejection by the craftsmen of bourgeois legality; for the coppersmiths were no revolutionaries. They did, in fact, acknowledge the tribunal's legitimacy, even going so far (as we have seen) as to complain of Fairfield's alleged infringement of the Act—though, given the circumstances, they would no doubt have preferred to have told Lloyd George (or the chairman) where he could put his tribunal. Yet the uproar, the challenge to Dalrymple,[20] the complaint of inefficiency on the part of the management, even the 'incredulous' laughter by the strikers when told that fines of £5 for each day lost through the strike could be imposed, do not imply, as Hinton suggests, that 'they found it extremely difficult to grasp the full import of compulsory arbitration and the illegality of strikes'.[21] It is more convincing to believe that they were simply tailoring their tactics to the circumstances. They were, in fact, subtly negotiating with the tribunal, though admittedly not according to any pre-determined plan. None the less, by exerting vocal pressure they were perhaps hoping that the tribunal chairman, in his exercise of a novel and unfamiliar

[17] Ibid., p. 50.
[18] McLean, *Legend of Red Clydeside*, p. 41.
[19] *Glasgow Herald*, 3 Aug. 1915.
[20] The other assessor was John Thomson, general secretary of the Associated Blacksmiths.
[21] Hinton, *The First Shop Stewards' Movement*, p. 114.

authority under trying circumstances, might accommodate himself to, or even be bullied into, the intense atmosphere of negotiating brinkmanship and plea bargaining. As we argued earlier, this tactic succeeded and the men undoubtedly felt that they had escaped lightly; indeed, that they had achieved victory, moral or otherwise. For had not one of the strikers jumped up at the hearing and, pointing to Cleghorn, proclaimed, 'It is *we* who are trying you!'?[22]

One of the most fascinating questions presently preoccupying social historians is the issue of working-class attitudes to law. The evidence from the coppersmiths' episode suggests a strong propensity on the part of trade unionists summoned as a group not to be cowed by the reputation of the law as a dignified institution. If this fell far short of a challenge to the legitimacy of the State, none the less the accused, with tenacious resolve, were prepared to undermine the authority of the tribunal; to show scant respect for the status of the tribunal chairman, to haggle, and to harass; in short, to resist authority by verbal abuse. But there was no refusal to be tried by, for example, turning their backs to the court and refusing to plead, as Irish revolutionaries might do. Their approach was pragmatic, multi-faceted, and opportunist. They would use the law to advance their own interests, and ridicule the law's agents if the same objective could be gained by such steps. Without wholly transforming the tribunal into an arbitration panel discussing grievances (instead of adjudicating upon them), they were able to manipulate the tribunal chairman into compromising his position far more effectively than if a less hostile, and more contrite, attitude to the charges had been adopted by them. Thus munitions tribunal hearings might sometimes oscillate between, on the one hand, stereotyped courts of law dispensing summary 'justice' and, on the other, joint negotiating committees seeking to resolve 'problems' of industrial relations. Features of both these models were to be found displayed in tribunal practice as it alternately tried the stick and the carrot (as indeed, up to a point, did Government labour policy in general). The coppersmiths'

---

[22] MUN 5/48/300/9, 'Minutes of Conference with Shipbuilding Employers' Federation. The Application of the Munitions Act etc. . . . August 12, 1915'. Fred Henderson, president of the Federation (SEF) was most offended, telling Lloyd George, 'He was one of the principals of the firm. That is not very nice.'

tactics corresponded to this image of the tribunal as a hybrid institution. They tried negotiation *and* they accepted, in the final analysis, the tribunal's tattered authority to fine them a paltry sum. It is this ultimately pragmatic approach to tribunal proceedings, whereby disruption was combined with instrumentalism, which characterized the more notable proceedings in Glasgow in 1915–16.[23]

THE SHIPWRIGHTS

Even more than the coppersmiths' case, that involving the Fairfield shipwrights gave the impetus to change in the 'nasty, brutish and short' history of the Munitions Act. Here, indeed, was an incident which undeniably justifies the description 'trivial';[24] so much so that the detailed events within the yard, leading up to the tribunal prosecution, do not merit more than the briefest recitation here, even though their ramifications extended to Parliament, even though rank-and-file organization was mobilized on an extensive footing, and even though trade unions on Clydeside were, unusually, drawn closer together by the event.

The potted version of events[25] reveals that two shipwrights singled out by a manager for loitering on board a ship were handed their cards and money together with pass-out checks on which were written, 'not attending to work'. These checks were, in fact, taken by the men as leaving certificates which they

---

[23] After the hearing, most of the strikers returned to work the following day. See *Glasgow Herald*, 4 Aug. 1915. Some 10 days later, Sheriff A. O. M. Mackenzie, sitting as arbiter, ruled against the men's complaint, leaving them exposed once more to the encroachment of the plumbers in the copper shop. See *OHMM*, vol. IV, pt. II, p. 49. No report of the arbitration is cited in the *Labour Gazette* despite the obvious importance of the case. Perhaps such a mention would have reminded readers of the embarrassing discord at the tribunal. According to the employers' newspaper, however, the outcome had had a 'most salutary effect on the working relationship of employed and employers and of one branch of artizans to another'. See the *Shipbuilder*, XIII (Oct. 1915), 169–70.

[24] McLean, 'The Clyde Workers' Committee, the Ministry of Munitions and the Suppression of the "Forward": An Alternative View', *Scottish Labour History Society Journal*, No. 6, Dec. 1972, 55; id., *Legend of Red Clydeside*, p. 41. There is no mention of the dispute in the published history of the Shipwrights' Union. See David Dougan, *The Shipwrights*, Newcastle, 1975. The strike, of course, was unofficial and condemned by the union executive.

[25] *OHMM*, vol. IV, pt. II, pp. 51–2; *Glasgow Herald*, 4 Sept. 1915, for the full details.

expected would have to be shown to prospective employers
before they could obtain new work. After a dinner-hour meeting
of shipwrights, H. M. MacMillan, the shipyard director, agreed
to remove the offending words 'under protest', but refused to
reinstate the two dismissed shipwrights, Andrew White and
Hugh Walker. In response, 426 shipwrights took industrial
action; the Ministry of Munitions was informed the following
day, and a week later, twenty-six of the strikers, mostly shop
stewards who were considered to be the ringleaders, were
prosecuted.

According to the historians of the Ministry of Munitions, the
men were spoiling for a fight over the Munitions Act. They
wrote

> But it must be remembered that these men on the Clyde are not cool
> and calculating, but impulsive and swayed by sentiment. . . . The
> threat to strike . . . can only be explained as the result of a temper eager
> to provoke a conflict on the flimsiest pretext and with suspicion against
> every disciplinary action of the management as a tyrannical exercise of
> power under the cover of the Munitions Act.[26]

It is more probable, however, that it was both the Ministry of
Munitions and the Fairfield management who, scandalized by
the coppersmiths' fiasco, were intent on a confrontation over the
Munitions Act. Lloyd George, for example, had told the
shipbuilding employers a few days after the coppersmiths'
hearing that the ministry would consider prosecuting in
'suitable cases . . . where we could make sure we could make a
real example'.[27] From the point of view of the Government and
employers, what could be a more appropriate opportunity than
an apparently irrational strike of skilled craftsmen who were
crucial to the war effort; where the management were portrayed
as willing to offer significant concessions; and where the men at
the centre of the dispute had been found seemingly neglecting
their work? As the *Official History*, undoubtedly seeking to
capture dominant departmental opinion at the time, commented after the war, 'Drastic action was necessary, though it
might involve a general stoppage. But determined repression (it

---

[26] *OHMM*, vol. iv, pt. ii, p. 52.
[27] MUN 5/48/300/9.

was thought) would go far to kill the unrest on the Clyde.'[28] The Fairfield shipwrights' case was to be the showdown.

From the outset, the trial[29] was marked by a pronounced lack of decorum, with the spectators frequently interrupting proceedings with their voluble interjections and raucous laughter directed against the firm's witnesses. Even the strikers' solicitor could not resist injecting an element of sarcasm into his contemptuous dismissal of the prosecution's case. Thus, to a shop steward[30] questioned by the prosecutor as to his knowledge of the existence of the statutory strike prohibition, the solicitor remarked victoriously that 'As a matter of fact, you have been so busy working that you have not had time to read the Munitions Act.' Moreover, as to the conduct of the management, he insisted that 'if at this time of crisis every smart under-manager was to go out of his way to dismiss men for every trifling fault, then there would be nothing but trouble in labour circles.'

It was now time for Sheriff Fyfe to sum up the proceedings. He first pointed out that considerable latitude had been allowed by him deliberately in order that the circumstances giving rise to the strike might be explored (Professor Gloag, it may be recalled, had doggedly struggled in the coppersmiths' case, to resist this descent into 'irrelevance'). Moreover, Fyfe noted, much evidence had been presented to demonstrate that the two dismissed shipwrights, White and Walker, were competent and had given long service to the firm.

He believed that, but their personal character was not a factor in the case at all. They were not being tried for any personal misdemeanour. What they were charged with was that in concert with others, they went on strike because a difference arose between the shipwrights in Fairfield and the management. And this was contrary to the Act. They

---

[28] *OHMM*, vol. IV, pt. II, p. 52. It should be noted that while there was no monolithic ministry view on labour policy in general and on prosecution policy in particular, none the less the view of Beveridge and his immediate colleagues at the ministry, such as Charles Rey, was in favour of vigorous enforcement of the Act at this juncture. See Harris, *William Beveridge: A Biography*, Oxford, 1977, pp. 212–13.

[29] *Glasgow Herald*, 4 Sept. 1915, for an extensive account of the trial. The assessors were Robert Baird, secretary of the Coalowners' Association and Sam Bunton of the ASE. The prosecutor was J. Turner MacFarlane, the Ministry of Munitions reports officer (and a qualified solicitor). The accused retained J. Geoffrey Hunter, a local solicitor, to defend them. Fyfe was on the bench.

[30] This was Charles MacPherson, a lay official of the union and one of those eventually imprisoned.

were not concerned with whether or not the dismissal of these two men was reasonable or not. That was not relevant to the present complaint. The only thing which was relevant was the fact that the shipwrights came out on strike because the management refused to reinstate two men. Whether they should be reinstated was a question which was not referred to the Board of Trade under section 2 of the Act, and the strike in connection with that matter was therefore illegal. No-one could pretend ignorance of the Act of Parliament which expressly forbade strikes during the period of war. Reasons for going on strike matter nothing under this Act of Parliament. Men might have a grievance or they might not. The tribunal had nothing to do with that. Like everybody else in this country, the accused were subject to the special war laws. They were, in their workshop, as much bound to obey orders as the soldier in the field. This statute was their commanding officer and its emphatic command to them was 'thou shalt not strike'. They had deliberately disobeyed this command, and they must take the consequences.

The striking feature of this lengthy passage is of course the calculated manner in which Sheriff Fyfe carefully skirted around the *merits* of the dispute. Despite the 'open forum' in the earlier part of the proceedings, he now had no intention of becoming embroiled in a heated debate on the reasonableness or otherwise of the two men's dismissal, or whether or not the Board of Trade would have ordered a reinstatement. He knew that once he entertained such questions in his decision he would find himself in dangerous waters. Therefore, his technique of structuring the issue around the narrower question of whether the accused had struck illegally in breach of the Munitions Act was a mechanism designed to ensure that any concluding references were channelled along *his* terms of reference. The criteria of relevance were legal, not social. To the extent that he retained control over the structure and content of court room dialogue, he could, accordingly, hope to maintain *social* control over the proceedings. For in matters of *legal* content he was, of course, supreme. He did in fact achieve his objective subtly and, indeed, impressively. By allowing scope for initial discussion of the background to the case, he ensured that the men's perspective was at least ventilated. But at the end of this long two and a half-hour hearing, Fyfe's forceful personality and domineering presence enabled him to convey an uncompromising message with due gravity and solemnity.

Lecturing the accused on the predictable theme that to strike in wartime was a crime againt the nation and against their comrades in the trenches, he concluded by imposing fines of £10 each on the fifteen who had pleaded guilty and on the two shipwrights who had denied the charge but who had been convicted on the evidence.[31] Twenty-one days were allowed for payment, failing which the alternative was thirty days in prison, an announcement which, for the last time during this prolonged hearing, was received with hoots of laughter by the spectators.[32]

Fyfe's speech was indeed a striking display of an inflexibly legalistic approach to industrial relations problems. One suspects, however, that he was well aware that he was employing a particularly blunt instrument unsuited, normally, to the frequently complex and emotive issues which constituted the industrial relations landscape. Indeed there is little doubt that he was expected by the Ministry of Munitions to launch a determined judicial effort to stamp out industrial disorder on Clydeside and that he responded as desired by the ministry. Clearly a thoughtful tactician, he diplomatically paid lip-service initially to an exchange on the causes of the strike but then called an immediate halt to this diversion, and gambled on a strictly legal, punitive approach. Adopting the lawyer's technique to control the shape of court discourse, his speech stressed that relevance was a judicially constructed, not a 'socially' constructed, concept; and he was determined that his concept was to prevail. This was not, perhaps, because as a lawyer he had been trained to conceive of relevance in a particular way, but because, tactically, after the coppersmiths' affair, it probably seemed to offer the best prospect for success in the sense both of maintaining decorum and respect for law, and of deterring others from engaging in similar conduct.

Thus the severe performance of a hardened sheriff adjudicating upon a *ministry* prosecution was in stark contrast with the previous disastrous experience of a private mass prosecution

---

[31] The case against a further 9 accused, including 3 Canadians, was withdrawn.

[32] Those found guilty included John Arbuthnot, Patrick Brogan, Hugh Coulter, David Fleming, Donald Fraser, Robert Harper, John Hempkins, Alexander Houston, Thomas Houston, Albert Knight, George Lang, Norman McLeod, Charles MacPherson, Peter Stirling, John Tait, and John Turner. Virtually all of them lived in Govan. See *Glasgow Herald*, 4 Sept. 1915.

during which Gloag was seen to wilt under the pressure of the aggressive coppersmiths. Fyfe was made of sterner stuff and clearly relished the task of beefing up the tribunal hearings and of intimidating other potential strikers.

Yet, though predictably full of praise after the trial for Fyfe's masterly display of ruthless law enforcement, the *Glasgow Herald* none the less struck a more cautious and conciliatory tone. It recognized that

> In some recent instances, there has doubtless been an amount of tactlessness on the part of employers or their representatives which has acted like salt in raw flesh. The Act was not passed in order that it might be flourished by foremen and others endowed with delegated power as if it were an Egyptian whip for the back of Israelite brickmakers. It was devised as a means for getting the most out of employers and their foremen as well as out of their squads of skilled and unskilled labourers. It knows no distinction between the wearers of broad cloth and the wearers of overalls. To the extent that that may have been forgotten, there must be an instant repentance, for the man who contributes to the exasperation of another, which leads to the striking of the latter, is under the same band of guiltiness.[33]

This, of course, was the message which Fyfe attempted to convey on numerous occasions: that the effectiveness of the Munitions Act, and the success of the national endeavour, depended not solely on the coercive enforcement of the Act against workers, but also on 'unity' reflected in firm but 'enlightened' management attitudes to labour. If employers, therefore, were discovered abusing the Act, then it was Fyfe's mission to shame them into rectification. The lengthy newspaper editorial did, indeed, appear to glimpse this insight, signalling a remarkable concession by an establishment-oriented voice which strongly reflected the views of professional and business strata in Glasgow. Yet, while it concluded that 'For the moment, the men seem disposed to think that further defiance of the Act is useless', it also portentously added that 'We await the sequel to yesterday's trial with some anxiety.'[34] Such caution was justified. For, as mentioned earlier, the subsequent imprisonment of three of the shipwrights who had refused to pay their

[33] See *Glasgow Herald*, 4 Sept. 1915.
[34] Ibid.

fines led to a crisis of massive proportions[35] which resulted in rapid amendment to the Munitions Act.[36] Here was a further example of labour legislation as the forcing-house of social change.

THE LOBNITZ CASE

Chronologically separating the two Fairfield cases was the prosecution of twenty holders-on (riveters' assistants) at Lobnitz shipyard in Renfrew, who had struck on 30 July and remained out till 2 August.[37] The men had sought an allowance of a shilling a man per day on the ground that workmen elsewhere were receiving this amount. They had approached the assistant foreman riveter, Hugh Gillen, who had informed them that since the managers were at that time absent on a trial trip, he could not grant the increase. What led to the strike, however, seems to have been the manner in which this information was conveyed to the men. For the workmen's representative at the tribunal, W. G. Sharp of the Boilermakers' Society, contended that the men's demand had been received with a 'lack of discretion' on the part of the firm. In fact, he continued with due understatement, 'It appeared to him that the member of the firm referred to [i.e. Gillen] was not in a very good mood that morning, and told them to get out of the works, and they took him at his word.'

So once again the accused's representative was faced with the daunting task of offering a defence to a charge whose factual basis could scarcely be denied. Yet the very fact that, as we shall see, paltry fines of just 5s. were imposed on each striker is, it is suggested, a testimony in part to the skill with which Sharp conducted that defence. For as well as stressing the provocative attitude adopted by the company's foreman, Gillen; as well as

---

[35] See n. 8 above.

[36] For its importance in the amendment campaign, see Rubin, 'Enforcement of the Munitions of War Acts', ch. 2.

[37] *Glasgow Herald*, 10 Aug. 1915, for details of the case and quotations. See also *Forward*, 14 Aug. 1915. The assessors were John Brown, general secretary of the Ironmoulders' Union, and Robert Baird, of the Coalowners' Association, who also sat as assessor at the shipwrights' trial.

regretting the loss of valuable working time—'The men realised now that it was not going to be advantageous to their interests to stop work'—Sharp also felt it appropriate to employ mildly disruptive tactics, which contained faint echoes of the Fairfield coppersmiths' hearing.

In the first instance, he objected to the fact that the prosecutor was an employers' association representative, Andrew Duncan,[38] who was the assistant to Thomas Biggart the secretary of the Clyde Shipbuilders' Association (CSA). Nothing less than a Crown prosecutor, as distinct from a private individual, would satisfy him. Next, he lashed out at 'trial by newspaper', in that the Glasgow press had announced that charges had been brought even before the summonses had been issued. Sharp demanded to know who had been responsible for 'thus blackening the men in the eyes of the public before they had a chance to defend themselves'. He even turned his hand to a spot of legal juggling, claiming (not without merit) that at the time of the alleged offence the men had not been engaged on munitions work, as statutorily defined.

Of course, all this sparring was conducted with a view to softening up the tribunal and the prosecutor. For the object was surely to minimize the penalty which would inevitably be imposed, an object scarcely prejudiced by Sharp's effort to distance himself from his members who, as *unofficial* strikers, were not viewed by him in a wholly virtuous light.

Thus it was that modest fines were imposed on each striker because, said Professor Gloag, the men soon returned to work and, he added, because they possibly 'did not understand the absolute necessity of the workmen of this country submitting to the conditions of the Act'. But a further explanation is, surely, because Sharp was prepared to stir things up, seeking also to place part of the blame on the shoulders of the employer. In these endeavours, his tactics could hardly be described as unsuccessful.

There was, in fact, no immediate reaction to the prosecution, in the sense of a heightened tension at the firm, nor further

---

[38] Duncan was an assistant solicitor in Biggart's law firm. He later became secretary of the SEF and eventually joined the government during the Second World War. See Wigham, *The Power to Manage: A History of the Engineering Employers' Federation*, London, 1973, p. 47.

industrial action. The Boilermakers' Society journal even failed to mention the incident. The ingredients certainly differed from those present in the Fairfield cases; and, of course, no one was imprisoned. Yet Sharp's spirited and somewhat unorthodox assault on the status and credibility of the tribunal proceedings offered a modest example of controlled aggression for constructive aims in an otherwise legally unpromising situation.

BEARDMORE, DALMUIR

However, as if to compensate for the less obtrusive 'profile' which Lobnitz presented in the annals of the Munitions Act, the shipbuilding yard of Beardmore at Dalmuir (near Dumbarton) featured prominently in proceedings undertaken under the Act. Beardmore has attracted considerable attention among labour historians, due principally to the activities of David Kirkwood, convenor of shop stewards at the company's Parkhead Forge works. Kirkwood's immodest account of his personal relations with the company chairman, Sir William Beardmore, his claims to leadership on the Clyde Workers' Committee, his dealings with Lloyd George, and his eventual deportation constitute fragments of the permanent Apocrypha of Red Clydeside.[39] However, Dalmuir, with its predominantly shipbuilding rather than engineering base, was less affected by the concerns which so animated the CWC. It was not so much the perceived threat of dilution in the sense of the possible replacement of skilled men by less-skilled female employees which exerted a disruptive influence on domestic industrial relations. For dilution of this nature scarcely impinged on the shipyards.[40]

The more prosaic interpretation is that wage grievances remained the principal concern of the labour force at Dalmuir,

---

[39] For his own account, see David Kirkwood, *My Life of Revolt*, London, 1935. Less flattering reminiscences are offered in Gallacher, *Revolt on the Clyde*, and in Harry McShane and Joan Smith, *Harry McShane: No Mean Fighter*, London, 1978. For the importance of Beardmore as a wartime producer, see J. R. Hume and Michael S. Moss, *Beardmore: The History of a Scottish Industrial Giant*, London, 1979.

[40] W. R. Scott and J. Cunnison, *Industries of the Clyde Valley during the War*, Oxford, 1924, pp. 85–6; Alastair Reid, 'Dilution, trade unionism and the state in Britain during the First World War', in Steven Tolliday and Jonathan Zeitlin (eds.), *Shop Floor Bargaining and the State*, Cambridge, 1985.

while the statutory demand for the removal of *any* practice which 'tends to restrict production or employment' was of only marginal signficance at Beardmore's yard. None the less, when legal conflicts did arise, a number of them, including those described in this chapter, were spectacular confrontations.

DALMUIR GUN-MOUNTING DISPUTE

Apart from those proceedings involving shipbuilding employees, the prosecution of engineers at Beardmore's gun-mounting department was, as Hinton observes,[41] the first prosecution of striking munitions workers in Glasgow. Moreover, like the Fairfield cases discussed so far, the 'stay-in' strike was untypical in that it did not originate in a wage-rate dispute. None the less, the case had at least one feature in common with many hearings, including the Lobnitz case. This was that the very presence of the Munitions Act undoubtedly encouraged the employer to undertake a specific disciplinary move in respect of his workforce, which he would, at most, have been hesitant or reluctant to implement in the absence of the Act's coercive provisions.

Though the participants' versions of the events differed, it seems that to enable shop stewards at the firm to attend a meeting addressed by Lloyd George in St Andrews' Hall in Glasgow on Christmas Day 1915, it was arranged that they could be paid their wages a day earlier, that is, on the Friday at 5.15 p.m., instead of on the Saturday as was customary.[42] However, the stewards in the gun shop had gained the impression, which they said originated from the instructions of Slade, the departmental manager, that they could collect their pay at 4 o'clock. This claim was denied and early payment was refused, whereupon James Logan, one of the stewards, allegedly told David Cameron, the firm's accountant, 'Good God Almighty, you can surely do me a favour like this, and I will do

---

[41] Hinton, *The First Shop Stewards' Movement*, p. 149.

[42] *Glasgow Herald*, 6, 10 Jan. 1916 for the account of the case. Cf. *Woman's Dreadnought*, 15 Jan. 1916. The ministry instructed the Solicitor-General for Scotland, T. B. Morison, KC, to lead the prosecution. The strikers retained a local solicitor, R. G. Carson, who also employed counsel, J. A. Christie.

you a favour some day.' Logan then saw Archibald Campbell, the general manager, but apparently used such 'disrespectful' language to him that he was dismissed on the following Tuesday. The next day, the men conducted their stay-in strike which lasted until the Friday.

During the trial itself, there were some notable exchanges. The strikers' counsel, cross-examining Slade, the departmental manager, asked, 'Can you tell us what was the violent language used to Mr. Campbell?' 'I can't recall the words,' came the reply. 'It can't have made very much impression on your mind, Mr. Slade,' counsel retorted, to bursts of loud applause from the spectators. Another prosecution witness, a pay clerk, recounted that Logan, on seeing a number of men lining up at the pay office the day before his dismissal, had told them that they were 'a damned lot of idiots waiting there for their money. Why not rush the window and take it?' According to Campbell, the general manager, that outburst was the culminating reason for Logan's dismissal. 'It was quite impossible to suffer such insubordination,' he told the court. His insistence that Logan's dismissal was for disobedience and for intolerable disrespect was, in fact, advanced by the company as its answer to the men's allegation that Logan had been victimized as a shop steward engaging in trade union activities. Both Slade and Campbell were adamant that this was not so.

FYFE (*the tribunal chairman*). You told us that Logan was of pronounced trade union proclivities. Have not all shop stewards these proclivities?

SLADE. I suppose they have. Some can be very reasonable and some can be very unreasonable.

FYFE. You are not suggesting that a man should be dismissed merely because he is an active trade unionist?

SLADE. No. If he is active and confined himself to that only, we welcome the shop steward. They are a benefit to us.

FYFE. Well, I just want to remove the impression that you were dismissing him because he is an active trade unionist.

Turning to Campbell, Fyfe enquired, 'You have ascertained from your staff that he was regarded as an unsettling influence in the shop?'

CAMPBELL. I have had it reported to me that he took up so much of his time with matters of that kind that he rarely got much work done.

It was a well orchestrated attempt by Fyfe to lead Campbell and Slade through potentially dangerous ground which would threaten to elevate Logan to the status of martyr in defence of the right of trade unionists to organize in the firm. Instead, Beardmore was portrayed as an enlightened and progressive employer, fully recognizing the advantages of the shop steward system so long as it was conducted by 'reasonable' men. In this light and in the light of the evidence of Logan's behaviour and advocacy of force in respect to the pay office, their hope was that the public would be persuaded that the firm was not anti-union, or even anti-shop steward. One suspects that few observers' opinions on this matter would have been altered one way or another by such testimony. None the less, so far as the tribunal was concerned, Logan's protestations of innocence—'I have never had any ill words with Mr Campbell yet'—were hardly convincing. Nor were his denials of involvement in any disturbances at the pay office or in the strike itself remotely persuasive. Another shop steward, James Boyd, who had gone to see Campbell, Slade and Beardmore, 'in what we term the harem ("Laughter")', in order to intercede, had had no success. 'Sir William Beardmore very near ate us. He said that under no consideration [sic] would he accept a deputation.' Not even the compromise proposal of reinstatement plus a tribunal hearing against Logan alone, presumably under the Ordering of Work regulations dealing with questions of factory discipline, would be considered by the management.

Thus, lacking evidence to sustain the accusation of victimization, Logan and the strikers were enmeshed in a frustrating situation. No doubt Logan *was* 'disrespectful' and uttered rash remarks. But there is no explanation as to the source of the story that the original paying-out time had been altered from 5.15 to 4 o'clock. Either Logan had invented the story or the management had spread a false rumour possibly hoping thereby to provoke a situation enabling them to deal finally with a shop steward whom the management, as we saw, claimed was an 'unsettling influence in the shop'. If so, then Logan naïvely walked into the trap.

The frustrations felt by the strikers, as they saw themselves being outmanoeuvred from the witness box, certainly spilled over to infect their workmates watching from the public benches. Indeed, the resultant uproar which accompanied the hearing is indicative of the way in which it was not only the litigants who were embroiled in the struggle. The spectators, also, were deeply involved, thereby 'enriching' the atmosphere in which the tribunal hearing was conducted, in much the same way as a prize fight might be promoted.

For some time before the proceedings began on 5 January 1916, the court was crowded by workers supporting the accused, and a strong force of policemen was present.[43] When the Solicitor-General and his junior counsel, M. P. Fraser, entered, there was a good deal of hissing; while on the arrival of the sheriff (a partisan boxing referee?), very few of the crowd stood up, contrary to the custom in courts of law. Even the reading of the complaint by the tribunal clerk (master of ceremonies?), T. F. Wilson, was greeted with ironical applause.

With his reputation for severity firmly established since the Fairfield shipwrights' case, Sheriff Fyfe immediately launched into a stern warning. If there was any expression of feeling, he cautioned, he would clear the court, an utterance which drew further wry applause rather than the instantaneous silence which he was no doubt seeking. 'I think I know the working men pretty well, and a word is quite enough for you. You also know me and you know I mean what I say,' he continued, dispensing *bonhomie*, threats, and bluff in equal measure.

This interaction between tribunal officials, the accused, and the spectators did indeed reach bizarre heights at one stage early in the proceedings, when the strikers' solicitor sought an adjournment so as the better to prepare his case. But Sheriff Fyfe would only assent to the request if the men returned to work. The word of any one of those present at the hearing, declared Fyfe, would be acceptable, whereupon the solicitor pointed out the men's union representative in the audience. But almost immediately one of the accused stood up and repudiated the official's authority to bind the men. Only if Brother Logan were reinstated the following day would work recommence. So Fyfe set about asking each of the accused individually. Yet this ploy also had no effect as soon as the union official signalled to the first accused to answer in the affirmative. As the *Glasgow*

---

[43] On the chief constable's arrangements, see Hinton, *The First Shop Stewards' Movement*, p. 136.

Herald,[44] with sober understatement, noted, 'it was evident that the men in the court did not approve of this course.' To retrieve the situation, therefore, one of the delegates suggested that Fyfe might permit a meeting of the men to be held. What then ensued could well have been written for a Gilbert and Sullivan comic opera. For Sheriff Fyfe, legal counsel, and trade union officials immediately went into a tight huddle, whispering agitatedly to each other. Eventually, a nod of approval to the accused was followed by the spectacle of Fyfe and his entourage of officials and lawyers ceremoniously trooping out of the chamber. But even the disappearance of the procession down the corridor failed to satisfy the accused strikers left behind in the chamber. For they could see that the *police* were still hovering at the back of the courtroom. It was therefore noisily hinted that the latter should likewise vacate the premises, which, to their embarrassment perhaps, they somewhat furtively did. At last it appeared that the accused were free to conduct their unorthodox business. But *still* they were restless in the silent chamber, either overawed by the imposing surroundings, or, more probably, suspicious of possible eavesdroppers. So the staged withdrawal was now completed as they, too, made their exit to seek the privacy of one of the side-rooms in the building.

Possibly nothing to parallel this spectacle had occurred prior to (nor, perhaps, subsequent to) the event in question in the history of legal administration. To offer a court side-room to litigants to agree upon terms of settlement might be a relatively common event. But for a judge to vacate the courtroom itself for the convenience, not of civil litigants, but of large numbers of men accused of committing a crime (for to strike was a criminal offence under the Act) was surely unique. Moreover, transient though it may have been, it was none the less a success for the rank and file whose insistence not to be bound by the dictates of the union officials was even given legitimacy by Fyfe's action in acquiescing in the men's demands to consult workshop representatives.

The outcome of the meeting was an agreement to return to work until Saturday when it was hoped that the trial would recommence at 2 p.m. Fyfe, however, suggested that since the

---

[44] *Glasgow Herald*, 6 Jan. 1916.

hearing would be lengthy, they ought to start in the morning after the men's breakfast-break at work. To laughter from those present, he added that 'the men would have time to have a wash up and be at the court to enjoy themselves by 10.30.' It is, of course, fascinating to note the striking similarity in style between Lloyd George and Sheriff Fyfe in respect to the way in which they tended to address working men. This was, indeed, entirely appropriate, given that the first named was the architect of the Munitions Act and the latter was its most vigorous exponent.

The resumed hearing on the Saturday did, none the less, pass unmemorably. Fyfe expressed some mild criticism of the tactlessness of the pay office, discovered some obscure ground on which to cross swords with the prosecuting counsel, T. B. Morison, delivered his ritual denunciation of strikes in wartime, and having imposed what he genuinely thought to be a modified fine of £5 on each striker, in view of the 'exceptional' circumstances of the case, finally resolved to 'let the matter take its course'. In the event, the Ministry of Munitions subsequently made an abortive effort to extract a statement of regret from the men, and when this failed, did not press for payment of the fines, which remained unpaid.[45]

The Dalmuir hearing thus joins the lengthening catalogue of open displays of working-class ridicule of such sittings, and of the strenuous efforts exerted by the tribunal chairmen to deploy sufficient 'muscle' to appear to vindicate the power and authority of the Act, but not so much as to cause open rebellion or rejection of its legitimacy. For the point must be stressed that the men on trial did not refuse to recognize the authority of the tribunal. They instructed counsel and were prepared to defend the case on its merits. They may have opposed the Act, but not to the extent of refusing absolutely to participate in the proceedings of the tribunal. What they did seek to engage in, notwithstanding, was a course of calculated pressure, involving thrust and counter-thrust over the terms under which they would consent to be tried. It was perhaps not a complete

[45] Hinton, *The First Shop Stewards' Movement*, p. 136; Humbert Wolfe, *Labour Supply and Regulation*, Oxford, 1923, p. 132.

'capture' of a legal institution by working people,[46] but it was a highly significant transformation of the court process none the less. As mentioned previously, the munitions tribunal appeared to have been structured on characteristics both of the ordinary courts of law and of the threats and bluffs informing the practices of tense joint negotiating committees. The Dalmuir hearing possibly represents one of the highest 'achievements' of this combination.

Why Sheriff Fyfe was prepared to tolerate the gradual incursion of 'social' reality into his legal domain, thereby loosening his grip on the proceedings, is not readily apparent. His stubborn insistence, when issuing his judgment in the previous Fairfield case, that the tribunal was not concerned with the reasons causing men to strike, is noticeably missing in this hearing. Perhaps the crowd, including the mass meeting outside the court house, unnerved him in a manner not experienced during the shipwrights' case, with the result that his resolve was weakened, rendering him more amenable to conciliatory gestures. Perhaps the ministry had suggested that he should 'go easy' on the strikers, though there is no documentary evidence in support. Moreover, events subsequent to the Fairfield decision had shown that pompous remarks stressing that legal criteria were the only valid criteria were not always the most judicious ploy. The conduct of the Dalmuir proceedings, indeed, had developed, with the connivance of the chairman, almost into a collective bargaining session. An abject surrender of the law was inconceivable, a tactical retreat with honour tolerable. This perhaps explains Fyfe's uncharacteristic decision to 'impose the penalty and let the matter take its course'. For given the strategic importance for the war effort which the Beardmore gun-mounting shop represented, he could present the authorities with the knotty problem of extracting the fines—if they so dared—and let *them* risk a further confrontation. As to threats of imprisonment in the event of failure to pay, that possibility was

---

[46] In late 1915, Sheriff Lee, responding to massive protests outside his court against eviction hearings brought by Glasgow landlords against their tenants, phoned Lloyd George to press on him the urgency of a remedy. The Rent and Mortgage Interest (Restriction) Act 1915 was passed within three days. The event has been widely documented. See, for example, Hinton, *The First Shop Stewards' Movement*, p. 126; Joseph Melling, *Rent Strikes*, Edinburgh, 1983, pp. 74–103.

expediently and carefully omitted from the tariff of punishments.

THE DEPORTATION STRIKE PROSECUTIONS

For a number of reasons, it is entirely appropriate that the present chapter should conclude with an account of the prosecution of those participating in the 'deportation strikes' of March 1916. As well as marking a crucial watershed in the history of the Government's dilution campaign, the events surrounding the removal of a number of leading shop stewards from the Clyde district corresponded to important shifts in the character of the legal dimension to the history of the wartime labour movement in Glasgow. At the most general, but also most significant level, though grievances over the operation of the Munitions Act continued to be expressed,[47] the massive displays of unrest on Clydeside began thereafter to diminish, as the veteran militant trade unionist, Harry McShane, seems to confirm in his recent autobiography.[48] But there were other related indications. First, while the deportation strikes were the finale of the Clydeside shop stewards' resistance to dilution on Government work imposed on the Government's terms, they also symbolized the final curtain of the regime of the Glasgow tribunal chairmen Gloag, Gibson, and Andrew, whose extreme sensitivity, especially in the case of Gloag, encouraged the militants, in the view of the Ministry of Munitions, to pursue a policy of disruption.

Second, the Munitions Amendment Act, passed in January 1916, authorized the establishment of the Munitions Appeal Tribunal, presided over by the Court of Session Judge, Lord Dewar. Moreover, it was now laid down that in the munitions tribunal, the two lay assessors, if unanimous, could bind the tribunal chairman on any question of fact. Third, from this time, the appearance of women munitions workers before the tribunal became a more frequent, if not yet common occurrence, necessitating the additional appointment of female assessors.

---

[47] For arbitration delays, see chs. 5 and 6. For continuous criticisms of the leaving certificate scheme, see ch. 8.

[48] McShane and Smith, *Harry McShane: No Mean Fighter*, p. 77.

Fourth, a greater number of applications to the tribunals were emanating from the iron and steel trades (and, in particular, from labourers) rather than, as formerly, from the shipbuilding sector. Fifth, more and more cases before the tribunal were inextricably linked to military conscription, whereas this was not an issue for the tribunals to consider (though they did deal with cases involving military *recruitment*) prior to 1916. Sixth, the depth of coverage of the cases in the newspapers altered after this time, as the *military* tribunals attracted more attention. Additionally, there was a greater tendency to omit the names of firms and defendants appearing before the tribunals, even in important strike prosecutions. Presumably this was on the instruction of the censor. Whether the reason was to avoid passing on military secrets to the Germans, to prevent the British public from reading of labour unrest in their own country, which the authorities might think would adversely affect morale, or whether, finally, it was to save the managers of the firms, particularly in the large munitions companies, from any possible embarrassment arising from the cases (and especially from tribunal criticism of their conduct towards their employees) is not clear.

For all the above reasons, then, the deportation strike prosecutions mark an important watershed in the legal, as well as in the industrial, history of wartime Clydeside labour.

The immediate background to the strikes in the district was in fact the decision of the management at the Parkhead Forge works of William Beardmore & Co. Ltd. to refuse freedom of movement throughout the works to David Kirkwood, convenor of shop stewards and one of the leaders of the CWC.[49] A strike broke out at Parkhead on 17 March 1916 and rapidly spread to other works in the district. Over the next ten days several prominent CWC members, including Kirkwood, were deported from the district by the military as the Government sought to argue that the strikes were a political plot. The Government also widely advertized its intention to threaten the strikers with the Munitions Act and with DORA, notices to that effect having been posted in the affected workshops. Moreover, the decision of

[49] Hinton, *The First Shop Stewards' Movement*, pp. 155–60; McLean, *Legend of Red Clydeside*, pp. 78–85.

the ASE executive to condemn the strikes as 'unauthorised and unconstitutional', the refusal of strike pay, and the executive's instruction to the district committee to order the men to resume work[50] allowed the tribunal further leverage in handling the strikers firmly without the fear of incurring the wrath of the union. Indeed, said the *Glasgow Herald*,

There is also abundance of proof that they [the ASE] have been almost as amazed as outsiders at the Government's patience—it is a stronger expression in their mouths; for whilst it may be true in a sense that gravity is only a recent development, the sinister beginnings of the evil were not hatched in an impenetrable secrecy. Many have been the warnings to the Executive, but as in some other matters, a lack of courage has given strength to the forces of disaffection. . . .[51]

The local engineering employers likewise demanded that the Government 'put the fullest powers of the Defence of the Realm Act into operation against ringleaders'.[52] One significant feature, we may observe, is the emphasis which the employers, perhaps unconsciously reflecting a corporatist strategy for munitions production, consistently placed on the steps which the *Government*, rather than the employers themselves, ought to take to meet the threat posed by militants. For they perceived such issues as 'law and order', or even constitutional, questions. While the employers readily supplied the names of 'agitators and undesirables' within their establishments to the dilution commissioners, the evidence necessary for prosecution, they insisted, had to be obtained by the Government.[53]

That it was the Ministry of Munitions which prosecuted the strikers, rather than their employers, was therefore entirely consistent with the view taken of the strike by the employers; that is, that it was directed against the Military Service Act, all forms of Government control, the agreement of the ASE to dilution, and the Committee on Production's recent decision on a local Clyde wages question.[54] These were all features which

[50] *Glasgow Herald*, 27 Mar. 1916.

[51] Ibid.

[52] North-West Engineering Trades Employers' Association (NWETEA), *Minute Book No. 7*, 23 Mar. 1916. A sub-committee was also delegated to meet the government's 'dilution commissioners' to press the need for prosecutions. See ibid.

[53] Ibid., 27 Mar. 1916.

[54] Ibid., 23 Mar. 1916. This was also the argument put by Christopher Addison, Lloyd George's deputy in the Commons. See McLean, *Legend of Red Clydeside*, p. 81.

pointed to a political campaign, rather than to a domestic industrial relations issue. The protestation of the CWC that 'the trouble at Parkhead is purely local, and is no part of any general policy' clearly failed to convince.[55]

The trial itself took place in two sessions, the first hearings being conducted on 29 March in the thick of the struggle. Ten of the accused were from Beardmore's Parkhead Forge, ten from the Dalmuir gun-mounting shop and a further ten from the North British Diesel Engine Works at Whiteinch. The neat symmetry was a product of Sheriff Fyfe's suggestion that a representative number be selected from the principal sites affected, in order, so he told the tribunal, 'to cause as little inconvenience as possible'.[56]

For the occasion, the strikers had been able to obtain the services of Rosslyn Mitchell, the 'lawyer dandy'[57] and confrère of David Kirkwood. It may indeed have been an inspired choice, in the sense that Mitchell was not prepared to let proceedings run an uncontroversial course confined to the eliciting of stark answers to the uncomplicated question whether these accused had in fact breached the Munitions Act by participating in an illegal strike. Instead, he harried the chairman, Sheriff Fyfe, and the ministry prosecutor, J. Turner MacFarlane, by raising gratuitous and obstructive preliminary pleas designed, no doubt, to deflect attention from the substantive legal question whether the men had committed the alleged offence. When he could go no further in undermining the prosecution case prior to addressing this question, he simply refused to participate any more in the proceedings.

Thus he first attempted to question MacFarlane's credentials authorizing the latter to prosecute, an objection which Fyfe dismissed as 'impertinent'. Next, he applied for a postponement of the hearing on the ground that the most important witnesses for the defence were precisely those who had been removed by the military authorities. They alone could speak on 'interviews

---

Ironically, this analysis should have *prevented* proceedings under the Munitions Act, since the definition of a strike under Section 19(b) only covered action over an employer's terms of employment. It was the *CWC's* view of the strike's objective which, by contrast, met the criteria of Section 19(b).

[55] *Glasgow Herald*, 30 Mar. 1916.
[56] Ibid.
[57] Arthur Marwick, *The Deluge*, London, 1973 edn., p. 74.

and other matters relative to the facts'. Any attempt to conduct a hearing in the absence of these witnesses could only lead to a 'burlesque trial'. Mitchell, however, protested too much. It was, of course, his intention throughout to orchestrate the proceedings in this way. For a 'proper' trial would only confirm the 'legitimacy' of the men's guilt. By portraying the proceedings as 'burlesque', the legitimacy of the verdicts themselves might appear to be compromised or sullied.

However, on being pressed by Fyfe that a postponement was generally permitted only where the accused returned to work, Mitchell replied that the 'whole atmosphere had changed since the stoppage in question,' as a result of the deportation of the shop stewards. For, he continued, 'six of the men who knew about it had suddenly been kidnapped from their homes, and were now hidden away from the defence. Indeed, he did not know what men would be available as witnesses next week. He did not know when his men would disappear,' he added, to roars of laughter from the large and vociferous crowd watching the proceedings. Thus a stalemate was reached, as no return to work was remotely likely at that juncture.

In reviewing Mitchell's tactics, it is clear that he had little interest in ascertaining the correctness or otherwise of the legal charge. His object was rather to dramatize the event with a view to depriving the final verdicts (that the accused were 'guilty') of that conventional legitimacy which the theatre of judicial proceedings is designed to promote. Finishing with the rhetorical flourish that 'there were men who regarded it as of more importance that the military should not be permitted to take away men in the midst of the night from their houses than that munitions should be produced,' he finally made his dramatic exit, announcing that he proposed to take no further part in the proceedings.

Since the defence offered no evidence, Sheriff Fyfe once more embarked upon his solemn lecture. Yet he seemed to invest it with a deeper political significance than in previous condemnations of strikers in wartime. For no doubt he was conscious of the climactic nature of the cases before him. Thus he declared that

Their solicitor had been perfectly frank, that they were out to defy the law and the Government. You have taken up the attitude that a certain shop steward is to manage the work. . . . I venture to think that not only the law of the land but the common sense of the nation is against any such preposterous doctrine.

What was therefore novel was that by stripping away the façade of legal technicality Sheriff Fyfe had expressly disavowed the supposedly apolitical nature of legal formalism which underpins capitalist legal relations. Of course, within the context of a corporatist-inclined munitions code, Fyfe made connections between law and policy every time he sat in judgment in a munitions tribunal. But this was conditioned by wartime exigencies. His political pronouncement in the deportation strike hearings was surely both descriptive *and* prescriptive of the legal foundations of an industrial society free from the ravages of war restrictions. Yet, ironically, his defence of a capitalist legal regime which would continue long after the experiment with war collectivism had expired was an outspoken political response on behalf of a system which was not, in fact, under threat. For although a number of the accused, during the second diet of hearings arising out of the deportation strikes, expressed a revolutionary motive informing their industrial action, it is clear that the strikes were confined to more parochial questions pertaining to Kirkwood's freedom of movement at Parkhead Forge. Political change played little or no part in the strikers' agenda. By misconstruing the situation and by obfuscating the motives of the strikers, Fyfe uncharacteristically allowed his rhetoric to get the better of him. For he used his judicial office as a platform from which to launch an explicitly political repudiation of what he wrongly perceived was the shop stewards' vision of the coming revolution.

Yet at the second round of tribunal hearings in the wake of the deportation strikes,[58] the sheriff was in fact confronted with the spectacle of three accused shop stewards who did indeed adopt a pronounced revolutionary stance during the proceedings. One of these individuals was an American, John Cuzins (or Cuzen), a member of the International Machinists' Union of America. In presenting his case to the tribunal, he had first attempted to

---

[58] *Glasgow Herald*, 14 Apr. 1916; AIMS, *Monthly Report*, May 1916, 72. About 60 men were tried on this occasion. Thirty-two were fined £5 each, about 25 established that they had been ill at the relevant time and several Belgians were excused.

widen the scope of the dialogue by pointing out the dangerous condition of the machine he had been operating. He was not in fact the first accused to raise this matter. Another American, Thomas Nolan, had testified that he had been informed in Philadelphia that Beardmore was to give them 'proper labour conditions'. Obviously sensing a threatened loss of control, Fyfe immediately stopped this line of argument, declaring, 'We are not concerned with labour conditions here.' Here again is illustrated the imposition of legally defined criteria of relevance whereby the 'secondary' reality of law elbows out the 'primary' reality of individuals' own experiences. Cuzins was no more successful in his endeavour than Nolan. So having failed to deflect attention to the company's failings, he expounded his own philosophy. He had come out in sympathy with the other strikers, for, he asserted, 'Men were justified in breaking the law if the law was against the men.' But such remarks were scarcely bound to impress Sheriff Fyfe whose response was to impose a hefty fine of £20 on Cuzins. Thus, 'Not only had he broken the law, but he had come before the tribunal and upheld the principle of breaking the law. That was an attitude which the tribunal could not regard otherwise than in a serious light. If [the] accused lived in a country, he must obey the law of the country.' Cuzins was followed into the dock by William Craig, a shop steward at Dalmuir. He also felt the men were justified in breaking the law, for which deed he did not feel in the least sorry. Indeed, since matters had, he added, quietened down in the district, this latest batch of prosecutions would only inflame tempers once more. Moreover, the authorities themselves had ignored the men's request that their grievances be addressed. Six weeks of inaction had elapsed, and, technically under the Munitions Act, strike action was permissible after three weeks' notification to the Board of Trade.

The revelation that constitutional steps had been taken in vain[59] persuaded Sheriff Fyfe to recall to the witness stand a third accused, David Hanton, a shop steward at Parkhead Forge. As one of Kirkwood's lieutenants, he had been directly

---

[59] The story is supported by the narrative account in the *Manifesto Issued during the Strike at Parkhead Forge 1916, by the Engineers—Addressed to Fellow-Workers in the District.* See copy in Scott and Cunnison, *Industries of the Clyde Valley,* app. xix; *Glasgow Herald,* 1 Apr. 1916; ASE, *Monthly Journal and Report* (executive council report), Apr. 1916.

Strike Prosecutions

involved in an incident at the New Howitzer Shop which had triggered the whole deportation episode, when the shop stewards sought to check the wage lines of newly imported female workers.[60] No permission to do so had formally been granted by the management, and this was used as the pretext to prevent Kirkwood's freedom of movement as convenor of shop stewards (given these facts, the selection of Hanton among the equal number of strikers from each factory casts doubts on whether there had been a random selection from each establishment).

Hanton had already been found guilty by the tribunal and fined £25 after having replied to Fyfe's questioning that in this instance, he too felt it was justifiable to break the law. As a shop steward, it was, for him, a matter of principle that he support the men striking over the restrictions imposed on Kirkwood; indeed, he still at the time of the trial adhered to that view. Fyfe was, however, governed by different principles. 'A man occupying the position of shop steward,' sniffed the worthy sheriff, 'instead of encouraging the breaking of the law, should try to see that the men obeyed the law. The tribunal regretted that a man who acted as shop steward should take up the attitude—which he still defiantly did—that going on strike on March 17 was justified.' However, on his recall to the witness stand, Hanton explained that the outstanding grievance to which the previous accused, William Craig, had referred concerned the non-union status of soldiers, themselves skilled engineers, drafted into the Forge to undertake turning and fitting. According to Hanton, the agreement to maintain a union shop was thereby breached, a matter reported to the authorities but not rectified after a long passage of time. In the light of this, he implied, the strike was surely lawful. Yet according to Sheriff Fyfe, that arrangement was superseded by the dilution scheme which made provision for wholesale workshop changes; and given this premiss, it was logical for him now to conclude that 'Whether the men belonged to a union or not is a matter of absolute indifference.' Thus by sleight of hand,

[60] Labour Party, *Report of the . . . Deportation in March 1916 of David Kirkwood and other Workmen . . .*, London, 1917, esp. paras. 60–71. Hanton later stood unsuccessfully for the post of Glasgow district secretary of the ASE, a position won by Harry Hopkins of the Govan Trades Council. See *Glasgow Herald*, 11 Oct., 12 Nov. 1917; ASE, *Monthly Journal and Report*, Oct. 1917, 4.

the men's original grievance was defined out of existence and the strike tainted with illegality. There was an unbridgeable gap separating the two competing realities, reflected in the imposition of punitive fines on the one hand and the affirmation of the justice of the strike on the other.

We may observe, therefore, that the verbal interchanges during the hearing constitute remarkable examples both of the articulation of alternative realities *and* of the simultaneous and frank recognition by Sheriff Fyfe that the law could not possibly tolerate the 'preposterous doctrine' of workers' control. In the first instance, Fyfe repeatedly emphasized the primacy of legal autonomy: that is, that law was an independent institution, compliance with which was a fundamental and absolute obligation which could not be subject to any condition precedent. For the accused, however, 'legal reality' was refracted through 'social reality'. If the latter dictated a course of conduct at odds with the injunctions of the former, then the path illuminated by the latter must be followed if the issue in question were sufficiently grave to justify a departure from strict obedience to laws.

Yet, secondly, to insist on the artificial separation of legal reality from social reality was, at base, tactical. After all, the exercise of discretion conferred on judges frequently turned on assessments of what was deemed to be socially or politically practicable or desirable. Indeed, the munitions code itself inevitably embodied partisan policy objectives. Fyfe's outspoken defence of what were, in effect, capitalist property relations was not as sharp a break with traditional judicial utterances as might have been supposed. None the less, his repudiation of the idea of the workers 'managing the shops' was an admission of the partisanship of law as the idealization of the capitalist system which most judges, except the brash, such as Bramwell or Atkinson,[61] eschewed making. In a sense stepping

[61] For Bramwell (1808–92) and for Atkinson (1844–1932), see A. W. B. Simpson (ed.), *Biographical Dictionary of the Common Law*, London, 1984, pp. 14, 19–20. Bramwell was an 'exponent of rugged individualism', especially noticeable in mid-19th c. trade union cases. Atkinson, 'under the guise of restating the law . . . was able to inject his own extremely Conservative brand of politics'. The best known example concerned his attack on the 'eccentric principles of socialistic philanthropy' and the 'vanity of appearing as model employers' shown by George Lansbury's Poplar Council in the 1920s. See *Roberts v. Hopwood* [1925] AC 578.

out of the context of wartime corporatist law, Fyfe's self-proclaimed neutrality, and his loyalty only to the rule of law as the embodiment of that neutrality, thus suffered a revealing lapse. In this respect, by striving to emphasize the primacy of 'legal reality' while rejecting as 'preposterous' a programme for workers' control, the tribunal hearings paradoxically both supported and exposed as a fallacy the ideology of the law as an institution wholly autonomous of dominant class interests.[62]

CONCLUSION

It may be argued that the close inspection of the major proceedings of the Glasgow munitions tribunal recounted in this chapter ought to be of interest not only to the labour historian, but also to the analyst of court room procedure, and to those engaged in exploring working-class attitudes to law. The hearings themselves were no longer simply a forum for adjudication, but an environment within which displays of bluster, cajolery, bullying, and intimidation were employed in varying degrees by accused trade unionists or by their representatives. Yet such behaviour was rarely, if ever, pointless or negative. As tactical ploys, such displays were adopted precisely in order, as those unionists conceived it, the better to advance their or their members' interests. Indeed, when we analysed the fascinating verbal exchanges between tribunal chairmen and the accused or their representatives, we saw how the chairmen attempted in vain to prevent this transformation (and indeed to prevent disorder generally at the tribunal) by endeavouring to control the content of courtroom conversation by reference to legally defined criteria of relevance. They found

---

[62] It is not claimed that the stance adopted by the shop stewards was necessarily comprehended in these terms by all those participating in the strikes. We are dealing merely with how a number of strikers hauled before the tribunal, perceived the experience. Nor are we arguing for widespread popular support for these men's resistance to the law. They were indeed the minority who were prepared to make a principled stand. Bearing in mind, also, that the strikes did not enjoy overwhelming support among munitions workers on the Clyde, it is open to question whether these strikers' actions achieved popular legitimacy, let alone popular support. It is arguable, indeed, that the Fairfield coppersmiths' actions, in view of their union's support for behaviour which their secretary had described as 'quite legal', came closest to attaining such popular legitimacy.

difficulty, however, in holding back the efforts of determined adversaries intent on imposing on the proceedings *their* alternative reality. No matter how much trade unionists might bemoan and bewail the Munitions Act while they were at work, their attitude to it was transformed once they were congregated in the hall where the tribunal was meeting. *Now* it became the means by which they could enjoy a carnival atmosphere at the expense of the dignified pomposity of the law; perhaps, indeed, the tribunal was a surrogate for their own employers whom they might be inhibited from treating in a similar fashion. There is therefore no evidence from the tribunal proceedings analysed here that workers struck a reverential posture towards the institutions and personnel of the law. On the contrary, experience points to the tribunals as the object of ridicule, rather than of respect, a function, no doubt, of the chairmen's inability successfully to employ remedial devices in order to routinize and thus render impotent outbreaks of tribunal disorder.

However, the contempt of trade unionists for the proceedings was double-edged. For, in the final analysis, they were prepared not merely to *defend* cases vigorously with the assistance of lawyers and trade union officialdom; they were even prepared, as will be more fully elaborated in subsequent chapters, to go on the legal offensive and take their *employers* to court. There is little doubt that working-class attitudes to law were in this light complex, often opportunistic, and occasionally contradictory.

In evaluating the contribution of the Glasgow munitions tribunal to the policy objective of disciplining recalcitrant workers who went on strike or who otherwise engaged in collective behaviour prohibited by the Act, it is evident how unsuccessful was the effort of the authorities to stamp out repetitions of such conduct. Perhaps the penalties prescribed for Ordering of Work, that is, disciplinary offences (as distinct from strikes), were seen by all to be derisory; a maximum fine of £3 was laid down in the Act. Moreover, the Fairfield episodes, coming so early in the history of the tribunals, deprived these institutions of strong credibility as a deterrent to be feared by Clydeside labour. The more widespread was the militancy, the more forlorn were the efforts of the chairmen to change either attitudes or behaviour. The fact is that such judicial institutions were not always the most appropriate bodies to handle the kinds of disputes which continually surfaced at this time. A judicial forum must come down on one side or the other. It cannot engage in distributive justice or make allocations as an arbitrator might do; or reach compromises as a joint negotiating committee might agree upon. In the most crucial department, that of deciding on guilt or innocence, the tribunal was engaged in a zero-sum game. In respect of sentencing, it could exercise discretion, as it could when hearing leaving certificate applications. Clearly, it capitalized on this escape route as frequently as possible, in an attempt to pacify an unsettled Clydeside labour movement. But when this avenue was not open to it, then the tribunal's ruling that, for example, workers had committed an offence by striking illegally merely succeeded in prolonging a grievance and building up further resentment. While an arbitration award might dispose of an initial dispute, the tribunal only furthered it. While, in the final analysis, it is impossible to prove whether the existence of the tribunals resulted in the bottling-up of grievances which otherwise would have been forcefully pursued, the evidence of repeated conduct prohibited by the Act which is displayed in this chapter, and indeed, throughout the whole work, strongly indicates that where the prospects for successful arbitration were considered dim or non-existent by groups of workers, then the tribunals were no deterrent against industrial action. Indeed, it can be advanced that for many such groups, the existence of the tribunals failed even to cause them to contemplate the usefulness of arbitration. The testimony of many strikers that they were unaware of the provisions for compulsory arbitration or of the unlawfulness of strikes is, of course, evidence not of the state of their legal knowledge, but of their sheer indifference towards, perhaps even contempt for, its restraints. Against this determination, and recognizing the ultimate futility of their efforts to stamp out strikes and other breaches of works rules, the tribunal chairmen were reduced to attempts to control the conduct of proceedings by delimiting the content of permitted court room conversation. And when this ploy spectacularly broke down in dramatic and well-publicized circumstances, the tribunal chairmen were left to go through the motions in determining guilt or innocence, and in trying to preserve their own self-respect. This entailed the imposition, on occasion, of relatively harsh punishments, but it more frequently led, through the exercise of discretion, to the imposition of mild sentences, reflecting the chairmen's surrender to the stubborn reality that law was no weapon to suppress (though it could attempt to punish) industrial action. Law, in short, was not so much the restrainer of industrial conflict, as the amplifier.

CHAPTER 4

The *Other* Clyde 'Deportations'

INTRODUCTION

In articulating the theoretical framework within which to locate the application of wartime labour regulation, we emphasized in Chapter 1 that a corporatist perspective was the closest approximate description of central Government policy which it was possible to identify. Indeed, given a context within which policy indecision and trial and error were, to some extent, inevitable, and where the small band of senior Ministry of Munitions officials might not necessarily approach the implementation of a robust labour regulation policy with equal zeal, the existence of even an 'inchoate coherence' was surely remarkable.

What we propose to argue in this chapter is that the advancement of the broad contours of identifiable ministry objectives also possessed implications for the *legal* enforcement of the Munitions Act. Thus tribunal chairmen might be expected to adopt an approach to legal construction of the Act which reflected the executive's interpretation of the law, to the exclusion of any alternative construction. Moreover, to the extent that judicial officers retained discretion in decision-making, this, too, was to be exercised in accordance with executive wishes and priorities. The corollary of such an approach to judicial interpretation and enforcement of legislation was that the classical liberal doctrine of the independence of the judiciary was expected by the ministry to be held in abeyance for the duration. The doctrine of the separation of powers among the legislature, executive, and judiciary was temporarily expendable in the drive to force through the policy of the Munitions Act.[1] As a result, those Glasgow tribunal

[1] That the Diceyian doctrine of the separation of powers and the rule of law constituted an ideological myth during the classical, non-classical, and 'late' capitalist phases is itself a fruitful source of debate which cannot be explored here. Modern literature on the subject is too vast to mention, much of it inspired by E. P. Thompson's brief observations in *Whigs and Hunters*, Harmondsworth, 1977, pp. 258–69.

chairmen who considered themselves to be independent upholders of the rule of law and privileged to issue judgments 'without fear or favour' were destined to be both sadly deluded and sacrificed to a more instrumental and less idealistic policy. Indeed, the act of delivering a decision of which the Ministry of Munitions disapproved may perhaps have been marginally a greater crime in the eyes of the executive than the failure of Glasgow chairmen to maintain order in the tribunal. For tribunal disorder was experienced elsewhere in the country, but did not result in the replacement of the chairmen involved. Moreover, Sheriff Fyfe himself had presided over hearings which were far from tranquil. Yet the difference in this instance was that, unlike Gloag, Fyfe did not shrink from imposing severe punishments (even though they remained, none the less, within the statutorily prescribed tariff). No doubt the ministry reasoned that a 'hard man' (a type perhaps not unknown in a city like Glasgow) would be more likely to triumph over disorder than a manifestly weak one.

The fact remains that Gloag, Gibson, and Andrew were all removed from their chairmanships after just eight months on the tribunal bench. In Gloag's case, as we shall see, it was essentially because he lacked the strength of character to insist on punitive measures against aggressive munitions workers. In the case of Gibson and Andrew, their removal became imperative for the ministry once they began in the course of their judgments to peddle their own ideas of what Ministry of Munitions wages policy ought to embrace. Thus, just as a number of Clydeside shop stewards were deported when they sought to challenge the assumptions underlying the labour policies of the centralized State bureaucracy, so, too, did these tribunal chairmen become victims of those same civil servants for having had the audacity to assert their own brand of autonomy.

THE HOUNDING OF PROFESSOR GLOAG

The transformation of the tribunal hearings into running exchanges of biting ferocity which we noted in Chapter 3 rapidly became known to even the highest authority within the Ministry of Munitions. Early in August 1915, at a meeting with the Shipbuilding Employers' Federation, Lloyd George raised the matter of the Fairfield shipyard coppersmiths' prosecution. At the conclusion of that tribunal hearing, a number of striking coppersmiths, as we saw in Chapter 3, had been fined just 2*s*. 6*d*. each for having infringed the Munitions Act. As Lloyd George told the secretary of the shipbuilders' federation, Thomas Biggart, 'I thought that prosecution in Scotland was very unsatisfactory. I read a report of it, and I was very distressed about it.'[2] Biggart, who had attended the tribunal hearing, complained that Gloag, the tribunal chairman, had given too much latitude to the men and their representatives. Thus, he had, 'allowed the Union's representatives to pop up and down. There were also 30 or 40 men sitting in the front seat of the Court, and he allowed at least half-a-dozen of them to begin to raise points and ask questions, and of course the matter got out of hand.' However, it was not merely the *conduct* of the proceedings which offended Biggart who, as secretary also of the Clyde Shipbuilders' Association, had had many years experience negotiating with the local shipbuilding unions. It was that Gloag's terms for a resumption of work involving the imposition of a derisory penalty of just half-a-crown, resort to the status quo, and reference to the Board of Trade for an arbitration settlement,

did not commend themselves to those who felt that if the Act was to get a chance, such a glaring case ought to be dealt with in some decisive manner . . . [and] instead of narrating his view of the action which the men had taken, he intimated his half-a-crown fine, and then passed on to a few general remarks.

Biggart, like Llewellyn Smith, Beveridge, and Rey at the Ministry of Munitions,[3] clearly believed that a policy of bold prosecutions conducted both by the ministry and by employers individually would sufficiently deter other munitions workers from undertaking strike action and from committing works offences, but *only* if the initial prosecutions were widely shown to be successful.[4] The demonstrative effect of this Fairfield

---

[2] MUN 5/48/300/9 for this and subsequent quotes.

[3] Harris, *William Beveridge: A Biography*, Oxford, 1977.

[4] Biggart's legal background may have led him to overestimate the efficacy of the law. However, as secretary of a number of employers' associations in Scotland, including the engineers, shipbuilders, coppersmiths, brassfounders, dry dock owners, and structural

prosecution, however, could only be to encourage further rebelliousness. Though Biggart considered that the professor's performances at subsequent hearings, including the Lobnitz shipyard holders-on case, were adequate, there was no denying that Gloag's copybook was now blotted and that a careful watch over his handling of hearings was being maintained by the local ministry officials.

However, if, according to the *Forward*,[5] 'the Capitalist class are furious at the result of the trial,' the strongest condemnation emanating from the local ministry official, Paterson, was reserved for Gloag's handling of the Bridges case. This was a case involving a Weir's shop steward charged with molesting a fellow worker and brought before the tribunal at the end of October 1915.[6] What had actually occurred between Bridges and the worker is not clear, though the 330 men employed in Bridges's department at Weir's believed that all he had done was to ask the worker to show him his union card in accordance with custom. The case was clearly perceived, therefore, as one of victimization against a shop steward; and in this combative mood, the rank and file descended on the tribunal clearly intent on disruption. The sober tones of the *Glasgow Herald* offer one version of events. It reported that

The business . . . was conducted with some difficulty owing to the unruly disposition of a number of workmen who attended the court. They frequently indulged in demonstrations of approval or disapproval of the proceedings, and at times their conduct was so irregular that the intervention of the two police officers who were in attendance was necessary. The disturbances were not of a serious nature and the persuasion of a constable sufficed to restore order. . . .[7]

---

engineers, he ought to have been more aware of the limits of the law. The combination of Biggart's legal and industrial relations activity was no doubt aided by the fact that his firm, Biggart, Lumsden & Co., occupied the same building as the employers' associations. Despite amalgamations and other changes in organization, this remains the case to this day. For biographical details of Biggart, see the *Bailie*, CVI, No. 2751 (1 July 1925), pp. 3–4; and Wigham, *The Power to Manage: A History of the Engineering Employers' Federation*, London, 1973, pp. 46–7. During the war, he also acted for an organization entitled the Association of Controlled Establishments set up in 1916 to seek the minimization of liability for excess profits duty. See *Glasgow Herald*, 6 July 1916.

[5] *Forward*, 7 Aug. 1915, commenting on the *Glasgow Herald* editorial of 3 Aug.
[6] Hinton, *The First Shop Stewards' Movement*, London, 1973, pp. 118–9; *Glasgow Herald*, 26 Oct. 1915; *Forward*, 30 Oct. 1915.
[7] *Glasgow Herald*, 26 Oct. 1915.

The version given by the local ministry official, writing to the assistant general secretary Umberto Wolff at the ministry headquarters in London is, however, more dramatic. Paterson wrote that

When the *Lumgair* [i.e. Bridges] case was announced, absolute pandemonium reigned for several minutes. On at least half a dozen occasions, the proceedings were so riotous as to have justified the clearing of the court, but all that happened was a feeble attempt to call for order.[8]

But this was not all. A number of leaving certificate applications as well as further prosecutions were set down for the same hearing,

and each workman as he came forward to the bar was loudly applauded by his fellow workmen at the back of the hall. The employers, managers and time-keepers who attended to give evidence were greeted with booing and hissing. A similar outburst took place when any workman was refused his certificate, and in the cases in which certificates were granted, the men loudly cheered.[9]

This was too much for the respectable dignitaries of the tribunal. 'You are only delaying the Court with that nonsense,' pleaded Thomas Wilson, the tribunal clerk, while Gloag himself threatened to have a riveter committed to gaol if he did not cease interrupting the evidence being presented.

The spectacle at the conclusion of the hearing, especially the uproar following an announcement of the abandonment of the charges against Bridges, left a deep impression on Paterson, the ministry official. He was quick to allocate blame for the chaos. He complained that

This is allowed to happen with only one chairman of the munitions tribunals in the district, viz. Professor Gloag, who whatever his ability as an advocate and Professor of Scots Law in the Glasgow University is of such a highly strung, sensitive, self-conscious, nervous and mild disposition that he is constitutionally unfit to occupy the bench in any court that is *likely* to be attended from time to time by groups of unruly workmen. Yesterday afternoon was quite the worst court we have had yet but there have been others presided over by the same chairman which were allowed to be conducted in a most undignified manner.[10]

---

[8] LAB 2/47/MT107/1, Paterson to Wolff, 26 Oct. 1915.
[9] Ibid.
[10] Ibid. Italics in original.

Presumably, the coppersmiths' case was the other prime example. Part of the trouble was in fact Gloag's own physical shortcoming in the form of his pronounced lisp. While he did not become an object of unfair ridicule on this account, his speech defect did allow workers to exploit the situation. Thus a number of the coppersmiths alleged that they were unable to hear his judgment and asked him to repeat it. This he did both loudly and deliberately, but this served only to heighten the sense of occasion and encouraged the men to bawl back at him in a similar manner.[11]

Even without this added complication, Gloag's capacity for the job was clearly exhausted. Paterson therefore concluded, 'I accordingly recommend that some way be found at once to arrange that Professor Gloag does not sit as Chairman of any more munitions tribunals. Probably, the only way is to terminate his appointment as a Chairman; if so, I am afraid that course must be taken.'[12]

With this suggestion, Wolff concurred. But one problem was how to ease Gloag out of office without generating suspicion among munitions workers that he was being punished for having imposed light sentences in strike prosecutions, as against the heavier penalties prescribed by Sheriff Fyfe. A resignation and not a dismissal was obviously preferable. Wolff therefore suggested to his ministry colleague Beveridge that Gloag, as a dual chairman, ought to be relieved of the burden of the *general* tribunal which dealt with the strike cases.

He will no doubt see through this statement and will in all probability resign both offices which, except for the impression it might create among the workmen, would in itself, be a satisfactory conclusion. I could imagine, however, that secretly he could not altogether object to be relieved of a difficult office.[13]

Beveridge told much the same thing to the permanent secretary Llewellyn Smith some three weeks later, adding that Gloag's removal from *both* tribunals was necessary since the local tribunals also dealt with 'important' questions. Moreover, another chairman, probably Gibson, had urged Paterson to withdraw Gloag; otherwise he would resign. In the end, the

[11] *Forward*, 30 Oct. 1915.
[12] LAB 2/47/MT107/1.
[13] Ibid., Wolff to Beveridge, 27 Oct. 1915.

same difficulty of how to administer the *coup de grâce* troubled the ministry officials. As Beveridge wrote, 'I have considered what would be the gentlest way of dispensing with him but can find no subterfuge. We cannot say there is not enough work because we may very well have to find another Chairman if we dispense with him.[14] They might suggest to Gloag that a regular, practising lawyer was required. But whatever explanation was given, it was 'better to write and say that on the whole the work is not well suited to him'.

Two draft letters were accordingly prepared, apparently by Keenlyside, head of the munitions tribunal section at the ministry, but never sent. One merely asked him how best to rectify the disturbances, while no doubt hoping he would take the hint and resign. The second was polite but firm and read

I understand that you have been experiencing some difficulty owing to the pressure of a disorderly element among those who attend the sittings of your Tribunals. I fully realise that the position of Munitions Tribunals in this regard is not an easy one. They have behind them no historic tradition to inspire respect. They have at hand no well recognized means of enforcing it. Moreover the Act under which the tribunals are constituted is viewed in some quarters with suspicion and even with hostility. In these circumstances a heavy burden is thrown upon the Chairman who not only has to decide new problems of great difficulty, but has at the same time to contend with disturbing factors which would be quite foreign in an ordinary Court of Law. The spirit of unrest is apparently prevalent in the Clyde area. ... Open manifestations of disrespect for the tribunals (such as have occurred, I am told, in Glasgow) may do much to counteract the salutary effect upon the public of the good work which they undoubtedly perform.

It is on these grounds that we have come to the conclusion that the Chairman of a busy Tribunal—particularly in a district such as Glasgow—should have considerable experience of the exercise of disciplinary powers. I therefore venture to suggest, though with great reluctance, that you may think it well, in the light of these considerations, to resign your appointments as Chairman. . . .[15]

Of course, insisted the ministry, no criticism of Gloag's legal qualifications, 'for which we in the department have the highest

[14] Ibid., Beveridge to Llewellyn Smith, 17 Nov. 1915.
[15] Ibid., Draft letter, Keenlyside (?) to Gloag, c. mid-Nov. 1915 (?).

respect', was thereby implied. Also unthinkable on the part of the ministry was the 'existence of any suspicion that your judgments have in the smallest degree been influenced by these disturbances'. The reality was different. Gloag's legal qualifications pointed to his donnish character, which failed to meet the ministry's dictatorial needs; while the ministry's comments on his judgments were the very opposite of the truth. They well knew that he had been intimidated in strike cases into imposing lenient penalties.

For some days the matter rested while Gloag took a short vacation. On his return, however, Paterson in Glasgow resumed the campaign against him, writing to Wolff and describing Gloag's performance at a local tribunal on 29 November. 'It does not appear', wrote Paterson,[16] 'that he has come back in any way strengthened by his rest.' Thus he explained that the local assistant ministry prosecutor, James Matson, had had a 'bad' case, with evidence clearly showing that a workman had been guilty on frequent occasions of bringing drink into a controlled establishment. Matson reported that he had heard Gloag tell the assessors that a £3 maximum fine would be appropriate. The workmen's assessor immediately protested and Gloag responded by dropping the amount to £1. The workmen's representative still shook his head and suggested 10 s. Finally a figure of 15 s. was agreed. Fortunately, wrote Paterson, the court was not a heavy one, with no particularly contentious cases. There was therefore little difficulty in keeping order. However, since the tribunal was sitting daily, he feared that awkward cases would arise in the future where further 'scenes' would occur. 'If this happens', he concluded,[17] 'I shall be greatly surprised if you do not receive at once the resignation of one of the other two chairmen, if not both.' The essence of the case against Gloag, then, was his weakness in maintaining order in the tribunal and his pusillanimity in imposing sentences. It was not that he disagreed on policy grounds with what the ministry was attempting to achieve through the tribunals. It was simply that he lacked the strength of character and an adequately ruthless streak to force through an unpopular policy with

---

[16] Ibid., Paterson to Wolff, 30 Nov. 1915.
[17] Ibid.

sufficient severity. His decisions—whether an individual had committed an Ordering of Work offence; whether groups of workers had, in law, participated in an unlawful strike; whether a leaving certificate had or had not been unjustifiably withheld by an employer—were not necessarily at odds with the wishes of the ministry.

Indeed, there is a certain irony in a leaving certificate decision of Gloag's issued during the same session which heard the Bridges case.[18] Though the facts were disputed at the hearings of the Balfour–Macassey Commission set up in October 1915 to enquire into the causes of labour unrest on Clydeside,[19] it seems that three riveters had been hired at the Scotstoun West yard of Barclay Curle shipbuilding company, in order to work at the company's neighbouring dry dock at Elderslie. Subsequently, the firm wished to transfer them back to the Scotstoun site, but the men adamantly refused to change sites again. Instead they applied for leaving certificates, which the company withheld. When the tribunal hearing came on, the CSA, representing the employer, argued that the case involved an important point of principle, the right of an employer to transfer an employee from one department or one site to another.[20] Clearly, the grant or refusal of a leaving certificate by the tribunal would be seen by employer and union as determining the legitimacy of an employer's claim to deploy labour as he saw fit. As the Boilermakers' official, Bill Sharp, later told the Balfour–Macassey enquiry, 'a big principle, in our opinion, is established here. If the firm had got away with this, they would be simply trying it on with other people.'[21] The issue of leaving certificates therefore seems almost incidental, except that this question was likely to have been one of those matters which prior to the war the employers might have been unable to resolve in their favour as beyond dispute and negotiation. The war, or the controls vested in the Munitions Act, afforded them the opportunity, it appeared, to attain that which had been beyond their reach in peacetime. But one should not misconstrue Gloag's decision in refusing the certificates. The employers may have perceived the matter as raising the principle of managerial prerogative and

[18] *Glasgow Herald*, 26. Oct. 1915.
[19] On the commission, see ch. 8.
[20] *Glasgow Herald*, 20 Oct. 1915; ASE, *Monthly Journal and Report*, Nov. 1915, 47–8.
[21] MUN 5/80/341/3, 'Clyde Munition Workers: Minutes of Evidence', p. 43.

thought that the munitions tribunal would be a suitable forum wherein to vindicate that doctrine. But such a perception was not necessarily shared by the tribunal personnel themselves. Their criterion was the 'national interest', informed by corporatist sentiments which accorded scant regard to the private claims of employers and of trade unionists alike. The tribunal's *ratio decidendi*, in rejecting the riveters' claims, did not correspond to the inference—the legitimation of managerial prerogative—which the employer would prefer to have drawn from the outcome. In this respect, Gloag was loyal to tightly drawn ministry and corporatist objectives.

Indeed, when similar cases arose in Newcastle around the same time, the tribunal *granted* certificates to the shipyard workers involved. Thus at Armstrong Whitworth's Elswick yard, those threatened with transfers to the company's sites at High Walker, Selby, Manchester, and the Clyde district were granted their clearances; while, the following month, the proposed transfer of men from Palmer's shipyard at Hebburn to the firm's site at Jarrow fell through on the grant of their leaving certificates.[22]

Thus on some matters, Gloag could be as harsh and uncompromising—indeed, more so—as tribunal chairmen elsewhere. It was, however, his method of suppressing conflict and his theory of deterrence which, the ministry concluded, were found wanting.

As we noted earlier, the draft letter inviting Gloag to resign was not sent. Instead the removal was postponed pending a general review of the performances of all tribunal chairmen.[23] For already there had been hints of dissatisfaction with the other local tribunal chairmen, Gibson and Andrew,[24] while in

---

[22] *Glasgow Herald*, 25 Nov. 1915.
[23] LAB 2/47/MT107/1, Wolff to Payne, 16 Dec. 1915.
[24] Walter Payne, another senior ministry official in London, had noted that if the ministry were to 'dispose' of Gibson and Andrew, they would require to appoint chairmen 'of an altogether different stamp', outside the sphere of Glasgow solicitors of whom Gibson and Andrew were 'quite fair types'. The only name suggested was George Neilson, LL D, stipendiary magistrate for Glasgow and a former procurator-fiscal. He was used to a large number of cases a day, with a grasp of court procedure, was 'absolutely fair' and was 'not at any time inclined to allow too much nonsense'. It is probably that Neilson's name was suggested by the Glasgow tribunal clerk T. F. Wilson. Payne's comments were undoubtedly in response to Wolff's general review of the chairmen which he completed in early Jan. 1916. See ibid., Payne to Wolff, 28 Dec. 1915.

Coventry, Professor Frank Tillyard,[25] who held the chair of Commercial Law at Birmingham University, was also attracting adverse ministry criticism. In the event, the outcome of this initial review in early January was to confirm the removal of Gloag, though only after the passing of the forthcoming Amendment Act, but also to recommend no other changes despite Tillyard's 'appalling decisions'.[26]

Over the next month various permutations were put forward to fill the place to be vacated by Gloag. Sir Thomas Munro, one of the Clyde 'dilution commissioners', was invited to hear leaving certificate cases but declined on account of his dilution work. Fyfe then suggested that Andrew and Gibson could be left to handle the 'domestic' work involving leaving certificate cases, while he would take on all the prosecutions. T. F. Wilson, for his part, considered that *any* changes would invite worker criticism. Even Gibson himself wrote to Wolff on 24 January 1916 to oppose 'the seeming clothing of the Tribunals with anything savouring of further *judicial* authority [which] would, in my humble opinion, be distasteful to the workmen and might be resented by them'.[27]

Gibson was certainly ambitious, suggesting that Andrew take on the leaving certificate cases while he would hear the prosecutions, a proposal which he considered to be justified by his background as a magistrate. Indeed, not only did he intimate that a post as stipendiary chairman of the Scottish tribunals would be welcome; he also later proposed in June 1917, that is, some fifteen months after his removal, that he be reappointed to the tribunal in the event that Sheriff Fyfe were to be appointed Sheriff-principal of Lanarkshire.[28] The latter was not in fact promoted, but it is an indication of Gibson's lust for office that he wrote to the ministry without evident embarrassment.

However, by the time of Gibson's letter of 24 January, his own

---

[25] Tillyard's publications included *Industrial Law* (1916) and *The Worker and the State* (1923), a version of which was published by the National Council of Labour Colleges in 1936.

[26] LAB 2/47/MT107/1, Wolff to Beveridge, 6 Jan. 1916. Why two professors on the tribunal list should have been singled out as especially inept might invite wild and improper speculation.

[27] Ibid., Gibson to Wolff, 24 Jan. 1916.

[28] Ibid., Gibson to Ministry of Munitions, 30 June 1917.

goose (and that of Andrew) were already being cooked. The whispering campaign against the two chairmen was apparently instituted by Bartellot, the Admiralty representative on the Clyde. Andrew was the first target, though it was Gibson who was subsequently to bear the brunt of adverse ministry criticism before both chairmen were eventually removed.

JAMES ANDREW AND THE BARCLAY CURLE CAULKERS

Seven caulkers employed by the Barclay Curle shipyard sought leaving certificates from the firm on 9 September 1915. They alleged that the firm was attempting to reduce their working rates of pay from $1s. 4d.$ to $10\frac{1}{2}d.$ an hour, and that by refusing certificates, the company was hoarding labour.[29] According to the firm, these men were employed at Elderslie Dry Dock and were the entire staff of caulkers available at the dock. They were mostly on urgent Government work, which sometimes came in intermittently. As a consequence, they might be idle occasionally for short periods. It was, however, important from a 'national point of view' that the men be available when the work *did* come in. The firm was therefore willing to pay them a stand-by time rate of $10\frac{1}{2}d.$ an hour, whether working or not. Moreover, the firm supported its case by producing a letter from Bartellot asking it to maintain under all circumstances a full staff ready to take in hand immediately any vessels arriving for urgent repairs.[30] Indeed, Bartellot had advised that a destroyer was due to arrive that night for repairs after a collision. 'In spite of this', he complained, in reporting the case to the ministry, 'the discharges were granted and the firm was left without caulkers.'

Why had the tribunal given a decision which, according to Bartellot, 'in the interests of the service, should not be allowed to stand'?[31] Bill Sharp of the Boilermakers' Society, who represented the men, told the tribunal that he could 'place them in situations tomorrow' where they would be continuously employed on Government work. Clearly the men wished to maximize the opportunities which a tight labour market was

[29] *Glasgow Herald*, 10 Sept. 1915.
[30] BEV, iii, 1, fos. 2–6.
[31] Ibid.

currently offering them and were thus not prepared to meet the company half-way by accepting a guaranteed rate. In any case, Sharp trumpeted patriotically, the men did not wish to be idle.

The employer's practice of labour-hoarding, facilitated by a refusal to grant leaving certificates, was a running sore with trade unions which they later ventilated before the Balfour–Macassey Commission. Andrew presumably therefore recognized that such a practice was likely to promote widespread unrest if not nipped in the bud. He therefore granted the men's certificates and left the firm to 'work out their redress by some other process'. It was the sort of decision bound to infuriate employers who, in fairness, could hardly predict when urgent ship repairs would be required but who were none the less obliged to maintain a labour force in readiness. On the other hand, under the guise of the national interest, they were attempting to force through a reduction in wage rates under the umbrella protection of an act which purported to prohibit such changes without ministry authorization. It is symptomatic of the blinkered vision of the Admiralty represenative, Bartellot, that his explicable outburst against Andrew's decision displayed no acknowledgement of the employer's provocative action.

We can see immediately that the nature of the criticism directed against Andrew differed from that levelled against Gloag. In the case of the former, a policy difference between the chairman and the ministry arose. In Gloag's case, as we have seen, it was, rather, his inept handling of rowdy sittings.

This difference over matters of policy was most pronounced in the case of Gibson's handling of tribunal hearings. There were two main areas of dissatisfaction on the part of the ministry. First, there was the matter of leaving certificate applications by a number of Canadian workmen. Second, there was the issue of labourers' wage rates.

CMDR. GIBSON AND THE CANADIAN WORKMEN

During the war, large numbers of Canadian and American workers came over to the Clyde district to help the war effort.[32]

---

[32] For example, a large contingent of 265 mechanics from British Columbia had been recruited by George Barnes, the former general secretary of the ASE, and had arrived in Glasgow at the beginning of Aug. 1915. See *Glasgow Herald,* 3 Aug. 1915.

While many were in receipt of wages in excess of that earned by the local workforce,[33] many more of the overseas workers had expected higher earnings than they actually received. One agency, for example, indicated that the standard rate with overtime would bring the average weekly wage to £6. But when they found it difficult to earn half as much as this, they frequently sought jobs elsewhere.[34] Many of these workers were recruited on six-month contracts, at the expiry of which they sought leaving certificates in order to move elsewhere. A number of the larger employers were, however, reluctant to lose their services, and so the certificates were withheld, thus requiring the workmen to resort to the tribunals. In pursuing this policy the employers were encouraged by the ministry, which felt that if a sympathetic attitude was displayed to a few overseas applicants, then hundreds of other Canadians would submit applications to go elsewhere. Such large-scale shifting of labour, it was considered, could hardly be beneficial to munitions production.

Eventually these matters were aired in a number of significant cases, principally involving Weir's of Cathcart and Beardmore's Dalmuir works. In mid-September 1915, for example, a number of American engineers at Weir's applied for leaving certificates on the completion of their six-month contracts.[35] The firm, which had been paying the men a halfpenny an hour above the district rate, resented having to bear the expense of bringing the men from the United States only to see them move elsewhere after six months. If they desired to return to America, declared the company, then no objection would be lodged. The men's representative, the ASE branch secretary William Brodie pointed out, however, that despite their standard rate the Americans found difficulty in supporting their dependants back home, in view of the high cost of living in Glasgow. For this reason, they desired to seek better paid employment elsewhere in the United Kingdom. In the end, the tribunal agreed to grant

[33] One of the factors behind the rank-and-file dispute originating at Weir's of Cathcart in Feb. 1915, and which eventually led to the establishment of the Clyde Workers' Committee, was the engineers' claim to parity with workmen imported from abroad. See ch. 3, n. 2.

[34] *OHMM*, vol IV, pt. II, p. 63. The case of Robert Peebles, recruited by the White Star Line for Beardmore, is probably the archetypal case. See *Glasgow Herald*, 5 Oct. 1915.

[35] Ibid., 17 Sept. 1915. Four days later, 2 more Americans from Weir's received certificates from the tribunal. See ibid., 21 Sept. 1915.

the certificates, though the reasoning appeared to imply that on the expiry of the contracts, the firm could not lawfully prevent the men leaving. The implication for ministry policy was that even the criterion of the 'national interest', in the shape of the struggle against wage drift (which would increase the overall financial cost of the war) and against labour mobility (which could disrupt production schedules), could not impair the men's plans to leave the firm if they so desired. The fact that another 200 fellow Americans worked at Weir's under these six-month contracts indicated, moreover, the potential damage to ministry objectives which the tribunal decision might inflict.

Indeed, at a third such hearing later in the same week, also involving American engineers at Weir's, the ASE district delegate Sam Bunton asked whether nothing could be done to prevent a repetition of such cases.[36] He believed there were still about fifty to be dealt with and that the company was proposing to object in every case. The chairman agreed that Weir's obstructive tactics were unhelpful given that the cases were virtually identical, but no doubt their posture signified deep frustration, especially at having to pay a £10 bonus to each man on the completion of his contract.

Yet, undeterred, the firm came back to the tribunal the following day to oppose the grant of certificates to a further six Americans.[37] It was, it said 'extremely sorry to be unable to give effect to the suggestion made at the previous day's court'. It did not wish to be vexatious or to waste the tribunal's time, but it felt it had not been acting unreasonably in trying to retain the services of the men. Perhaps the tribunal's message finally got through to the company when the chairman, Andrew, insisted that the previous decisions provided a precedent which had to be followed. For no more applications from American engineers at Weir's were entertained by the tribunal. Instead, the focus of controversy turned to Beardmore's Dalmuir works where 250 American riveters had formed the Overseas Mechanic Union, which had been holding meetings each week.[38] Their dissatisfaction had indeed begun to spill over into all departments of the

---

[36] Ibid., 23 Sept. 1915.
[37] Ibid., 24 Sept. 1915. Interestingly, Brodie was the workmen's assessor in this case.
[38] MUN 5/80/341/3, pp. 339–45, 363–7, 559–76.

works, and their grievances eventually came to a head in February 1916.

Apart from the case involving Robert Peebles (see n. 34), Beardmore had already had an unfortunate tribunal experience with some Canadian workmen when, in December 1915, it was compelled to withdraw objections to the desire of Canadian caulkers to leave the firm, a matter to which we will refer in Chapter 5.

The episode in February 1916, however, concerned seven more Canadians who had completed their six-month stints and who were now seeking certificates from the tribunal.[39] Though Gibson felt that they were entitled to leave the firm when their contracts expired, he was sensitive to the employer's likely reaction. But his call to the men to remain with the firm as a patriotic gesture was sharply rebuffed with the riposte that 'They had had it thrown in their teeth on different occasions during the last six months.'

What was the reason for this almost grovelling posture assumed by the chairman? Possibly it was a response to background pressure by officials at the Ministry of Munitions, exerted with a view to 'beefing up' the attitudes of the Glasgow tribunal chairmen towards leaving certificate applications by overseas volunteers. Beardmore, for example, had contacted the manager of the Clydebank Labour Exchange to enquire whether leaving certificates were required to be granted to Canadians brought over by the Board of Trade and who had completed their six-month stint.[40] The answer given on 9 February was that if the men proposed to remain in the United Kingdom then certificates ought to be granted. If, however, Beardmore required their continued services, then the firm was entitled to refuse clearance lines. However, we saw above that the practice of the tribunals in previous similar applications did not correspond to the view that employers were acting reasonably in refusing certificates. Thus, when Cmdr. Gibson ruled in favour of the Canadians just three days after Beardmore had received contrary advice, the local ministry representative, Paterson, was enraged and Beardmore livid. Paterson wrote to

[39] *Glasgow Herald*, 14 Feb. 1916.
[40] LAB 2/63/MT167/1.

Wolff that day (Saturday 12 February 1916), pointing out that the Labour Exchange manager's advice to the company originally emanated from the Board of Trade in London.[41] What was worse, Paterson's assistant Cramond had seen Gibson prior to the hearings and had told him that the decisions in these seven Canadians' cases would govern hundreds of other cases at Dalmuir and elsewhere. He left the meeting with Gibson, under the impression that 'Gibson now understood'. But, as he ruefully reported back, all seven certificates were granted that day,

and Beardmore's know many other Canadians now applying, and A. J. Campbell, General Manager at Beardmore, has announced he is sick of the Government, the Ministry of Munitions, the Munitions Act and the munitions tribunal, and that unless by 4 p.m. on Monday he has got a direction from the Ministry of Munitions to withhold leaving certificates, he will grant these in every case despite the dislocation to be caused to Admiralty and munitions work.[42]

Paterson ended his noted with the following plea: 'I know that the Ministry is reluctant at any time to give directions to Chairmen of Munitions Tribunals. If, however, an exception cannot be made in this case, the only alternative, I am afraid, is to terminate Cmdr. Gibson's appointment.'[43]

In the matter of directions, the ministry was in some difficulty. It had been the practice for leading tribunal decisions to be circulated to chairmen with a view to inducing uniformity, a process furthered by the commissioning of Treasury Solicitor opinions.[44] But this was a long way short of the nobbling of a judge, or even of the 'executive re-writing of a judgment'.[45] Wolff recognized the ministry's dilemma when he wrote to Beveridge two days later.[46] It was, he indicated, 'impossible' to give directions to tribunal chairmen in terms of Paterson's request. The Canadians' contracts were for six months only; and therefore it seemed reasonable to state that the men were free to leave at the end of the period. Hopefully, thought Wolff, the

---

[41] Ibid., Paterson to Wolff, 12 Feb. 1916.
[42] Ibid.
[43] Ibid.
[44] MUN 5/353/349/1.
[45] Cf. the attempt of the Foreign Office in 1932 to doctor a decision of the Judicial Committee of the Privy Council, in A. V. Lowe and J. R. Young, 'An Executive Attempt to Rewrite a Judgment', *Law Quarterly Review*, xciv (1978), 255–75.
[46] LAB 2/63/MT167/1, Wolff to Beveridge, 14 Feb. 1916.

appeal court, shortly due to be inaugurated, could iron out difficulties if a question of law or mixed fact and law were to arise.[47] This answer was hardly likely to satisfy either Paterson or Beardmore. Indeed, whether any 'question of law or mixed fact and law' was involved in Gibson's decision is extremely doubtful. If, therefore, not all ministry officials were prepared to condemn Gibson in this instance[48] (he did, after all, seek to issue decisions consistent with those given earlier by Andrew in similar cases) his—and Andrew's—utterances in another clutch

[47] J. Turner MacFarlane, the ministry's reports officer who, as a practising solicitor, attended tribunal hearings to procure summaries of cases and note important decisions, was confident, after meeting the new Scottish Appeal Court judge, Lord Dewar, that the latter would 'exercise very tactful discrimination' in handling cases. This probably meant that unlike Gibson and his colleagues, Dewar would seek to avoid embarrassing the ministry and the major employers on which it heavily depended. For example, in one case involving the transfer of workers at Beardmore from night to day shift, Sheriff Fyfe had ruled that this was not a change in the rate of wages which required prior ministry approval. (See also ch. 5, n. 23.) The ministry, wishing this decision to become a binding precedent on all tribunals, suggested that in the absence of either party's taking the matter to appeal, where the decision would become binding, the ministry itself ought to do so. Dewar thought this was an undesirable step but agreed that if other similar cases came before him, he would support Fyfe's view. Thus were bureaucratic-centralist preferences given effect by at least one pliant judicial officer. See LAB 2/63/MT167/6, MacFarlane to Payne, 19 Apr. 1916. Arthur Dewar (1860–1917) ; born Perth, son of John Dewar of the whisky distillery company. Advocate 1885; KC 1901; extra Advocate-Depute on Glasgow circuit, 1892–5. Solicitor-General for Scotland, 1909–10; Liberal MP, South Edinburgh, 1899–1900 and 1906–10; appointed Court of Session judge 1910. See *Dod's Peerage, Baronetage and Knightage of Great Britain and Ireland, for 1914*, p. 367; *Scottish Law Review*, xxxiii (July 1917), 190–2. Shortly before his death, he received what must surely have been the supreme accolade, a ringing paean from the parliamentary scourge of the Ministry of Munitions, the Radical MP, William Pringle. During a debate, Pringle agreed that the Munitions Appeal Tribunal had, 'worked very well, because it has not confined itself strictly to legal considerations'. He was here referring to Dewar; for he added that the English Appeal Tribunal was, 'not so satisfactory, as the Chairman [Atkin] always took the view that he is restricted to an appeal at law'. See HC Deb., 5th ser., vol. 92, Cols. 2763–4, 27 Apr. 1917. Atkin is considered by the legal establishment to have been one of the 'greatest' judges of the past 200 years. He chaired the *Committee on the Relations between Men's and Women's Wages* (1918), prompting Beatrice Webb, a fellow committee member, to observe in her usual charming style that he, 'heartily disliked me; I rather liked him. He was a precise and courteous little person.' See her (unpublished) diary entry, insert in Sept. 1919, undated. For more 'respectable' versions of Atkin see, for example, *Dictionary of National Biography 1941–50; Who Was Who, 1940; Law Quarterly Review*, LX (1944), 355. For a recent biography, see Geoffrey Lewis, *Lord Atkin*, London, 1983.

[48] In his note to Beveridge on the Canadians' case, Wolff did concede that Gibson was, 'not really a satisfactory Chairman', but this view reflected Gibson's performance in the labourers' cases. See LAB 2/63/MT167/1, Wolff to Beveridge, 14 Feb. 1916.

of cases heard during the same month of February 1916 sealed
his, and his colleague's, fate.

That which finally consigned Gibson and Andrew to the
tribunal scrap-heap was their misplaced humanitarianism and
solicitude for groups of workers at the very bottom of the
munitions pile. These were the labourers, mostly employed in
the Lanarkshire steel and iron works, whose pitiably low wages,
calculated on time and not on piece-rates, shocked and outraged
the tribunal chairmen. That such wage rates, which averaged
around 25*s*. for a fifty-seven hour week, were determined,
almost certainly on a customary basis,[49] with the approval of the
Board of Trade only served to enhance the displeasure which the
chairmen felt for a public policy which both tolerated such
pathetic wage levels and placed obstacles, such as the leaving
certificate scheme, in the path of those labourers determined to
extract themselves from their exploitation. Thus, as in the case
of the Canadian workmen at Beardmore, the actions of the
chairmen in seeking to alleviate the financial burdens of the
Lanarkshire labourers, seemed tinged with the features of a
moral crusade. The ministry, as we shall see, however, had no
time for such sentimentality.

The specific problem confronting the labourers was that,
unlike the vast majority of employees in the iron and steel
industry who benefited under the sliding scale arrangement for
wages, the former were straight time-workers.[50] Whereas
increased effort and output on the part of puddlers, millmen,
gas-producermen, charge wheelers, enginemen, cranemen, and
firemen—80 per cent of all iron and steel workers—would be
reflected in increased wages, the same was not true of the time-
rated labourers. Already at the bottom of the earnings league in

[49] Cf. S. J. Hurwitz, *State Intervention in Britain: A Study of Economic Control and Social
Response, 1914–1919,* New York, 1949, p. 121.

[50] For detailed consideration of the earnings background, see Rubin, 'The
Enforcement of the Munitions of War Acts 1915–1917, with Particular Reference to
Proceedings before the Munitions Tribunal in Glasgow, 1915–1921', Warwick Univ.
Ph.D. thesis (1984), pp. 292–4, where the source material is cited.

the industry, their only prospects for improvement, at a time of steeply rising food prices, were to persuade a reluctant Board of Trade to consent to a general wage improvement, or to transfer to different occupations. To an extent, some movement did occur during the war as labour in higher-paid steel and iron occupations became scarcer. Thus men might be transferred from ordinary labouring at between 4*s.* and 5*s.* 6*d.* a shift to a new job, possibly involving the use of simple pneumatic tools, at wages ranging from £2. 17*s.* 6*d.* to £5. 5*s.*[51] But these would be the lucky ones whose employers instigated the transfers. Less favoured labourers could only better themselves by appealing to Gibson's and Andrew's tribunals to overturn their employers' refusal to grant them release. If the applications failed, their plight would become acute, with little prospect of favourable treatment from the Board of Trade arbiters. For example, on 15 February 1916, that is, a few days after the first applications by Lanarkshire labourers for leaving certificates were submitted to Gibson's tribunal, a court of arbitration comprising Sheriff A. O. M. Mackenzie, Sheriff-principal of Lanarkshire, George Pate, and the miners' leader, Robert Smillie, rejected a claim for 2*d.* an hour made on behalf of bricklayers' labourers and general labourers in West of Scotland steel works.[52] Nine months later, the steel labourers' unions managed to wrest a paltry ½*d.* an hour out of the government wage-fixing body, the Committee on Production.[53] When, just nine days after this award was announced, Herbert Beard, a local employer and president of the West of Scotland Iron and Steel Institute, declared that high wages in the iron and steel trade had led to limitation of output and to increases in 'frivolities and indulgence in amusements', he cannot have been referring to the labouring class.[54] Eventually the iron and steel labourers did benefit from an almost indiscriminate extension of a 12½ per cent government

[51] S. W. Rawson, 'War and Wages in the Iron, Coal and Steel Industries', *Economic Journal*, xxvi (June 1916), 174–82, at 180.

[52] *Labour Gazette*, Mar. 1916, 111. Perhaps the Iron and Steel Workers' Society launched a campaign to exert pressure on the authorities wherever it could, a campaign which included the lodging of tribunal application. If so, this strategy might be dubbed 'collective bargaining by litigation', on which, see ch. 5.

[53] Ibid., Dec. 1916, 485. From Aug. 1917 a rise of 3*s.* a week was granted. See *Glasgow Herald*, 4 Aug. 1917; *Labour Gazette*, July 1917, 265; ibid., Aug. 1917, 309. For those in the Workers' Union, see ibid., Apr. 1917, 157; ibid., Dec. 1917, 470.

[54] *Glasgow Herald*, 9 Dec. 1916.

award of October 1917, (ch. 6, n. 14), which had originally been granted to skilled munitions workers on hourly rates, who had seen their semi-skilled supervisees on piece-rates earning greater sums than they.[55] While the award to the labourers was no doubt merited, it was the misfortune of Gibson and Andrew to recognize the former's plight too early, as the following tribunal cases, and the ministry's ferocious reaction, indicate.

The first of the cases was heard on 7 February 1916 when seven labourers at Stewart & Lloyds steel works applied for leaving certificates.[56] Their representative, Robert Climie of the Workers' Union, told the tribunal that several of the men were paid 4*s*. 6*d*. a day and one had been offered 15*s*. elsewhere. Gibson, however, declined to grant most of the certificates on the ground that the labourers were in receipt of Board of Trade approved rates. None the less, he continued,

They had heard a great deal since the Munitions Act had come into force about the huge wages being earned by munitions workers, and he thought it would be well that the public should understand the situation, and see both sides of the picture. Personally, he had been aware all along of the rate of wages being earned by labourers, and while it was unfortunately not a matter which came under the cognizance of that court, and they were unable to deal with cases of that kind, there was nothing to prevent him sympathising with the men in the position in which they found themselves.[57]

The second case, heard two days later,[58] did not directly involve labourers employed in steel works but is significant for the explicit condemnation by Gibson of the underpayment made to an engineman, William Gough, employed at Barclay Curle shipyard. Working eighty-seven and a half hours on night shift and eighty and a half hours a week on days, Gough reckoned that his pay, which the employer stated was 44*s*. including holidays, was grossly inadequate. In response, Gibson declared that he did not wish to encourage men to leave their employment, but in the present case Gough was clearly 'very much underpaid'. If he found a job elsewhere, Gibson told him, his leaving certificate application would receive sympathetic

---

[55] Wrigley, *David Lloyd George and the British Labour Movement*, Hassocks, 1976, pp. 219–21; Hinton, *The First Shop Stewards' Movement*, pp. 243–4.
[56] *Glasgow Herald*, 8 Feb. 1916; *Coatbridge Leader*, 12 Feb. 1916.
[57] *Glasgow Herald*, 8 Feb. 1916.   [58] Ibid., 10 Feb. 1916.

consideration. We can see immediately the seeds of the ministry's discontent in its realization that its carefully prepared schemes to prevent the movement of labour was under threat from its own agents of policy enforcement. But there was more to come.

For the third of Gibson's 'trilogy' of allegedly horrendous decisions was heard the following day and concerned an application by another Stewart & Lloyds labourer, William Barbour, who wished to leave his employer.[59] His trade union official, Owen Coyle of the Iron and Steel Workers' Society, told the tribunal that Barbour, a family man, was earning 25*s.* for a fifty-seven-hour week, whereas he had been offered a job elsewhere at 30*s.* for a similar week. He used to rely on overtime to supplement his income but this was no longer available. When Gibson was told by the firm that the rates in the district were less than 25*s.* (they were 24*s.*), he commented, 'Then all I can say is that in circumstances such as these, it is a scandal. To my mind, these small wages are due to the fact that the labourers are not sufficiently organized.'[60] Gibson had now compiled his own judicial obituary by his comments in the labourers' cases and his handling of the Canadians' hearing earlier. Indeed, while all the manoeuvring within the ministry over the replacement of the chairmen was obviously a closely guarded secret prior to the actual assumption of office by the new local tribunal chairmen, Sheriffs Fyfe and Craigie, the *Forward* prophetically hinted at things to come. Commenting on the Barbour case, it wrote that 'If Cmdr. Gibson continues to affront Capitalism like that, he will get his own Clearance Certificate one of these days. In the meantime, however, he is giving the workers more confidence in the munitions tribunals.'[61]

James Paterson, at the ministry's local office in Glasgow, now set in motion the final act of the drama. Writing to Wolff on 12 February 1916, he referred to Gibson's 'irresponsible utterances on wage questions', and pointed specifically to his remarks in 'the Coatbridge case', that is, in the Stewart & Lloyds labourers' cases.[62] Hitherto, Paterson had 'pled' with his superiors to retain

[59] Ibid., 11 Feb. 1916.
[60] Ibid.
[61] *Forward*, 19 Feb. 1916.
[62] LAB 2/63/MT167/1, Paterson to Wolff, 12 Feb. 1916.

Gibson as the best of the trio. Now he would have to alter his opinion unless the ministry could direct Gibson to cease his 'outbursts' on matters with which he was not acquainted and in respect to which no evidence had been presented to him. Paterson went on to explain that R. D. D. Barman, the managing director at Stewart & Lloyds, had spoken to him, 'using language which he felt constrained to convey to the ministry'. He added that 'It is certainly no part of the function of the Chairman to let himself loose on questions of wages and so stir up a great deal of discontent in the district.'[63] The fact that Gibson was aware that the men were receiving wage rates approved by the Board of Trade made 'his succeeding remarks nothing short of impertinence. He has no right whatever in any way to criticize the scales of wages,' especially where both sides had been able to make representations to the Board of Trade.

Sir George Askwith, the Chief Industrial Commissioner, was also in an angry mood. Writing from Glasgow to the ministry's permanent secretary Sir Hubert Llewellyn Smith, and enclosing press cuttings of Gibson's statements, Askwith insisted that 'it is not practicable to sit in this City hearing [arbitration] cases affecting thousands of men and refusing applications when these idiots at the head of Government Tribunals are airing their views on wages.'[64]

The die was now cast, and the ministry, finally deciding the following week to dispense with their services, at last wrote to the three chairmen on 1 March, giving them one month's notice. Paterson, though 'delighted to learn' that the letters of dismissal had been sent, remained concerned, none the less, lest there still be opportunities for further 'irresponsible outbreaks [*sic*] *re* what is a living wage for a wartime labourer'.[65] In respect to Gibson, his fears were, it seems, groundless, for in the last such case prior to the termination of office the tribunal chairman expressed no embarrassing criticism of wage levels. The case, heard on 22 March, concerned a young married man, also at Stewart &

[63] John King, an employers' assessor and secretary of the National Light Castings Association, had also written to complain of Gibson's comments at the tribunal. They 'are always quite gratuitous, but they have a most disturbing effect among the workers'. He wanted to know, 'if this is to be permitted to go on?' See LAB 2/47/MT107/1, King to Ministry of Munitions, 16 Feb. 1916.

[64] Ibid., Askwith to Llewellyn Smith, 11 Feb. 1916.

[65] Ibid., Paterson to Wolff, 3 Mar. 1916.

Lloyds, who had been with the firm for eight years, during which time he had received a rise of just one shilling a week.[66] His current wage was 4s. 6d. a day, and he had been promised munitions work with another firm which, on piece-rate calculation, would earn him about 10s a shift. Though the certificate was granted—a last defiant gesture by Gibson in the exercise of his judicial discretion?—the 'irresponsible outbursts' were noticeably absent. Perhaps the ministry's message was learned—too late.

But Paterson's fears that the period of notice granted to the chairmen might not be trouble-free did come close to realization in the case of Andrew. The latter had already distinguished himself just one week before receiving his dismissal notice, in a case involving John Ralston, a boiler feeder in Coatbridge whose rate of pay was 4½d. an hour. The firm, presumably Stewart & Lloyds again, would pay only Board of Trade rates, prompting Andrew, in granting the certificate, to announce that 'they would try and move the Board of Trade. They must endeavour to assist the men with such low wages. The earnings of the applicant did not represent a living wage at the present time.'[67] Perhaps Paterson failed to notice this case. Certainly, in his letter to Wolff on 3 March,[68] he did state that Andrew had followed Gibson in making explicit remarks about the inadequacy of 25s. for a labourer at Stewart & Lloyds. But he was undoubtedly referring to a case over which Andrew presided on 1 March, ironically the date of his letter of dismissal. The case was virtually identical to those already described, with Andrew declaring that 25s. was

far too little in these times of high prices for an active labourer working 59 hours a week. We wish the Board of Trade would allow you [the firm] to do something better, and there seems to be an indication in that direction from rules which have been issued today. I think we have no option but to let this man better himself.[69]

The next morning, Paterson explained to Wolff, there was a

---

[66] *Glasgow Herald*, 23 Mar. 1916.
[67] Ibid., 24 Feb. 1916.
[68] See n. 65.
[69] *Glasgow Herald*, 2 Mar. 1916. The rules referred to probably related to special arbitration panels to be set up to adjudicate on differences involving unskilled labourers under Section 8 of the Munitions Amendment Act 1916.

flood of applications to the management for leaving certificates from men in similar positions, and several of the shops in Coatbridge were 'upset'.[70] As he pointed out, 'Interference with Stewart & Lloyds interrupts other important controlled establishments in West Scotland.[71] Therefore we *must* tell the three not to make comments *re* wages.'

By this time, of course, their time was up, and their removal was merely a matter, for Paterson, of counting the days and keeping his fingers crossed.

Thus did Andrew join Gloag and Gibson in falling from grace. While attention focused on the deportation of the shop stewards (ch. 3), no one noticed the other evictions occurring simultaneously. If the Ministry of Munitions was embroiled in the difficulties of forcing through dilution; if the obstructiveness of both the leadership and the rank and file of the ASE in this regard was problematic; and if the deportation of the shop stewards of the CWC was the only drastic measure which could untangle that particular Gordian knot;[72] none the less, the ministry's treatment of its own tribunal chairmen clearly indicates that other critical considerations occupied its thoughts. Thus the maintenance of co-operation with major employers such as Beardmore and Stewart & Lloyds on matters wholly unconnected with the dilution campaign; the necessity to preserve intact both the contours and the principle of the district rate; and, finally, the imperative need to reiterate that there was *no* free market in labour were seen as being as crucial to the war effort as any militant steps taken to advance dilution.

With Gloag, Gibson, and Andrew gone, the new local tribunal chairmen were to be Sheriffs Fyfe and Craigie, a clear reflection of the failure of the previous incumbents sufficiently to

---

[70] LAB 2/47/MT107/1, Paterson to Wolff, 3 Mar. 1916.

[71] The firm had 3 tube works and 1 foundry in Coatbridge, though other iron and steel companies were also located there, for example, the Carnbroe Ironworks of Merry and Cunningham Ltd. For the Stewart and Lloyds establishments, see BEV VII, 23, fo. 287.

[72] For the conflicting interpretations on these questions, see Hinton, *The First Shop Stewards' Movement;* Davidson, 'Government Labour Policy, 1914–16; A Re-appraisal', *Scottish Labour History Society Journal*, No. 8, June 1974; McLean, *The Legend of Red Clydeside*, Edinburgh, 1983; Reid, 'Dilution, trade unionism and the state in Britain during the First World War', in Steven Tolliday and Jonathan Zeithin (eds.), *Shop Floor Bargaining and the State*, Cambridge, 1985.

'create the judicial atmosphere necessary in the Glasgow situation'.[73]

The 'judicial atmosphere' did of course relate predominantly to Gloag's handling of controversial strike prosecutions. The factors which also led to the removal of his colleagues were not as visible, but were none the less damaging to the credibility of ministry policy in enforcing the Munitions Act.

The preoccupation by Gibson and Andrew with the issue of a living wage for poorly paid labourers strongly indicates a sensitive and sympathetic attitude, which sometimes did, and sometimes did not, lead to the grant of a leaving certificate by the tribunal.[74] None the less, such expressions of sympathy for the plight of the low paid were highly disconcerting to the ministry. What to many observers might be justifiable comment in the wake of rising prices and increasing shortages of commodities was, according to the ministry, dangerous naïvety. By raising false expectations among labourers of rapid improvement and by indulging in emotional appeals to the authorities, the chairmen were exceeding their remit. The delicate policy undertaken by the Board of Trade conciliators and arbiters, designed to contain wages while simultaneously confining industrial conflict, would be threatened by such ingenuous and injudicious remarks.

The crux of the ministry's complaint was, in fact, not that the tribunal chairmen had invoked the moral doctrine of the living wage in order to publicize the case of the labourers. Such doctrine is not necessarily antithetical to policies containing corporatist nuances. Indeed, the aims of unity and order can be met by the application of the just wage. What infuriated the officials was the endorsement of the ideology of the *market* by the chairmen. For it was precisely market competition for labour which the Munitions Act was designed to curb. Yet here were ministry appointees sanctioning and encouraging the very antithesis of the policy they were charged with enforcing. So long as the labourers were in receipt of the district rate there could be no warrant for the grant of leaving certificates, which could only lead to bidding-up, instability, and general dissatisfaction—precisely that which was beginning to occur once the

---

[73] LAB 2/47/MT107/1, memorandum by Wolff, 24 Jan. 1916.
[74] For another similar instance, see *Glasgow Herald*, 12 Nov. 1915.

initial green light had been given in the shape of a favourable tribunal decision or *obiter dictum*. The purpose of wartime compulsory wage regulation was to discourage individuals and work groups from believing that their favourable market position was exploitable by demanding improved terms and conditions and by threatening to strike or to leave if they were not met. The practice of the tribunal chairmen was, however, tending to make a mockery of Government intentions which were based on centralized determination of such matters. For this reason in particular they were removed.

THE LABOURERS' POSTSCRIPT

Incredibly, however, the issue of low wages was also the subject of 'careless talk' indulged in shortly thereafter by Sheriff Fyfe himself, though no disciplinary steps against the latter appear to have been taken. Thus, in one case heard in mid-April, he criticized the lack of uniformity attaching to labourers' wage rates and suggested that a 'fixed standard' would 'save a lot of heartburning throughout the country'.[75] If the employers could not increase the wage of an applicant on 29s. a week who had been offered another post at 35s., he, Sheriff Fyfe, 'might consider he was entitled to his certificate if he applied again'. At the same sitting was also heard an application by a labourer on 24s., compelled to work ninety-three hours a week during the previous three weeks in order to provide adequately for his family. As his trade union representative told the sheriff, 'there would be nothing but unrest' among those labourers receiving less than the standard rate. What this implied was that the standard rate differed from the district rate, in that the latter was the irreducible minimum (probable 24s.) approved by the Board of Trade. Fyfe's observations were clearly directed toward rounding up the going rate.

Though criticized by the local engineering employers' association for this action,[76] Fyfe, for the moment at least, was

---

[75] *Glasgow Herald*, 17 Apr. 1916.

[76] The association wrote to him pointing out that the situation affecting those labourers appearing at the tribunal did not apply to labourers in the engineering industry. See NWETEA, *Minute Book* No. 7, 20 Apr. 1916.

not to be deflected. When, in another case, a building labourer employed by Messrs William Arrol & Co. applied for a certificate in July 1916, the applicant stated that his wages were 25s., whereas he could obtain 27–8s. elsewhere.[77] Though the labourer was receiving, according to the employers, the standard rate, Fyfe went so far as to recommend an actual figure of 27s. which he thought ought to be the minimum, and advised the company to contact the ministry about a proposed increase. 'It was true', he added,[78] that 'the tribunal had nothing to do with wages, but they might make a recommendation in cases where there seemed an injustice.' Perhaps encouraged by Fyfe's action in the above case, a group of labourers sought his opinion during a leaving certificate hearing the following month as to what constituted a 'fair and living wage'.[79] One labourer explained that he was being paid $5\frac{3}{4}d.$ an hour, plus 3s. 3d. war bonus, whereas the standard rate was $7\frac{1}{2}d.$ an hour; that is, his wage was almost 27s., excluding bonus, for a fifty-six-hour week. Perhaps Fyfe considered he had gone too far in the Arrol case; perhaps the ministry had communicated with him in unambiguous terms (no ministry documents dealing with this episode can be traced). Whatever the explanation, Fyfe was clearly less forthcoming on this occasion. The labourer's request, he declared,[80] 'might be a compliment to the Court, but they were not there to settle everything.' He was prepared to concede that the applicants were entitled to a rate which

enables a man to live. But whatever my personal opinion is, the point does not arise in this Court.

APPLICANT. You would not care to express your personal opinion?

FYFE. I have done so about fifty times already in the strongest possible terms, but it is not paid any attention to.

Fyfe seriously contemplated his tribunal becoming a wage-fixing body as the logical next step, once it had been recognized as a forum wherein to appeal specifically against low pay.[81] But until Parliament had authorized the change, Fyfe considered it

[77] *Glasgow Herald*, 13 July 1916.
[78] Ibid.
[79] Ibid., 16 Aug. 1916.
[80] Ibid.
[81] For details, see G. R. Rubin, 'Labour Courts and the Proposals of 1917–19', *Industrial Law Journal*, XIV (1985), 33–41.

his duty to arrest any encouragement of this development. It is surely for this reason that he remained coy in the above case. Thus, at a later hearing involving operative plumbers[82]—and in respect to whom the issue of low pay for labourers was irrelevant—he stated that

> One cannot, of course, but sympathise with workmen, especially the unskilled workmen, and of them more particularly that less intelligent class who belong to no union and have nobody to advise them about the Munitions Act under which they must submit to live and work during the war. But surely it ought to be obvious even to the meanest intelligence that for this tribunal to express in any individual case any opinion upon wages rates would lead to hopeless confusion.[83]

While the ministry's message was unambiguously conveyed in this last case, there is no doubt that some of Fyfe's earlier meanderings through those cases involving labourers were reminiscent of the practices of his former colleagues. Indeed, he perhaps exceeded the achievements of the involuntarily retired chairmen when, as we saw above, he himself proposed an appropriate figure for construction industry labourers. Even the disgraced trio did not venture that far, yet they were removed while he remained. Why this was so can only be inferred, given the absence of relevant ministry documentation.

First, as we have just seen, his earlier solecisms were soon recanted. Second, if it were decided that what is sauce for the goose is also sauce for the gander, and so Fyfe would have to go, how could the ministry publicly justify another change of chairmen on the tribunal? Indeed, could they expect to persuade a new incumbent to a position which smacked of the kiss of death? Third, though perhaps unlikely, the ministry may have reasoned that there was indeed a fundamental problem concerning labourers' wage rates which it was difficult to avoid discussing during hearings. Finally, and most crucially, Fyfe was simply too valuable to the ministry to permit his compulsory departure, which equity to Gibson and his colleagues perhaps demanded. For Fyfe's all-round track record as chairman bore favourable comparison with every other chairman on the ministry's list.[84]

[82] The case is cited in a different context in ch. 5.
[83] *Glasgow Herald*, 22 Nov. 1916.
[84] Cf. the 'Sam Crush affair', ch. 2.

Indeed, any sentimentality towards the claims of poorly paid labourers was conditional on their constituting the deserving poor. They would forfeit that claim if their actions to advance their cause assumed a more direct and forceful step than merely lodging leaving certificate applications. When ten labourers at a steel works were prosecuted for being absent without leave, the sympathy previously expressed for those earning only 24*s.* a week evaporated in a flash.[85] Informed by the employer that the men's action had caused almost forty other employees to be thrown idle, Sheriff Fyfe did not mince his words.

You are the kind of fellows that I should have the power to put in the Army . . . I am exceedingly sorry I cannot sent you straight to the front line of trenches in Flanders. You are traitors to your country. It is quite evident that you don't understand the seriousness of the position you have adopted. . . .[86]

This was more like the Sheriff Fyfe of old. For even if the advent of compulsory military service in 1916 had no doubt provided encouragement to the severity of his condemnation, it was clear that his previous aberrations had now ceased. His continuation in office was vindicated and centralizing tendencies reinforced.

[85] Ibid., 3 Aug. 1916.
[86] Ibid. Characteristically, he imposed light penalties of 10*s.* per man. Even Sheriff Fyfe appreciated the dangers of inflaming passions unnecessarily by imposing stiff fines on offenders.

CHAPTER 5

Collective Bargaining by Litigation[1]

INTRODUCTION

In November 1916, Sheriff Fyfe was confronted by a number of applications for leaving certificates submitted by a group of operative plumbers. The applications were, however, peremptorily refused. For the tribunal chairman was aware of an ulterior motive behind the plumbers' initiative. He stated that

We are daily endeavouring to impress . . . that settling wages disputes is not the function of this tribunal. If a man is getting the rate of pay recognised in the district for workmen of his class, this tribunal has no power to offer any opinion as to whether that rate of pay is sufficient in the circumstances of the times. That is a matter for the Board of Trade, not for a munitions tribunal. It is quite useless for men to deluge this tribunal as they are daily doing with leaving certificate applications based only upon the ground that the district rate of pay is insufficient for their needs.[2]

Sheriff Fyfe was astute enough to realize that the central issue in this case was not an unswervable determination on the part of the plumbers to leave their employment. Their intention was, simply, to force an upward shift in the wage rate provisions of the collective agreement applicable to their employment. The attempt by the plumbers to transform the tribunal into some kind of arbitration body or wages tribunal was thus emphatically rejected by the chairman. But in fact the gradual process of mutation, though never a complete transformation, had commenced almost from the outset of the tribunal's existence. Indeed, in mid-1917, Sheriff Fyfe went so far as to advocate a

[1] Matters pertaining to women's wages and to dilution of labour, including the change to different payment systems, are not dealt with here. For dilution, see ch. 9. For the experience of women before the tribunals, see Rubin, 'The Enforcement of the Munitions of War Acts 1915–1917, with Particular Reference to Proceedings before the Munitions Tribunal in Glasgow, 1915–1921', Warwick Univ. Ph.D. thesis (1984), ch. 10.

[2] *Glasgow Herald*, 22 Nov. 1916.

formalization of the process. He proposed the establishment of a modified version of the munitions tribunal as a local board of arbitration, whose awards would have legal effect, and which would be specifically designed to bypass the Board of Trade in London, with its centralizing and delaying tactics. In view of Sir George Askwith's hostility, however, nothing came of the idea.[3] Moreover, irrespective of the tribunal decision itself, the very fact that a wage grievance was being ventilated in open court— whether the formal hearing was a leaving certificate application, a strike prosecution, or an Ordering of Work complaint—could serve as a pressure point on the employer or the authorities to provide a remedy for the underlying issue.

The principal argument of this chapter, therefore, is that munitions workers were prepared to use the tribunal pragmatically and resourcefully as an aid towards the achievement of collective bargaining goals. Given the comparative accessibility of the tribunal in the context of an industrial relations system which prohibited strikes and industrial indiscipline and which imposed wage norms ratified by a centralized bureaucracy, munitions workers were prepared to commit factory offences, go on strike, accuse their employers of making unauthorized changes to wage rates, or of failing to comply with wage awards, even to threaten to leave their employment by lodging leaving certificate applications—all in order to expedite their wage claims.

Indeed, the dissatisfaction with compulsory arbitration as the war wore on made such steps even more rational in the circumstances. As one local newspaper correspondent wrote at length

Experience has shown that the Board of Trade procedure is hopelessly inadequate for the purpose of dealing with the innumerable little local questions which arise in every district, and which might for the most part be dealt with on the spot immediately they arise and before they grow into a source of serious trouble. The Board of Trade, with its present organisation of travelling Commissioner centralized in London and having the whole country for his field of operations,

---

[3] For the details, see LAB 2/805/IC5379, 'Memorandum putting forward Suggestions in favour of the Setting-up of Local Tribunals to deal with Industrial Unrest and to assist . . . Arbitration . . . , by T. A. Fyfe, August 1, 1917'; Rubin, 'Labour Courts and the Proposals of 1917–19', *Industrial Law Journal*, XIV (1985).

cannot possibly deal adequately with these questions, and employers and workmen know by costly experience of the last 12 months the weak points of the present procedure. Endless correspondence with London, irritating delays, waste of time and money travelling from Glasgow to London, and many other obstacles have made it difficult for the employers and workmen to use the existing Board of Trade procedure for the settlement of disputes. Occasional visits of the Chief Industrial Commissioner himself to Glasgow are not sufficient to enable him to deal promptly with the accumulation of small matters for which an immediate local hearing and a prompt decision are the most effective cure.[4]

Applications such as those of the plumbers could thus be construed as a protest against a cumbersome, unproductive, centralized system, an attempt to break the log-jam holding up progress, or an effort to shock employers out of the secure complacency which the prohibition of strikes and the imposition of compulsory wage regulation might have induced. However, as well as reflecting union members' preference for local autonomy as against centralized wage-fixing, the attempts to recruit the tribunals for their case, or even simply to employ the opportunity to express their case publicly, perhaps reflected a deep and continuing commitment to collective *laissez-faire*, more particularly to the element of *bargaining* inherent in voluntarism, even if this contradicted the absolute adherence to corporatist unity which remote union leaders had pledged in the first half of 1915. A market for labour might well be hedged round by legal restrictions, but local trade unionists, irritated by employers' opportunism, rose to the challenge by utilizing the law imaginatively. In doing so, they exhibited little compunction about sowing industrial disorder as a tactical step. The resultant litigation was a further stage in the process. Hence the description 'collective bargaining by litigation'.

It remains open to argument, as will be explored in the discussion of the 'tea-interval' dispute at Alexander Stephen's shipyard in Glasgow (see below), that such hearings might draw attention only to ostensible causes of disruption and not to more hidden fears and suspicions which perhaps underlay the manifest conduct of which munitions workers were accused or which prompted leaving certificate applications.

---

[4] *Glasgow Herald*, 24 Nov. 1916.

None the less, it is difficult not to interpret these various legal steps as an attempt to manipulate the legal system to influence the outcome of an instrumental, wage-related object. They were efforts to apply bargaining pressure at different stages of a prolonged struggle, employing law as a weapon in that struggle, and not as an end in itself. Given that other avenues were strewn with obstacles, a drastic situation of strict wage controls demanded the use of those remedies which lay readily to hand, a lesson well learned and applied frequently in practice, as we shall see. Thus, much as the Munitions Act may have been hated and conceived by some workers as an instrument of slavery, this opinion did not prevent trade unionists from attempting to make use of those of its provisions which enabled them to go on the legal offensive against employers. That they were often unsuccessful in respect to the verdicts may have added ammunition to the campaign to reform the Act in late 1915. But this would be to miss the point that positive gains could be made simply by forcing employers to defend claims made against them at the tribunals, or by exposing them, in prosecutions of workmen, to criticism from tribunal chairmen that their styles of management were inept or injudicious. For it must be recognized that, confronted with a constricting legislative provision, workers would be acting rationally if they attempted both to maximize their gains under an unfavourable system, *and* to minimize the constraints. Thus their conduct might pull in a direction different from that implied by public criticisms of the legislation, for example, by those expressed by Clyde munitions workers before the Balfour–Macassey Commission in October 1915 (ch. 8). There was no contradiction. They used the law where they could, for otherwise their positions might worsen. But they reserved the right to engage in propaganda, special pleading, and political agitation.

In developing this theme, we may point to a number of different, but ultimately related, objectives which trade unionists might pursue in tangling with the munitions tribunal. We can, initially, differentiate between the use of the tribunal as a final arbiter on the one hand and the use of tribunal proceedings as part of an extended and continuing process on the other. In the first category might fall those cases where trade unionists sought to establish a point of principle; or sought a definitive ruling from the tribunal on the applicability of the Munitions Act to specific groups of workers; or where they even wished to 'clear their name'. For example, in one case, rather than concede the right of their employer, Barclay Curle shipyard, to transfer them to a different site, three Glasgow riveters chose instead to apply for leaving certificates.[5] The grant of the certificates by the munitions tribunal signified for the riveters a rejection of the employer's assertion of managerial prerogative to shift staff at will.

In another case involving carters from Rutherglen, near Glasgow, who were in dispute with their employer over an arbitration award, the general secretary of the Scottish Horse and Motormen's Union, Hugh Lyon, advised his members to go on strike for the avowed object, as Lord Dewar said in the appeal tribunal,[6] 'of testing the question whether the men fell within the provisions of the Act, and not with the intention of defying the law'. If carters were held by the appeal tribunal to be engaged on munitions work, then the strike would be called off and he, Lyon, would pay the men's fines himself.[7]

In contrast to those cases which suggested the airing of a point of principle or tested the scope of the legislation, were those where workers sought to 'clear their names' or to register their protest against oppressive conduct (not usually involving questions of wages) allegedly perpetrated by foremen or managers. The object of lodging leaving certificates or, conceivably, of refusing to obey a lawful order, was to secure the termination of the managerial conduct to which objection had been taken, or even to score a point off the employer in the prestige stakes. Thus, sixteen engineers employed at a large munitions works in Glasgow's East End, presumably Beardmore's Parkhead Forge, sought leaving certificates in retaliation for allegedly insulting remarks about their competence made by one of the firm's managers.[8] Given the employer's desperation to

---

[5] Ibid., 20 Oct. 1915. The case was briefly discussed in a different context in ch. 4.

[6] Angela Tuckett, *The Scottish Carter*, London, 1967, pp. 135–7; *Glasgow Herald*, 16 Nov. 1916; *Preston et al. v. Knox*, 1917 SMAR 39–43, at 42, 13 Nov. 1916.

[7] In the event, both the sheriff and Lord Dewar ruled that carters engaged on the transport of raw materials to and from a controlled establishment, which was not, of course, their own employer, were covered by the Munitions Act (and therefore could presumably prosecute the employer for having failed to give effect to a wage direction of the Minister of Munitions).

[8] *Glasgow Herald*, 5 Sept. 1917.

retain his pool of skilled men, the engineers were able without difficulty to extract a public apology given at the tribunal, together with the company's testimony that they were 'the best type of workmen within their works'. Honour was settled in favour of the men by a tactical use of the legal process which the munitions workers themselves had set in train. The law could therefore be employed profitably to vindicate a status position, the disregard of which became a festering sore.[9]

The above cases sought to illustrate the point that munitions workers might invoke the law or infringe its provisions in order to mobilize the tribunal as a final arbiter or as a forcing-house to obtain an immediate settlement of an issue or grievance. In fact, such a tactic was only rarely employed. What was more common was to find that the pursuit of illegal industrial action, or the submission of leaving certificates, or complaints by employees of unauthorized alterations of wage rates represented further and more dramatic steps taken by munitions workers in a negotiating process which had probably commenced at an earlier stage but which was now perhaps bogged down. It was not simply a matter of drawing attention to 'legitimate' grievances which the other side had a 'duty' to rectify. Rather, the process was a purer version of 'collective bargaining by litigation' than the 'one-off' efforts of the previous category cited. The most vivid wartime example concerned the various steps taken by Beardmore caulkers, transferred by their employers to water testing. As we shall see in detail, this particular dispute dragged on for months, during which time the caulkers were prosecuted once for an Ordering of Work offence; they themselves unsuccessfully prosecuted their employer for allegedly altering wage rates unlawfully; and finally on three separate occasions, in December 1915, in January 1916, and again in May 1916, they submitted leaving certificate applications. Eventually an agreement was hammered out by arbitration conducted by Sheriff Fyfe.

Munitions workers, then, could initiate 'collective bargaining

---

[9] Cf. *Slack* v. *Barr*, heard in the Court of Session in Jan. 1918, when a worker claimed he had been slandered by an assistant manager who told the Committee on Production that the employee had been dismissed for want of skill. The court held that the statement was 'privileged' and thus not actionable. Almost certainly, the case involved George Barr, Beardmore's assistant manager. See *Labour Gazette*, June 1918, 24.

by litigation' by deliberately committing an offence under the Munitions Act; or they could mobilize the permissive provisions of the Act, involving the submission of leaving certificate applications, or the lodging of complaints that employers had either failed to implement a wage award or had made an unauthorized wage alteration. Indeed, as the Beardmore caulkers' episode will illustrate, they could even resort to a package of measures to press home their wage claims.

The first two examples, below, illustrate the ease with which munitions workers could manipulate the Act to their advantage without falling foul of its penal provisions. In the first case, involving a number of coppersmiths at Fairfield shipyard, the lodging of leaving certificate applications paid immediate dividends for the applicants, whilst at the same time operating as a clear reminder to the company of the issues which had informed the celebrated confrontation some months earlier.[10] The district secretary of the National Society of Coppersmiths, Alexander Turnbull, had submitted twenty-five applications to the tribunal on behalf of his members at Fairfield.[11] The coppersmiths complained that as a result of the firm's subcontracting some of the work to private firms, their services were not being fully utilized. The unspoken assumption was, of course, that a policy of hiving off some of the coppersmiths' work to subcontractors was inconsistent with the company's previous claim that there was a shortage of coppersmiths, thus necessitating the employment of plumbers.

Perhaps fearing the embarrassment which such a revelation in open court might cause it, the firm held a meeting with Turnbull in the morning before the hearing was due to take place. As a result, Turnbull informed the tribunal that the applications were to be withdrawn. Though no further details emerge from the report, we can guess that Turnbull was able to extract a commitment from the company that there would be no further subcontracting if this had the effect of reducing the coppersmiths' skilled work load. Another possibility is that Fairfield would agree to the removal of any remaining plumbers in the copper shop in exchange for the withdrawal of the leaving certificate applications.

[10] Ch. 3.
[11] *Glasgow Herald*, 3 Mar. 1916.

Whatever agreement was hammered out, it seems that the lodging of the applications was a tactical move by the coppersmiths in a bargaining process, rather than an indication of a genuine desire on the part of the men to leave the firm. The use of the legal process in this sequel to the major confrontation involving the Fairfield coppersmiths was not to seek a specifically legal remedy in the form of the grant of certificates, but to prod the company into taking action on the men's grievances. Here, then, is a further example of the 'use of court action as a stage in a quarrel as a means by which one party indicated to another that matters had gone far enough'.[12]

The case also illustrates that not every grievance which resulted in a tribunal hearing directly concerned wages, though it is clear that such issues were central to the vast majority of such hearings. For example, in January 1916 ten workers employed in shell-making at Armstrong Whitworth's works at Alexandria near Dumbarton complained that the company had infringed the Act by reducing wages.[13] The complaint was that in December, the firm had changed the type of shell on which the men had been working. The piece-work price for the new shell was 4*d.*, instead of 5*d.* for the previous shell, although there was a difference of only eight to ten seconds in the time taken to manufacture them. In lodging their complaint, the men made clear that what they were seeking was that the price dispute should be settled. They were therefore willing to accept Sheriff Fyfe's suggestion that the case be withdrawn and submitted to the Board of Trade for arbitration. For it is unlikely that the men held much hope that the chairman's decision would finally settle the price question. The employment of the tribunal simply as a point of bargaining pressure was, we must assume, the more likely objective.

MUNITIONS WORKERS AS OFFENDERS

The point was made earlier that munitions workers were prepared to break the law and risk prosecution for unlawfully

---

[12] Olwen Hufton, 'Crime in Pre-Industrial Europe', International Association for the History of Crime and Criminal Justice, *Newsletter*, No. 4, July 1981, 21.

[13] *Glasgow Herald*, 20 Jan. 1916.

striking or for disobeying a lawful order, in order to bring their grievances to the notice of the employer or to the authorities. For by breaking the law deliberately, munitions workers were seeking to vindicate a right to which they believed they were entitled, and of which the public, or the Ministry of Munitions, ought to be apprised.

In one of the very earliest cases heard in Glasgow, twenty-four men employed by a firm of Paisley coachbuilders, Charles Glasgow & Co., had gone on strike on 24 July 1915, in pursuit of higher wages which they claimed had been awarded to them by arbitration.[14] The award in fact applied to the Glasgow district and the question arose whether the employers were a country shop. Other firms in Paisley, just seven miles from Glasgow, had consented to grant the award, but the Board of Trade initially declined to intervene. So the men struck without adequate notice and were eventually prosecuted before Professor Gloag at Glasgow on 5 August. While a number of the accused were found guilty and fined 5s. each or five days in prison, and the charge against another group was found not proven,[15] it seems that the applicability of the award itself was not actually resolved at the hearing. None the less, the men's industrial action, allied to the resolve of their union, the United Kingdom Society of Coach Makers, to pursue the matter further,[16] sufficiently persuaded the Board of Trade to take their complaint seriously. Lynden Macassey, the barrister later called upon with Lord Balfour of Burleigh to investigate the grievances of Clyde munitions workers, was asked to arbitrate and issued his award at the end of October, fully justifying the men's claims. He held that Glasgow rates, in accordance with the Fair Wages Resolution,[17] which sought to ensure that government

---

[14] *Glasgow Herald*, 6 Aug. 1915. According to the *Woman's Dreadnought*, 14 Aug. 1915, 298, only 16 appeared in court. Cf. *Solicitors' Journal*, LIX (1915), 696.

[15] Conceivably, a finding of not proven would have been incompetent in England. The sentence of a fine *or* imprisonment, as distinct from imprisonment in default of payment, was unusual. See comments in MUN 5/353/349/1.

[16] The local union official, Joseph Compton, travelled to the Manchester headquarters of the union to discuss a possible appeal, though no relevant legal machinery for appeals in fact existed at the time. See *Glasgow Herald*, 10 Aug. 1915.

[17] For the Fair Wages Resolution during the war, see, for example, Wolfe, *Labour Supply and Regulation*, Oxford, 1923, pp. 238–42; Brian Bercusson, *Fair Wages Resolutions*, London, 1978, pp. 142–56; *OHMM*, vol. v, pt. 1, pp. 35–6, 91–8.

contractors paid a 'fair' level of wages to their employees, were payable.[18] Direct action, though prohibited by law, was perceived clearly by the men as a justifiable step to prod the authorities and the employer to perform *their* constitutional duty. Not only did the coachbuilders believe in the justice of their action, but the subsequent decision of the Board of Trade undoubtedly vindicated their position. As with the 200,000 South Wales miners who struck in defiance of the extension of the Munitions Act to their trade the previous month,[19] crime paid.

Another example of the *genre*, though one where the outcome is perhaps less clear, concerned what the *Glasgow Herald*[20] described as a 'curious, Clyde dispute' involving twenty-four electricians at the shipyard of Messrs Alexander Stephen & Sons, Linthouse. According to the firm's chief electrician Henry Bremner, he had asked the men to work until 9 o'clock one morning just before Christmas 1915 but told them that he did not propose to pay them for the tea interval. In response, the men refused to work after 7.30 unless such payment was made. An impasse developed and the men remained unmoved by Bremner's threat to 'put their names before the Munitions Tribunal'. He suggested to the tribunal that the men's demand was made simply to comply with union instructions, though he conceded that the half-hour tea interval had previously been paid and, moreover, that the engineers were still being paid for this period. 'But', he added, 'we are now dealing with the electrical department.'

In the event, modified fines of 10s. were imposed on each of the men, with general approval expressed for a reference to arbitration. None the less, in what respects the dispute ought to

---

[18] *Labour Gazette*, Nov. 1915, 425. The employer, Charles Glasgow, was a 'typical employer, with whom Trade Unionists are unpopular'. See *Forward*, 14 Aug. 1915. He was also an extremely stubborn one. In another case, his refusal to release a youth for the Army angered the tribunal chairman, Cmdr. Gibson, who had been told by him that the youth had been recruited by the firm before the war. Gibson's response was to accuse him of selfish behaviour. 'You want to take advantage of an agreement made in January 1914', he told him, 'to hold a man against his services to his nation.' See AIMS, *Monthly Report*, Jan. 1916, 250. Here is a clear articulation of the 'corporate spirit'.

[19] Ch. 3, n. 14.

[20] *Glasgow Herald*, 13 Jan. 1916.

have been labelled 'curious' by the local newspaper is not immediately apparent. The union was clearly intent, on the surface at least, on resurrecting the old practice of payment for the tea interval, which had gradually been eroded by the employers, probably before the advent of the Munitions Act. Otherwise one would expect the union to have complained under the Act that an alteration in working practices had occurred which failed to meet the requirements of Schedule II to the Act in respect of recording the change. But no such complaint arose.

A more machiavellian interpretation is that the claim was connected with the campaign by the Electrical Trades Union to obtain recognition by the CSA of its working rules, which may well have included provisions relating to payments for meal breaks. After a rejection of the union's overtures in October 1915,[21] an arbiter finally ruled in July 1916 that, contrary to the employers' submission, the time was opportune for a consideration of general working rules.[22]

If, therefore, the dispute at Alexander Stephen & Sons was not purely a domestic matter (and the role of the union together with its strict instructions to its members suggest that a matter of important principle was at stake), then the incident perhaps signifies an attempt by the union to force the broader issue through the instrumentality of a narrower one. In this analysis, the tea interval dispute would lead to arbitration, where a wider question which embraced the general working rules might be opened up. Since the union eventually prised from the CSA a reluctant commitment to arbitration on the works rules, the tea interval issue, as a catalyst, became redundant in any case. If this analysis is correct, then it exemplifies once more the way in which a deliberate breach of the law by one party might be construed not as a 'mindless' flouting of the law of the land, but as a carefully planned attempt to mobilize the legal process in order to jog the other side into action to remedy the offender's grievance. Though perhaps speculative or circumstantial, such an interpretation remains appealing; and the dispute may not have been so curious after all.

---

[21] CSA, *Minute Book* No. 9, 4 Oct. 1915.

[22] Ibid., 21 July 1916; *Labour Gazette*, July 1916, 267.

1. Lieut. Commander Robert Gibson, R.N.V.R., F.F.I., J.P.
Chairman Munitions Tribunal, Glasgow District.

2. Professor William Murray Gloag, K.C.
Chairman of General Munitions Tribunal Sitting in Glasgow.

HARVEY LAMBETH.

3. Sheriff T. A. Fyfe, chairman of the munitions tribunals in Glasgow (sketched in 1901).

4. The "almost truculently self-righteous and jauntily disrespectful" coppersmiths prosecuted before the Glasgow munitions tribunal in early August 1915 (pp. 71–9).

5. The Lobnitz shipyard holders-on (riveters' assistants) prosecuted in Glasgow in August 1915 (pp. 85–7).

6. Crowds outside the munitions tribunal during the Beardmore (Dalmuir) gun-mounting department prosecution in January 1916 (pp. 88–95). Tom Johnston (inset) was editor of the Glasgow socialist newspaper, the *Forward*. He later became Secretary of State for Scotland from 1941 to 1945.

7. The audience listening to the trial of the gun-mounting department strikers, January 1916.

8. The Balfour-Macassey Commission of October 1915 in session in the Central Hotel, Glasgow. Lord Balfour of Burleigh is addressing a group of trade union officials. On his left is his co-investigator into the Clyde munitions workers' grievances, Lynden Macassey K.C. On his right is James Paterson, the Ministry of Munitions representative in Glasgow.

9b. W. G. ('Bill') Sharp, the Clydeside official of the United Society of Boilermakers.

9a. William Brodie and Sam Bunton, Clydeside officials of the Amalgamated Society of Engineers.

BEARDMORE CAULKERS

Not unexpectedly, given its size, Beardmore featured prominently in such hearings, the most significant being that of the Dalmuir caulkers who exploited a diverse repertoire of legal and non-legal steps in order to press their case.[23] Here, undoubtedly, was a prolonged dispute where the tribunal was employed pragmatically and opportunistically to further the aims of a group of workers.

The first stage in the dispute occurred when a large number of the firm's caulkers held a lunch-time meeting at the Dalmuir yard in September 1915.[24] However, the meeting, held to discuss the men's dissatisfaction with the current price list, ran over the scheduled time by just ten minutes and therefore ate into working time, whereupon the foreman, Henry Gascoyne, ordered the men back to work. As explained at the subsequent Ordering of Work prosecution of fifty of the caulkers, 'It was not so much what he said as the way in which he said it that irritated the men. He told them to get to their work or get outside the gate,'[25] whereupon most of the caulkers left the works at 4 p.m.

In fact, the foreman's peremptory instructions merely added a gloss to the grievance of the men which arose from the price list. Indeed, one specific aspect of the wage structure was at the root of the caulkers' unrest, and had already been raised with the Balfour–Macassey Commission enquiring into Clyde munitions workers' grievances. This was the transfer of caulkers to less lucrative and less pleasant work on water testing.

Thus, following the abortive lunch-time meeting in September with its resultant prosecution the next month, the caulkers decided to take the dispute a stage further. Eight of them lodged a complaint that Beardmore, by transferring them to water testing, was altering rates of pay without ministry approval, contrary to Section 4(2) of the 1915 Act. The hearing

[23] Other noteworthy cases of 'collective bargaining by litigation' involving Beardmore included the case of the engineers transferred by the company from night shift to day shift, with a consequent reduction in wages. See *Glasgow Herald*, 16 Mar. 1916. Another Beardmore case involved 23 sheet-iron workers who had applied for leaving certificates on the ground that their employer was selfishly hoarding labour. See ibid., 24 Mar. 1916. There is no evidence of a co-ordinated move to petition the tribunal.

[24] Ibid., 8 Oct. 1915.

[25] Ibid. The men were fined £2 each.

took place before Sheriff Fyfe just before Christmas 1915,[26] at a time when the Clyde already was in a ferment over a proposed and controversial visit of Lloyd George to the district. W. G. Sharp of the Boilermakers' Society, who, according to William Gallacher,[27] had gone to Newcastle on 22 December to meet Lloyd George prior to the latter's visit to Glasgow, was in fact at the Glasgow munitions tribunal that day, putting forward his members' case. Prompted by Sharp, one caulker named William Hill explained,

If the firm had agreed to pay the average rate of wages, there would have been no trouble. If there had been no Munitions Act, he would have left the employment of Messrs. Beardmore. He was forced into an unfair position by the Munitions Act. Four of the squad had been getting 1*s.* 4½*d.* an hour, and the other four were on piece-work, and were earning as high as 2*s.* per hour.[28]

On transfer to water testing, it was pointed out, the rate became 10½*d.* plus 25 per cent which was said to be equal to 1*s.* 1¼*d.*, or 3¼*d.* less. As the *Official History of the Ministry of Munitions* observed, 'transfers from highly paid work, such as caulking, to work, dirty, disagreeable and less well paid, such as water testing, were not accepted with any better grace because the Munitions Act threatened compulsion.'[29]

The dispute was not, therefore, about deskilling, that is, putting skilled men on unskilled work. Craft control was not being threatened, for the Boilermakers' Society maintained that water testing was caulkers' work, and must be done by them even though it was the 'lean' part of their work.[30] The complaint was, simply, that the water testing rate was too low for the dirty, uncomfortable, and hazardous work involved. The caulkers had tolerated the shortfall of 3*d.* an hour in the past without complaint. Now it seemed ripe to register a protest which had in fact been building up for some time and had influenced the decision to hold the works lunch-time meeting referred to earlier. However, for the second time, the law appeared to look

[26] Ibid., 23 Dec. 1915.

[27] Gallacher, *Revolt on the Clyde*, London, 1936, pp. 78, 81.

[28] *Glasgow Herald*, 23 Dec. 1915.

[29] *OHMM*, vol. IV, pt. II, p. 61.

[30] For a brief description of the work involved, see G. A. B. Dewar, *The Great Munition Feat*, London, 1921, pp. 146–7.

upon the caulkers with disfavour, though in dismissing their complaint, Sheriff Fyfe did add that 'The Court . . . considered that the spirit of the Munitions Act was that work should not be allocated in such a manner as to result in any man earning less than he had previously been earning.'[31]

Notwithstanding this second rebuff, the caulkers remained undaunted, for there was still the possibility of submitting leaving certificate applications as an alternative method of drawing attention to their grievance. On the very date of the above hearing, the first such leaving certificate was granted to a Beardmore caulker, George Aitken.[32] The day after that, a Canadian caulker sought a certificate, though in his case he claimed that he had had no experience of water testing.[33] Earning from £4 to £5 a week on 'ordinary' caulking work, he told the tribunal that it was not the reduction of wages involved in water testing to which he objected. However, despite this honourable protestation, both the tribunal clerk T. F. Wilson and the chairman Cmdr. Gibson dwelt on the issue of the threatened loss of earnings as the rationale for the leaving certificate application. Indicating that the company would be acting 'indiscreetly' if it insisted on the retention of the applicant's services, Gibson declared that 'At a time like the present, every man was worth his price. They had been getting good service from the applicant in the capacity he was originally engaged for, and he thought it would be in their own interest to agree to keep him at that work.'[34] The firm, taking the hint, accepted the chairman's advice. But what was still alarming it was that following Sheriff Fyfe's decision in the wage reduction case (above), it was now faced with leaving certificate applications from the eight caulkers involved in that hearing. And when this case was eventually heard by another tribunal chairman, James Andrew, it was held that a reduction of wages consequent on the transfer of the men from one part of the works and from one task to another justified the grant of leaving certificates.[35]

[31] *Glasgow Herald*, 23 Dec. 1915.
[32] Ibid.
[33] Ibid., 24 Dec. 1915.
[34] Ibid.
[35] Ibid., 20 Jan. 1916.

This decision, of course, placed the company in some difficulty since caulkers, threatened with a transfer to water testing, could simply resort to the tribunal without much fear of subsequent unemployment in a labour market where their skills were in constant demand. Perhaps to discourage a future tribunal chairman from issuing a similar ruling, or perhaps to reinforce the management's weakened authority, the Government's Committee on Production therefore suddenly rediscovered a long neglected reference to it of the caulkers' grievance, and issued a ruling in February 1916 which conveniently upheld the company's contention that it was not required to pay piece-work caulkers who had been transferred to water testing their average piece-work earnings.[36]

However, as this still left undecided the position regarding time-rated caulkers transferred to water testing,[37] the grievance rumbled on. Indeed, when the shipyard of John Brown & Co. of Clydebank made changes in water testing rates around May 1916, Beardmore's caulkers sought similar increases.[38] On being refused, sixty-five of them promptly lodged yet more leaving certificate applications.[39] This action, it appears, finally convinced the company to seek a permanent solution acceptable to the caulkers, though it needed the determined efforts of Sheriff Fyfe at the tribunal to push the two sides nearer to each other. For initially, William Mackie, the Boilermakers' official, had insisted that Beardmore should come into line with the rest of Clydeside, while George Barr, the company's assistant manager, remained adamant that an 'existing private arrangement' made in January 1912 should be honoured. Faced with this impasse, Fyfe offered to recommend a settlement, given that 'he could never think of granting all these certificates'. A subsequent meeting chaired by Sheriff Fyfe was therefore arranged, at which the company eventually indicated its willingness to *consider* fixing a uniform rate for water testing.[40] But even this concession fell far short of an agreement as to what those rates ought to have been. Indeed, it took another ten

[36] *Labour Gazette*, Mar. 1916, 113.

[37] Four of the 8 complainants in the wage reduction case before Christmas 1915 were time-rated caulkers.

[38] CSA, *Minute Book* No. 9, 29 May 1916.

[39] *Glasgow Herald*, 22 May 1916.

[40] CSA, *Minute Book* No. 9, 29 May 1916.

months of haggling before this festering sore finally subsided, when another arbiter, with delightful simplicity, decided that caulkers put on water testing should be paid time and a half.[41] Thus, having taken an unconscionable time a-dying, the whole episode of Beardmore caulkers transferred to water testing reveals clearly the relationship between important Munitions Act hearings in Glasgow and the pursuit of collective grievances. On a number of separate occasions, the men's wage dispute provided the foundation for proceedings conducted under different legal categories. Various sets of leaving certificate applications were submitted, one complaint by the employer was heard under the Ordering of Work regulations and one was lodged by the caulkers that the employers were unlawfully altering wage rates. On top of this, arbitration was arranged not once, but twice, with the matter finally being settled on the second occasion. The role of the Munitions Act in this extended drama was not to suppress the men's grievances but to provide an airing for them; perhaps even to offer an institutional framework where little of this nature had previously existed. The negotiating character of a prosecution or of an application for leaving certificates is thus vividly illustrated, while the unions' distaste for compulsory arbitration was matched only by the imaginativeness with which they sought to circumvent it.[42]

CONCLUSION

The broader context within which collective bargaining by litigation was conducted was one in which centralized wage

---

[41] *Labour Gazette*, Apr. 1917, 155.

[42] One writer has, however, claimed that 'Trade unions found compulsory arbitration more expeditious in settling disputes than the ordinary conciliation board procedure. It was much quicker to report differences under the Munitions Act at an early stage and get an award which was legally enforceable for a definite period of time . . . than to spend much time with employers in negotiations which might result in a deadlock leading to a stoppage.' See Ducksoo Chang, *British Methods of Industrial Peace*, New York, 1936, p. 91. None the less, such observations are in conflict with the evidence of trade union criticism of those frustrating delays attaching to compulsory arbitration proceedings, which in fact compelled the Government to amend the Munitions Act in 1916, and again in 1917. Indeed, Chang himself (at p. 75), notes these statutory responses to such criticisms. For examples of trade union complaints, see the *Trade Union Worker*, Feb. 1916, 3; ibid., Apr. 1916, 8.

fixing by the Committee on Production tended to result in the imposition of uniform levels of settlement. As can be seen from Table 5.1, in the period from February 1915 to September 1915, settlements (on a sectional or district basis) were frequently 4*d.* on time-rates and 10 per cent on piece-rates. From September 1915 to the spring of 1916, there was a tendency to refuse advances, thus obliging munitions workers to place a higher premium on local organization if improvements were to be gained. From the spring of 1916 to April 1917, various advances, commonly of around 3*s.* on time-rates, were awarded; while from April 1917, the institution of national settlements began to occur. Yet it is important to note that in all these cases, the awards were strictly defined as war bonuses, added on to wildly divergent pre-war base rates, which in turn reflected differences in gender, location, industries, occupations, levels of skill, and methods of payment. Thus as a result of the tendency towards the issuance of similar or identical rewards, the centralizing influence of compulsory arbitration and of numerous statutory arbitration tribunals still left an untidy picture containing anomalies galore.

Table 5.1 Committee on Production Cycle of Advances

Cycle	Approximate dates	Nature of advance
First	February to September 1915	4*s.* on time rates; 10% on piece rates
—	October 1915 to April 1916	No increases
Second	May to November 1916	3*s.* on time rates only
Third	April 1917 (national agreement)	5*s.* to time- and piece-workers
Fourth	August 1917 (national agreement)	3*s.* to time- and piece-workers
Fifth	December 1917 (national agreement)	5*s.* to time- and piece-workers
Sixth	June 1918 (national agreement)	3*s* 6*d.* to time- and piece-workers
Seventh	November 1918 (national agreement)	5*s.* to time- and piece-workers

Source. Henry Clay, 'Government Control of Wages in War-Time' in Henry Clay, *The Problem of Industrial Relations*, London, 1929, p. 37.

With roaring price inflation[43] merely compounding wage-earners' sense of injustice, one immediate consequence of the Government's insufficiently sensitive wages policy was that the munitions tribunal, like the factories themselves, was now working flat out. For given the boost to employers' confidence by the trade unions' *formal* renunciation of their right to strike; given the existence of the leaving certificate scheme; and given the provision in Section 4(2) of the Munitions Act which required the approval of the Ministry of Munitions before alterations in wage rates could be implemented,[44] employers could afford to adopt a dismissive attitude, initially, to legitimate wage demands.[45]

Thus it is against a background where munitions workers were frustrated in their endeavours to capitalize on their enhanced market superiority that one must appreciate the pragmatism and opportunism which informed their alternate uses of direct industrial action and direct legal action. For it was an imaginative strategy which succeeded in standing that notorious and inhibiting measure, the Munitions Act, on its head. In fact, if not in form, the munitions tribunals were seen to offer a unique opportunity, albeit born of desperation, to fashion a new instrument of wartime wage determination, the technique of collective bargaining by litigation.[46]

---

[43] Retail food prices by 1 Jan. 1917 were 87% above the July 1914 figure, whereas a year earlier they were 45% above the figure at the outbreak of the war. Food prices thus rose 29% in 1916, though of course wage rates and earnings were also rising. Only in the fourth year of the war, however, did wage rates begin to catch up with the rise in the cost of living. For these points, see *Labour Gazette*, Jan. 1917, 3–5; ibid., Jan. 1918, 5; A. L. Bowley, *Prices and Wages in the United Kingdom, 1914–1920*, Oxford, 1921, p. 106.

[44] Wolfe, *Labour Supply and Regulation*, p. 254, for the effect of Section 4(2).

[45] Cf. the complaint in the *New Statesman* that 'In one case, in a great industrial area, when the men applied for an advance in wages, the Employers' Association, by skilful dilatoriness, managed to put off the decision for three months, and then entirely refused to let the award be made retrospective, the result being a saving to the employers of many thousands of pounds for each week of delay.' See *New Statesman*, 7 Apr. 1917, 7–8. Even the advent of the 'cost plus' system of government contracting in Feb. 1916, whereby the employer was permitted to pass on to the contracting department any increase in his costs due to an increase in wages, did not have a noticeable effect on wage bargaining. Employers continued to dig in their heels, perhaps, as Lord Amulree (the former arbitrator, Sir William Mackenzie) engagingly put it, 'either from habit or from a regard to general public consideration and the finances of the State'. See Lord Amulree, *Industrial Arbitration in Great Britain*, Oxford, 1929, p. 144.

[46] That the government had reason to approve this development is considered briefly in the final chapter.

CHAPTER 6

Parkhead Revisited: Wage Frustration and Strike Prosecutions, 1916–1918

INTRODUCTION

As we have remarked earlier, the spring of 1916 marked a watershed in industrial relations on the Clyde. The deportation of the shop stewards had a calming influence on the industrial climate.[1] The seething discontent had abated, but, as we shall see, only to gain a respite. The munitions tribunal in Glasgow was under new management, though whether anyone outside the Ministry of Munitions noticed, is a different matter. Certainly the atmosphere *within* the tribunal showed a marked change from that under the old regime, whose indulgence had been its own undoing. The dilution programme was apparently proceeding apace, relatively unhindered,[2] though appearances, as suggested in Chapter 9, could be deceptive. Furthermore, the most glaring abuses under the Munitions Act had, on paper at least, been rectified in the Amendment Act of January 1916.[3] A Government-imposed wage freeze which had prevented the Committee on Production, the wartime arbitration body, from issuing general wage awards, now began to thaw.[4] Moreover, the experience of almost one year's working of the munitions tribunal suggested the tactical possibilities which it might offer workers as an aid to collective bargaining. Thus, despite the restrictions which lay at the core of the Munitions Act—the prohibition of strikes, the restraints on labour mobility, the pursuit of labour discipline, compulsory arbitration and the drive towards centralized wage determination—the lesson

---

[1] According to Scott and Cunnison, *Industries of the Clyde Valley during the War*, Oxford, 1924, p. 151, 'Open activity in opposition to the Munitions Act ceased from that date in the Clyde district'.

[2] Ibid., p. 153.

[3] For leaving certificate changes, see ch. 8.

[4] Wolfe, *Labour Supply and Regulation*, Oxford, 1923, p. 246; also Table 5.1 above.

seemed to be that, in favourable circumstances, legal proceedings against an employer, or even direct industrial action, might ultimately bear fruit in the shape of improved terms of employment. But despite the favourable signs pointing to a new *modus vivendi*, dark clouds loomed on the horizon. Military conscription began to occupy the centre of the stage of social and political concern; despite modifications, the leaving certificate was still strongly resented by workmen as an intolerable shackle; working conditions became more exhausting as the pattern of the war shifted: the Somme 1916, then submarine warfare. During 1916, in particular, there was a rapid rise in the cost of living. It is true that the increase in average weekly wage rates for nearly six million workpeople in 1916 was 6*s*. (and 10*s*. to 12*s*. for some of those in munitions work) and that this ignores increased earnings due to more regular employment and overtime. However, as previously mentioned (ch. 5), by 1 January 1917 retail food prices were 87 per cent above the July 1914 figure, whereas a year earlier they were 45 per cent above the figure at the outbreak of the war. Food prices thus rose 29 per cent in 1916,[5] and food shortages began to occur thereafter.[6] It was easy to associate such movements with profiteering and with the conspicuous consumption of the rich. In short, the sources of tension, the pressure for increased wage demands, were still present. If socialists were not slow to draw attention to 'The Huns at Home'[7] or to the profits of patriotism,[8] then the acknowledgement by the capitalist press[9] in 1917 of 'Excessive Retail Prices in Glasgow' suggested that not many in the second

---

[5] *Labour Gazette*, Jan. 1917, 3–5.

[6] Hinton, *The First Shop Stewards' Movement*, London, 1973, pp. 236–7.

[7] Thomas Johnston, *The Huns at Home During Three Years of the Great War*, Glasgow, c. 1917.

[8] See, for example, the comments of George Dallas in the *Trade Union Worker*, Mar. 1916, 8; ibid., July 1916, 8. Cf. Glasgow Trades Council, *Annual Report 1917–18* (1918), 28.

[9] *Glasgow Herald*, 3 Oct. 1917. The Lord Provost of Glasgow, Thomas Dunlop, urged the workers to eat just half a potato with each meal, as he had claimed to be doing. He became known as 'Half-a-spud' or 'Half-a-Potato' Dunlop. See Gallacher, *Revolt on the Clyde*, London, 1936, p. 188; McShane and Smith, *Harry McShane: No Mean Fighter*, London, 1978, p. 96.

city of the Empire would be impressed by the fact that the rate of increase in food prices had slowed down that year.[10] Against this background of economic pressure, wage disputes continued to erupt; and, as a consequence, the munitions tribunal in Glasgow, like the munitions factories themselves, was working to capacity. Those trade unionists who felt inhibited by the anti-strike clauses and by the 'slavery' provisions of an act which, in David Kirkwood's words, 'cut clean athwart the political economy of the hour',[11] continued to lodge complaints that employers were altering their wages or were failing to honour arbitration awards.[12] However such inhibitions were not universal, so that in spite of their optimistic hopes after the Clyde deportations, the authorities and the munitions tribunal found themselves still wrestling with the challenge of strikes on Clydeside.

The following account, therefore, will analyse Sheriff Fyfe's handling of strike prosecutions after the spring of 1916, a relatively unexplored period of wartime Clydeside's labour history. For with the removal of the shop stewards from the scene in March and April 1916, the attention of historians has tended to shift elsewhere. Perhaps it was assumed that until the deportees' return from banishment in June 1917, the industrial labour movement in Glasgow fell asleep from the spring of 1916 till May 1917, and that at that point its slumbers were disturbed just long enough to signal its refusal to participate in a near-countrywide strike movement that year, known as the 'May Strikes' (ch. 9).[13] In fact, significant industrial unrest continued in spite of the emasculation of the CWC following the shop steward deportations, and flared up at regular intervals. The culmination during the war was a nationwide movement, with its counterpart in Glasgow under the influence of the now

---

[10] *Labour Gazette,* Jan. 1918, 5. Only in the fourth year of the war did wage rates begin to catch up with the rise in the cost of living. See Bowley, *Prices and Wages in the United Kingdom, 1914–1920,* Oxford, 1921, p. 106.

[11] Kirkwood, *My Life of Revolt,* London, 1935, p. 101.

[12] For details, see Rubin, 'The Enforcement of the Munitions of War Acts 1915–1917, with Particular Reference to Proceedings before the Munitions Tribunal in Glasgow, 1915–1921', Warwick Univ. Ph.D thesis (1984), pp. 315–24.

[13] McLean, for example, has recently claimed that, 'After March 1916 . . . industrial militancy on the Clyde was to be absent for three years.' See McLean, *The Legend of Red Clydeside,* Edinburgh, 1983, p. 90.

revitalized CWC, to extend to all classes of munitions workers a general $12\frac{1}{2}$ per cent award which had been paid in late 1917 to skilled time-workers.[14]

The argument of this chapter is that the pattern of decision-making adopted by Sheriff Fyfe's tribunal in deliberating upon strike prosecutions tended, despite occasional lapses, to reinforce corporatist notions of patriotic unity and order. Thus he would condemn both unofficial strike action *and* 'irresponsible' trade union leadership. But he was sanguine enough to impose hefty fines only where continued recalcitrance was established. For his decisions were strongly influenced by his recognition that industrial unrest was endemic and could only to a limited extent be attributed to malevolent or revolutionary sentiment. He knew that he was condemned to an unenviable existence, struggling to hold back the tide of discontent which the pressures of war were whipping up. His role oscillated from that of stern deliverer of penal thunderbolts to that of self-conscious sympathizer with those strikers fined nominal amounts by the tribunal for striking out of sheer frustration and exasperation. But it was also as a conduit for the channelling of grievances that his tribunal performed a useful role in advancing the government's interests. He syphoned off some of the complaints that might otherwise have exploded in more direct action. He may thereby have relieved some of the burden from the shoulders of the arbitration machinery, though he also redirected issues into the lap of Sir George Askwith, the Chief Industrial Commissioner, if he thought that no immediate answer was called for. He thus played it by ear, though subject to certain overriding precepts. One might say that in this respect, he matched the State bureaucracy at large, and achieved ultimately the same kind of success as the whole munitions enterprise.

[14] The $12\frac{1}{2}$ per cent award was to rectify the anomaly whereby time-based skilled munitions workers who were 'setting up' machinery for less-skilled workers to operate, found they were earning less than their less-skilled co-workers who were on piece-work. The ambit of those falling within the award was constantly being widened, in order to meet further demands for inclusion. Even unskilled workers benefited from the subsequent payment of a compensatory award of $7\frac{1}{2}$ per cent. The $12\frac{1}{2}$ per cent award caused tremendous disruption in industrial relations, and the timeworkers' 'grievance' was reflected in a number of munitions tribunal hearings, examples of which are cited below. For general discussion of the award, see *OHMM*, vol. v, pt. 1, pp. 167–93; Wrigley, *David Lloyd George and the British Labour Movement*, Hassocks, 1976, pp. 219–22.

STRIKE PROSECUTIONS 1916–1918

Isolated strike action over wages came to the attention of the munitions tribunal during this period. For example, two mill workers struck against a reduction in their work load, and consequently in their wage packets, brought about by the company's decision to allocate an extra man to the work.[15] Since the court declared that those trade unionists guided by Owen Coyle, district secretary of the Amalgamated Society of Steel and Iron Workers, would be 'well advised', and that the employer brought the case 'as a matter of discipline . . . with no desire to punish these particular men', the strikers were admonished. Similarly, an employer's conciliatory remarks led to a lenient fine of 10s. imposed on fourteen brass foundry labourers who had struck in pursuit of a comparability claim in June 1917.[16]

However, despite the refusal of Clydeside trade unionists to participate in the widespread 'May Strikes' in 1917 (ch. 9), the Glasgow area's remarkable record for industrial militancy on a grand scale had not fallen completely into abeyance after the shop steward deportations. A number of major stoppages occurred during this period, not all of which, for instance, a major iron moulders' strike of September 1917, resulted in prosecutions. The following, however, are the more significant strikes which eventually landed on Sheriff Fyfe's lap.

In one case heard in July 1916, six riveters and three holders-on had gone on strike at a Paisley shipyard (possibly Bow, MacLachlan and Co. Ltd.) in protest at their transfer from work on single-screw to twin-screw mine-sweepers.[17] The transfer represented a reduction in rates of between 20 and 25 per cent in view of the larger and heavier dimensions of single-screws. But despite their grievance, the men eschewed Board of Trade intervention and struck work. The result was a severe lecture delivered by the sheriff and stiff fines (which he none the less described as lenient) of £10 and £5 in the case of the six found guilty. He also, however, issued a stern rebuke to their trade union official (probably William Mackie of the Boilermakers'

[15] *Glasgow Herald*, 14 Sept. 1916.
[16] Ibid., 9 July 1917.
[17] Ibid., 22 July 1916.

Society) for not discouraging them from their illegal conduct, despite the latter's protestation that it would be 'ill advice to try to compel these men to go in'. It seems plausible that Sheriff Fyfe's animated stance in this case—he also condemned the employers who had 'stood rather on their own dignity'— was due to the capacity of the non-technical layman to relate directly and intimately to the particular munitions work in question, the construction of a mine-sweeper. Perhaps unspecified caulking or the manufacture of optical instruments would not have had the same vivid impact on the imagination.

This point becomes clearer in a strike prosecution case heard shortly thereafter. This involved fifteen caulkers employed by D. & W. Henderson Ltd. who had been asked to move on to a meat-carrying vessel, certified as war work by the Board of Trade, once they had completed a job on a Government transport ship.[18] A dispute broke out over the method of payment, the men preferring a time-rate with a percentage to the employer's offer of piece-rates. Apparently the matter was a long-standing grievance which had not proved amenable in the past to a temporary agreement proposed by the management. The strike, however, broke the deadlock; Sheriff Fyfe succeeded in persuading the men to return to work; a nominal fine of £1 was imposed; and arbitration finally arranged which very rapidly conceded most of the men's claims.[19]

The men had also taken the 'precaution' of lodging leaving certificate applications whose hearing was arranged for the afternoon of the strike prosecution. They pointed out that they had specifically been hired on repair work, but were now being allocated to merchant work, which they deemed a breach of contract. Sheriff Fyfe realized the difficulty. For, 'To grant a clearance certificate on the application before him would be to make a laughing-stock of the previous Court, which had fined the men for going on strike rather than do the work assigned to them.'[20] He therefore sought refuge in the artificial reasoning that the leaving certificate applications made no mention of breach of contract, but only of a disputed transfer, an argument which clearly angered the men's representative, William

[18] Ibid., 2 Sept. 1916.
[19] *Labour Gazette*, Oct. 1916, 393.
[20] *Glasgow Herald*, 2 Sept. 1916.

Mackie of the Boilermakers. 'And all the time the employers will be laughing up their sleeves', he protested. But the deed was done. The men had already been fined for striking. The tribunal could hardly be expected to grant certificates in *those* circumstances, though the venom of Sheriff Fyfe's condemnation of the Paisley shipyard workers in the previous case was noticeably absent here. A delay to a meat-carrying vessel at that time scarcely conjured up the same image of provocative behaviour as a refusal to work on a particular type of mine-sweeper. A year hence and attitudes might have been different as food shortages reached a critical state.[21]

But it was in the previous month, August 1916, when three major strike prosecutions followed rapidly one after another, that a reminder of the pent-up frustrations of munitions workers at the ineptitude of Board of Trade arbitration was forcefully underlined. The first case involved a two-day stoppage by seventy-two foundry and dressing shop labourers employed at the Steel Company of Scotland's Parkhead Works.[22] Alex Haddow, secretary of the Parkhead branch of the Steel and Iron Workers' Society, told the tribunal that an application for an increase of 2*d*. an hour had been on the table since 14 April. A conference had been arranged in May, but no settlement achieved. Finally the men gave fourteen days' notice and struck on 7 and 8 August.

The tactic which Sheriff Fyfe seemed now to be employing was not to lambast the strikers for their traitorous behaviour, a prominent feature of the earlier months of the legislation. Instead, his anger was directed to the failure of 'responsible' trade union 'leadership' to deflect the rank and file from their illegal path. Haddow was singled out for having, like the official in the Paisley shipyard case (above), fomented the strike. This attempt at a public humiliation was also extended to an individual employee, George McDade, who had initially written to the management 'upon private paper' informing them of the fourteen-day strike ultimatum.[23]

---

[21] Cf. Lloyd George in Jan. 1918, in Wrigley, *David Lloyd George and the British Labour Movement*, p. 218.

[22] *Glasgow Herald*, 14 Aug. 1916.

[23] McDade replied by writing to the newspapers, pointing out that he had merely acted as minutes secretary at the branch meeting which voted on the ultimatum. See ibid., 16 Aug. 1916.

A policy of blaming the militant leaders for having led otherwise docile and law-abiding employees to take industrial action was now evolved, so that 'He was not blaming the men so much as the leaders in this case'.[24] Officially, therefore, there was a conspiracy to cause industrial unrest. It mattered not that the Parkhead labourers were low paid, earning 28s. 4d., as Haddow's full-time officer, Owen Coyle, pointed out to the tribunal.[25] It mattered not, as Haddow replied to Fyfe's reminder that the union was 'under discipline', that 'Discipline is a very fine phrase, but when it is all on one side I don't like it'.[26] Moreover, it mattered not, as even Sheriff Fyfe admitted, that

'One could not sit there without being impressed with the fact that the machinery of arbitration was cumbrous and dilatory; . . . undoubtedly it was a misfortune that the pressure in that department made it inevitable that a great deal of time must elapse before a dispute of the kind must be settled.'

Within the sphere of Sheriff Fyfe's legal reality, however, such considerations were irrelevant. 'He was not concerned as to whether the machinery could be improved or not . . . it was there and it could be adopted and it was the quid pro quo which was put in expressly as the other side of the stipulation that a strike was illegal.' Clearly the insensitivity of such remarks might otherwise have been breath-taking in their effort to devalue the material conditions under which the men were working. Yet the very fact that a policy was adopted of laying blame on individual trade union officers surely suggests that even the sheriff acknowledged the justice of the men's case, if he disapproved of their methods. This was a dilemma which had rarely surfaced when strikes occurred in 1915 and early 1916. Then, both means and end were equally condemned. Now, however, the early signs of war-weariness, plus the added privations brought about by the rising cost of living, perhaps

---

[24] They were thus fined only £1 each. Fyfe's approach should be compared with the Minister of Munitions, Christopher Addison's, simultaneous statement to the Commons that the troubles on Clydeside, which he claimed had now passed, had been fomented by a small number of individuals who were conducting a campaign which was also directed against the trade unions. See HC Deb. 5th ser., vol. 85, 15 Aug. 1916, col. 1728.

[25] Coyle was apparently absolved of any blame in the matter by Sheriff Fyfe who, as we have seen, admired his qualities as a union official.

[26] *Glasgow Herald*, 14 Aug. 1916 for this and subsequent quotations.

impressed themselves, if barely imperceptibly, even on Sheriff Fyfe's hardened brow.

Indeed two days later, another batch of fifty-five strikers from the firm's Hallside works were before the tribunal under similar circumstances, and again were represented by Owen Coyle.[27] The message expressed the previous Saturday was reiterated at this Monday sitting. For while the sheriff bemoaned the delays accompanying the attempt to solve local disputes, he could not close his eyes to the fact that 'Whether the delay was long or short, the strike was not to be used as a weapon to enforce labour conditions'.

The imposition of a modified penalty of £1 was possibly the least he could do to indicate his sympathy for the men's dilemma (as well as to treat them equitably with the Parkhead labourers fined the same amount two days earlier). Otherwise he himself might have been accused of failing to discourage recurrences elsewhere.

But in fact he *was* on the bench again two days later in Grangemouth to try a further group of munitions workers accused of striking unlawfully. On this occasion, the case involved a number of riveters in dispute with their employer, the Greenock & Grangemouth Dockyard Company, over the proper wage rate for shell-plating a merchantman ordered by the Admiralty. However, instead of modified sums, punitive fines of £20 were imposed on each of the strikers found guilty.[28] The large amounts seemed to reflect Fyfe's anger at those accused who had engaged in a 'disgraceful exhibition of perversity' by refusing to give an undertaking to the tribunal that they would return to work pending a Board of Trade settlement. But the amounts were also probably influenced by the fact that only a fortnight earlier another munitions tribunal in Edinburgh, chaired by Sheriff Fleming, had imposed fines of £10 and £15 on ten other riveters in the same firm, who had also struck over a wage dispute.[29]

Three strike prosecutions in one week certainly hinted at something more than an accident; indeed, considerably more

[27] *Glasgow Herald*, 15 Aug. 1916.
[28] Ibid., 17 Aug. 1916.
[29] Ibid., 31 July 1916.

than carelessness. Though 'epidemic' was too strong a word, none the less diagnosis and treatment were still urgent. Of course, it was not necessary to go so far as to formulate a controversial diagnosis which pointed to the one-sided nature of a law against strikes which failed to punish *employers* for intransigence over local disputes, or for contriving a deadlock by adopting an attitude of complacency towards employees' wage grievances.[30] It was sufficient that the munitions tribunal chairman acknowledge that the existing system was flawed. Thus at the Hallside hearing (above), Coyle had taken up Fyfe's remarks on the cumbersome procedures hitherto required in order to mobilize the Board of Trade and the Committee on Production. Coyle therefore suggested that a 'wages court' modelled on the local munitions tribunals be established, which could expedite the examination of grievances and reach decisions within a week or a fortnight. Such an innovation, he believed, would reduce the amount of irritation, often resulting in strikes, which accompanied the exasperating delays in reaching settlements.

The idea, as we saw in Chapter 5, was taken up by Sheriff Fyfe, but he failed to convince Sir George Askwith of its utility.[31] The only concession made by the Government was that to prevent the possibility of positions becoming too deeply entrenched when both sides refused to trigger the arbitration machinery, the Government itself could, from 1917, refer a dispute to the Board of Trade in order to mobilize Askwith's department.[32] But of course such suggestions were only palliatives which did not touch the core grievance—that the value of money was being eroded as rapidly as it was being earned and that the normal mechanism of market competition had been interrupted; besides which, the deterrent effect of punitive labour legislation had its limitations whether in time of war or in peacetime. No amount of tinkering with statutory arbitration provisions could dispute this finding.

[30] Cf. the view of the *New Statesman*, cited in ch. 5, n. 45.
[31] See also Rubin, 'Labour Courts and the Proposals of 1917–19', *Industrial Law Journal*, xiv (1985).
[32] Munitions of War Act 1917, s. 6(2).

STRIKES AT BEARDMORE

By the last quarter of 1917, therefore, an air of militancy pervaded Clydeside. According to Gallacher, 'Strikes were an almost everyday occurrence',[33] while the local Ministry of Munitions official in Glasgow, contemplating the ferment in the factories, was reporting that 'everything points to a big movement in October'.[34] A number of forces were at work including the presence of a revitalized CWC following the return of the deportees, the skilled time-workers' grievance which was to lead to the troublesome $12\frac{1}{2}$ per cent award; the liberating influence of the proposed abolition of leaving certificates; the Government drive for increased output accompanied by the extension of piece-work, and the premium bonus payment system which generated suspicion. More general features identified in the regional reports of the Commission on Industrial Unrest, such as high food prices and the unequal distribution of food, the operation of the Military Service Acts, housing shortages, and general exhaustion could also be cited.[35]

Into this whirlpool of industrial ferment stepped the munitions tribunal in Glasgow, intent on promoting industrial order in place of anarchy, on promoting 'responsible' trade unionism, on patching up differences between major employers and their strategically important labour forces in such a way as to preserve those managerial prerogatives consistent with the ministry's corporatist aims, and, if possible, to offer *some* positive hope for trade unionist applicants, even if only the prospect of further arbitration. Finally, it saw its task as the discouragement of rank-and-file militancy which repudiated the constitutionalism of trade union officials.

The major episode which offered the tribunal the opportunity to pursue with vigour its moral crusade was the industrial action inspired by an 'Emergency Committee' of the Moulders Union at Beardmore's Parkhead Forge, where the aim, as we shall see below, was to secure the extension of the $12\frac{1}{2}$ per cent bonus to all workers at the plant. As a prelude to its involvement in this agitation in the winter of 1917–18, the tribunal first adjudicated

[33] Gallacher, *Revolt on the Clyde*, p. 168.
[34] Cited in Hinton, *The First Shop Stewards' Movement*, p. 252.
[35] Cf. *Labour Gazette*, Aug. 1917, 273.

on a complaint lodged by the Workers' Union against Beardmore's shell factory in Paisley.[36] According to Robert Climie, the union's representative, 300 men at the factory had, for six weeks, been deprived of an output bonus granted to them by an arbitration award.[37] The company explained that it had written to the Board of Trade some ten days after the award, objecting to certain aspects, and two weeks after that, the union had been told that no bonuses would be paid until the doubt was resolved. This, said the company, did not amount to a failure to pay the award; but in any case, it would be implemented forthwith. The union none the less pressed for a penalty, and a week later Sheriff Fyfe imposed a fine of £100 on the company, having calculated that at £5 a day per employee, the firm was theoretically liable to a fine of £54,000.[38]

The rationale of the chairman's decision was that the company had flouted the arbitration provisions of the Act which represented the quid pro quo for the prohibition of strikes, and that it was improper to enter into correspondence with the Board of Trade over the interpretation of the award without first seeking the approval of the other party, the Workers' Union. Of course, Fyfe might have added that the major concern was that no excuse should be offered to munitions workers to take industrial action.[39] Therefore, it was plainly imperative that there should be no delay in giving effect to awards, particularly those which, as in the present case, were considered by the tribunal to be unambiguous. It was difficult enough to restrain workers from taking action in response to delays in submitting claims to arbitration without having to tempt fate once an arbitration award had actually been issued. Presumably, reasoning of this nature underlay the exemplary fine of £100 imposed on the company which overshadowed by far any previous monetary penalty announced by the tribunal. Here was a further illustration of Fyfe's drive to project the legislation as 'impartial' as between the 'two' sides of industry, and to show

---

[36] *Glasgow Herald*, 11 Oct. 1917.
[37] Cf. *Labour Gazette*, Oct. 1917, 347 which refers to a bonus award which matches all the details cited in the tribunal report, except that the firm's Dalmuir plant and not the Paisley factory is mentioned. The failure to mention the shell works is probably an accidental omission in the Labour Ministry's publication.
[38] *Glasgow Herald*, 18 Oct. 1917.
[39] Cf. the leading article in ibid.

that both were subject to 'equal' sacrifices under the scheme. Employers, also, were to be subordinated to the overriding needs of the state and would incur punishment if in breach of the corporatist goals of unity and order. A prominent local shipowner, William Raeburn, might bewail that since a three week strike of ironmoulders in September and early October had not been prosecuted,[40] then there must be 'veritably one law for the employer and a different one for the employed. . . . Because it is quite easy to catch an employer and make an example of him, but it is a very different story when you have thousands of workmen to deal with!'[41] None the less, the ideological potential of a decision such as that involving the Beardmore shell factory at Paisley can be clearly gauged from an anonymous reply to Raeburn's complaint. This, in contrast, argued that

the one thing which has gained for the local tribunal in this district the respect and confidence of both employer and workman is the fearless manner in which the Munitions Act has been applied to both classes concerned, and the impartial way in which transgressors have been dealt with, irrespective of whether they were employers or workmen.[42]

Whether such sentiments were broadly shared after the Clyde deportations and whether the imposition of a £100 fine on Beardmore was perceived as contributing to a spirit of unity are difficult to confirm. None the less, one feature is clear. That is the prominent role which Beardmore played in the history of the Glasgow munitions tribunal. There is, indeed, a certain irony in the speech of James Maxton, the ILP pacifist, to the Labour Party conference in 1916, when he declared that 'In Parkhead Forge, where the men were well organized under a capable leader, there were practically no cases of men being brought before the Tribunal because the employers at Parkhead knew that, Munitions Act or no Munitions Act, if injustice was done to any of the workers, work would cease.'[43] Admittedly, much of Beardmore's litigation had emanated from Dalmuir and that the case just discussed originated at the Paisley works of the firm.

[40] For the ironmoulders' strike, see ibid., 28 Sept. 1917; Hinton, *The First Shop Stewards' Movement*, p. 251.
[41] *Glasgow Herald*, 22 Oct. 1917.
[42] Ibid., 25 Oct. 1917. Cf. Fyfe's own comments at p.35 above.
[43] Labour Party, *Annual Conference Report 1916*, 129.

However, Parkhead itself was hardly immune from legal confrontations, as is indicated by the prosecution of David Hanton and nine others at the Forge (ch. 3, above), in the wake of the deportation strikes.

The strike movement in 1917–18 similarly was rooted in Parkhead where rank-and-file organization was being resurrected. As Harry McShane has recently noted, the howitzer shop was a particular hot-bed of militancy. 'The men and the shop stewards there were among the most militant in Parkhead Forge. You could always rely on them to back you up; in fact it was difficult to keep them in sometimes because they stopped work for the most trivial reasons.'[44] Yet of prosecutions of striking Clydeside munitions workers in pursuit of the $12\frac{1}{2}$ per cent bonus there were none; merely one paltry Ordering of Work prosecution against a number of youths in Motherwell long after the troubles had subsided.[45] Instead, the munitions tribunal was called upon simply to determine, in the wake of two of the succession of strikes at the Forge, whether non-strikers laid off as a consequence of the industrial action were entitled to compensation when the company closed the works.

What had happened was that in the last few days before Hogmanay, the bricklayers and steel workers in the howitzer shop had walked out in pursuit of an extension of the $12\frac{1}{2}$ per cent.[46] This was followed by a dispute[47] involving the gas-producermen in the Millmen's Union (i.e. the British Steel Smelters, Mill, Iron, Tinplate, and Kindred Trades Association). As it had not been settled by 8 January 1918, the date for the resumption of work after the New Year holidays, those non-strikers who presented themselves for work that day were sent home, a process repeated on subsequent days. These included 159 ironmoulders, members of AIMS, who needed a supply of

[44] McShane and Smith, *Harry McShane*, p. 88.

[45] Twenty-three young steel workers aged between 15 and 17 were prosecuted under the Ordering of Work regulations for absenting themselves without leave on one night in Mar. 1918 as part of their campaign for an extension of the bonus. They were fined between 20s and 30s. It is difficult to imagine a clearer indictment of the failure of the law to stamp out mass rank-and-file activity. See *Glasgow Herald*, 29 Mar. 1918.

[46] Hinton, *The First Shop Stewards' Movement*, p. 253.

[47] This was probably the issue referred to by Hinton when the bonus was extended to iron and steel workers at Parkhead in such a way as to merge with existing bonuses so that the net gain was just $6\frac{1}{4}$ per cent. Therefore the dispute continued. See ibid., pp. 253–4.

gas for the melting of metal for the foundry.[48] A complaint by them was then lodged with the tribunal to the effect that the management had not merely *suspended* work, for which specific action there was now no statutory remedy since the repeal of the leaving certificate scheme (ch. 8), but had *terminated* the men's contracts by laying them off. And since under Section 3(1) of the 1917 Act, each side was required to give a week's notice or payment in lieu in order to end the contract, the union's president, James Fulton, claimed compensation for his dutiful members. The legal arguments were complex but the substance of Sheriff Fyfe's decision was that the management's action *had* amounted to a termination by it of the men's contracts for which a week's wages in lieu of notice were due. This decision was issued on 5 February. But by this time a further stoppage had occurred as a result of the management locking out steel workers who were threatening an overtime and weekend working ban and who had left the British Steel Smelters' Union in protest against the failure to obtain the full 12½ per cent. The Moulders' Emergency Committee which had led the stoppage in September, now struck in support of the breakaway steel men, and again large numbers of non-striking workers, about 300 in different trade unions, were laid off[49] and claimed compensation.

Though the first decision of 5 February was now under appeal to the Munitions Appeal Tribunal in Edinburgh, Sheriff Fyfe could hardly issue an inconsistent ruling in this second hearing conducted three weeks later. But the most striking feature of his judgment[50] was the manner in which he used the tribunal as a platform from which the Emergency Committee's activities might be condemned. He clearly pictured himself as waging a moral crusade in which 'responsible' trades unionism was to be fêted while unconstitutional militancy was to be publicly pilloried. His munitions tribunal was not to be simply a crude measure of repression, but was, through the educative effects of bold pronouncements, to impart a message of loyalty to the 'corporate spirit'. Thus, he declared that

[48] AIMS, *Monthly Report*, Mar. 1918, 26; *Glasgow Herald*, 6 Feb. 1918.
[49] Hinton, *The First Shop Stewards' Movement*, p. 254.
[50] *Glasgow Herald*, 27 Feb. 1918.

The intervention of this so-called Workers' Committee was quite unnecessary, and if it did not represent any substantial section of the workers, its intervention was impertinent, and was disloyal to the general body of workers as well as their own trade unions and to their employers. He was of opinion that this committee represented probably no-one but the so-called delegates who comprised it, or at best a very trifling proportion of the thousands of workers at Parkhead . . .[51]

Adding that all the tribunal applicants had disavowed the Emergency Committee and that none had 'had any complicity in the threat-to-cease-work propaganda of that committee', he accordingly awarded them compensation.

It is difficult to resist the conclusion that Fyfe's judgment, though on technical grounds later overruled by Lord Hunter in the Appeal Tribunal,[52] was informed by a belief that the authority of official trades unionism would thereby be enhanced if individual trade unionists who repudiated the Emergency Committee's actions, could be rewarded in such a way. Certainly his legal argument was open to serious questioning, so much so that even counsel for the trade unions, when the case went to appeal in Edinburgh, agreed that it was not worth defending.

His judgment none the less conformed to the distinct pattern of promoting order in industrial relations by reinforcing the structure of responsible and officially recognized trade unions, and by seeking to eliminate causes of tension wherever this could be achieved without violence to the national interest as he understood it. It need hardly be said that Beardmore's sectional interest in minimizing labour costs determined their resistance to the non-strikers' claim and further explains why the question was taken to appeal by the company. But more difficult to explain is the view of the Ministry of Munitions which was represented at the appeal hearing. Thus 'The Solicitor-General who at the outset stated that the position of the Ministry was that of neutral, characterised the judgments both in reasoning

[51] Ibid.

[52] Ibid., 29 Mar. 1918; AIMS, *Monthly Report,* July 1918, 128–9; *William Beardmore & Co. Ltd.* v. *George Miller et al;* idem. v. *Daniel Brawley et al.,* 1918 SMAR 115–22, 28 Mar. 1918.

and result as unsound, and submitted that they ought to be reversed.'[53]

It appears that, once again, the ministry's need to maintain the co-operation of Beardmore in the war effort was a pressing concern, as we have already noted (ch. 4) in the affair involving Cmdr. Gibson and the Canadian leaving certificate cases. Shortly after Fyfe's first judgment on 5 February, Sir George Askwith had a meeting with Sir William Beardmore during which the latter objected that Fyfe's ruling had 'upset all acknowledged law and custom'.[54] Not only would Parkhead incur expenditure of £50,000 in lay-off pay, but 'if the principle worked, it was a direct inducement to other sections sympathetically to lay off'. Askwith sought to calm down the industrialist by remarking that he presumed Sir William 'would employ the best counsel of the Scottish bar', who would advise whether any further appeal by way of case stated might be made in the event of Lord Hunter's upholding Fyfe's decision. Askwith clearly saw the force of Beardmore's complaint, suggesting to his departmental colleagues that Fyfe's judgment 'would of course be a direct inducement to a small section of men to cause a strike and for another section to lay off and obtain pay for nothing'. It was therefore considered vital, at least for public consumption, for the appropriate Government departments not only to endeavour to prevent such a potentially calamitous decision (Askwith was even thinking in terms of a rushed amendment to the Munitions Act) but to be *seen* to be taking a leading role. Thus despite severe reservations about kowtowing to a man whose pride, the Ministry of Labour advised the Cabinet, 'should be put in its proper place',[55] in this instance an obsequious policy was followed. Evidently, the pacification of the leading Clydeside industrial baron was held to outweigh a possible risk of resentment by loyal workers at a ruling restricting the entitlement of large numbers of non-striking trade unionists to a week's lay-off pay. Indeed, the Government officials might have

[53] AIMS, *Monthly Report*, July 1918, 128.

[54] LAB 2/213/IC1173, 'Sir William Beardmore & Co; Munitions of War Act; Memorandum by Sir George Askwith re interview with Sir William Beardmore . . . February 8, 1918'.

[55] Rodney Lowe, 'The Demand for a Ministry of Labour, its Establishment and Initial Role, 1916–1924', London Univ. Ph.D. thesis (1975), p. 81, citing a Ministry of Labour memorandum on 'The Labour Situation on the Clyde, February 15, 1918'.

reasoned, had not such workmen already amply displayed their 'loyalty' by presenting themselves for work while wholesale stoppages were occurring elsewhere? It is, none the less, strongly arguable that the more 'mature' Sheriff Fyfe, with his epic battles with the Fairfield shipwrights and deportation strikers far behind him, was now closer to the pulse of the Clydeside labour movement than was the Ministry of Munitions. Experience both of previous tribunal hearings and of the evidence presented to the frenetic sittings of the industrial unrest enquiry, concluded some months earlier, undoubtedly mellowed his outlook and surely influenced his ruling in this crucial case.[56]

CONCLUSION

The strategy pursued by the Glasgow munitions tribunal in handling strike prosecutions and related cases between the spring of 1916 and the Armistice was one conditioned by a number of factors deemed necessary by the tribunal to the maintenance of corporate unity. Strikes which Sheriff Fyfe considered lacked sufficient provocation would be harshly treated, especially where repetitions of forbidden behaviour occurred. Where arbitration delays were identified, however, his sympathy with strikers' predicament could clearly be

[56] A case raising the identical question to that posed in the Beardmore clash was *H. McGinnes et al.* v. *Bow, MacLachlan & Co. Ltd.*, 1918 SMAR 129–31, 2 July 1918. When the platers at this Paisley shipyard struck on 12 Feb. 1918 in sympathy with the platers and riveters in other Clyde shipyards, the platers' helpers were consequently laid off for a week and no compensation was recovered. The moulders' lockout at Parkhead had actually ceased the day before, but the shock waves were still passing through the Clyde district. For the case of a bricklayer's labourer at Parkhead Forge whose claim dragged on through the courts, possibly into 1921, see *Glasgow Herald*, 3 Nov. 1920; LAB 2/697/SD436; MUN 4/6393. The labourer, George Brown, disputed the amount of the arbitration award granted by Sir Thomas Munro as part of the $12\frac{1}{2}$ per cent movement and cited as defenders in the action, the Ministries of Labour and Munitions, the Iron and Steel Trades Confederation, the Amalgamated Society of Steel and Iron Workers, and the employers' association, the Scottish Steel Makers' Wages Association. He eventually lost his case and the Ministry of Munitions finally abandoned its efforts to recover its costs of almost £50, as Brown appeared to have been financed by his fellow workers at the Forge. Finally, the ASE district delegate reported ruefully in Jan. 1919 that claims for the $12\frac{1}{2}$ per cent and $7\frac{1}{2}$ per cent were still being received. But as the relevant provisions of the Munitions Act had been repealed, there was little hope of such claims being met. See ASE, *Monthly Journal and Report*, Jan. 1919, 21.

discerned. In particular, where prominent employers, such as Beardmore at Paisley, had been caught manipulating arbitration awards to their advantage, Sheriff Fyfe boldly imposed an exemplary fine. His strategy also encompassed the condemnation of 'irresponsible' trade union leadership as well as unjustifiable unofficial action. But he reserved his greatest venom for political 'agitators'. The munitions tribunal certainly had had few contacts with, in the words of the Scottish industrial unrest commissioners, the 'revolutionary element within the unions [which was] trying to undermine the authority of the official executive councils and district committees in order to further their own extreme views'.[57] When, however, such opponents of the 'corporate spirit'[58] were prosecuted by the tribunal, they were severely dealt with; while on numerous occasions, the authority of official trades unionism was cultivated and reinforced by Sheriff Fyfe. Thus the Parkhead Workers' Emergency Committee was, in a most blatant fashion, treated contemptuously by the sheriff as a wholly unrepresentative, fractious, and impertinent body, whose attempts to 'speed up the union officials' by industrial action he condemned vociferously. In contrast, the lodging by union officials of complaints of failure by employers, such as Beardmore at Paisley, to implement awards only served to lock the mass of the rank and file within the unions tighter into the existing legal framework of government-sponsored munitions production.

But how was it that, after the deportations, strikes did not dissolve into oblivion during this period, as they had done in the first six months of the war? Certainly, the professional pundits believed that the Government labour policy evolved by the end of 1915 had nipped the strike 'problem' in the bud. Thus, the air of confidence with which the civil servants at the Ministry of Munitions reported proudly to Lloyd George in early December 1915 on their prowess in *preventing* stoppages,[59] was to disintegrate only slowly as the war progressed. Humbert Wolfe, for example, considered that the situation concerning strikes was 'more steady' in 1916 than in 1915,[60] while, according to

---

[57] PP 1917–18, xv, 133, para. 2.
[58] Ibid., para. 6.
[59] BEV III, 13, fo. 80.
[60] Wolfe, *Labour Supply and Regulation*, p. 133.

Christopher Addison, it was only a major stoppage in Sheffield in November 1916 over the conscription of a skilled engineer Leonard Hargreaves, who in fact possessed exemption from military call-up (ch. 8, n. 62), 'which broke the spell of industrial peace which fell on the workshops of Britain after the defeat of the Clyde strikes . . .'.[61] Various reasons for optimism were advanced, such as the modifications to the Munitions Act, the attack on the CWC, a favourable view of the military situation, and the working of the compulsory arbitration machinery.

But it is clear that such a judgment was premature. Even on Clydeside, 'cleansed' for a time of the subversive influence of the CWC, strikes erupted with a disconcerting frequency, as we have already recorded. 'Serious in 1916, the labour unrest seemed to be getting out of hand in 1917.'[62] It appears that about three-quarters of the 1,841 strikes reported to the Board of Trade during the period of the Munitions Acts concerned questions of wages.[63] No doubt a large proportion of such strikes were unlawful, theoretically rendering the strikers liable to penalties. But even as early as October 1915, following the South Wales strike and the Fairfield shipwrights' epic drama, 'There were those among the Labour leaders who were moved to point out that when they asked for amendments by constitutional methods, nothing was done, whereas a strike or a threat of a strike was electric in its effect.'[64] How much more so in the case of rank-and-file trade unionists pursuing more mundane wage grievances. As we have seen (ch. 2), even Sheriff Fyfe, in his capacity as industrial unrest commissioner, was driven to recognize this lesson. The fact was that conflict was endemic. Overwhelmingly, transient phenomena were blamed. It was 'no easy task to eliminate high prices, restrictions on personal freedom, industrial fatigue and lack of confidence in the Government and in some of the trade union leaders without creating a worse situation.'[65]

More radical critics attributed the labour ferment to

[61] Cited in Hurwitz, *State Intervention in Britain: A Study of Economic Control and Social Response, 1914–1919*, New York, 1949, p. 278.
[62] Ibid., p. 279.
[63] Michael Moses, 'Compulsory Arbitration in Great Britain during the War', *Journal of Political Economy*, XXVI (1918), 884–900, at 893.
[64] Wolfe, *Labour Supply and Regulation*, p. 130.
[65] Hurwitz, *State Intervention in Britain*, p. 279.

profounder causes. The *New Statesman* remarked, 'We have no panacea to offer for Industrial Unrest. The changing status of the wage-earner necessarily involves a further retirement, very gradually and possibly even slowly, from the position of autocracy in the factory which the employer has inherited . . .'[66] Whatever the analysis might be, and revolution was discounted on all sides, the Government's attitude to strikes was formally to ban them, hopefully to prevent them, and realistically to compromise over them. As the War Cabinet instructed in 1918, 'If an imminent strike appeared to be inevitable all the concessions asked for should be granted'.[67] It was an attitude probably shared by all the production departments of State which confronted industrial questions, though the disregard for principle would no doubt have appalled Askwith.[68]

Of course, a small number of strikers *were* prosecuted before the munitions tribunals, but after the deportation strikes hardly any stoppage of national significance resulted in such cases being brought. Prosecutions for minor infractions of the law against strikes were all that might be risked. As alternatives, where the Government alleged that stoppages contained a politically subversive element, then it might rely on 'public' opinion as expressed through the media to isolate the strikers, or even, on occasion, institute a prosecution under DORA.[69] In the case of the latter, however, the charges might rapidly be abandoned once the rank and file and the public, as in the May 1917 strikes (ch. 9), had been duped into believing that the Government was acting firmly against the political conspirators.[70] The reality was, as the *Glasgow Herald* recognized, that

In all their dealings with Labour, the Government seem to have two obsessions. The first is that the veil of secrecy must be drawn around every dispute, large or small, as long as possible: and the second is that the official policy must be that of cajoling and temporising, explaining here and beseeching there ... It is little wonder if in these circumstances the restless elements in Labour act as though they

---

[66] *New Statesman*, 23 June 1917, 270.
[67] Cited in Lowe, 'The Ministry of Labour, 1916–19; A Still Small Voice?', in Kathleen Burk (ed.), *War and the State*, London, 1982, p. 116.
[68] Eric Wigham, *Strikes and the Government 1893–1974*, London, 1976, pp. 37–8.
[69] Wolfe, *Labour Supply and Regulation*, p. 136.
[70] Cf. *Glasgow Herald*, 25 May 1917.

believed that the Government's bark would continue to be worse than their bite . . .[71]

Certainly, when measured against this unfavourable judgment of the Government's approach to labour crises, Sheriff Fyfe could justifiably claim a greater accomplishment. For his achievement was to combine successfully a policy of 'cajoling and temporising, explaining here and beseeching there', with a convincing demonstration that he could bite as well as bark.[72]

---

[71] Ibid., 19 May 1917.

[72] For a consideration of industrial action by, and tribunal proceedings against, women in Clydeside munitions works, see Rubin, 'The Enforcement of the Munitions of War Acts 1915–1917, with Particular Reference to Proceedings before the Munitions Tribunal in Glasgow, 1915–1921', Warwick Univ. Ph.D. thesis (1984), pp. 519–23.

CHAPTER 7

Time, Work Discipline, and Industrial Corporatism

INTRODUCTION

At the Trades Union Congress (TUC) in 1916, a resolution was proposed and passed unanimously, condemning the employers' system of fining workers in the textile and other industries. In particular, the mover of the resolution, J. W. Ogden of the Amalgamated Weavers, urged every operative 'to resist all attempts to make them assentors to and participators in the system', and not to acquiesce in the application of the fines to some charitable object. He concluded by stating that 'We object to any money being collected for that purpose in this way for our people. We say the employer has no right to take the money from his workpeople in the first instance.'¹ It was a bold and outspoken challenge not only to the procedures for punishing infractions of the textile employers' disciplinary rules; for it also sought to reject the managerial assumption upon which such a disciplinary code was built. In this respect, the resolution was distinctive. Generally speaking, the level of consciousness thus displayed at the TUC failed to inform the criticisms of trade unionists directed against the more immediate concern of the Ordering of Work regulations prescribing rules of factory discipline under the Munitions Act. Thus, on the one hand, the monthly and quarterly reports of local trade union officials during the war constantly bewailed the statutory disciplinary regime, with its object of establishing 'good order' and diligent working, and of stamping out or reducing levels of illicit smoking, gambling, drinking, sleeping at work, and, in particular, bad timekeeping. On the other hand, though still regularly infringing them, trade unionists *did* come to terms with the Ordering of Work rules, no doubt due to a combination of patriotic fervour and of the paucity of alternative strategies in

¹ Trades Union Congress, *Annual Report 1916*, 375.

the face of a determined and litigious management. Indeed, in one munitions tribunal hearing in Glasgow in February 1917, Robert Climie, an official of the Workers' Union, even complained, when one establishment decided it was more convenient to institute their own domestic disciplinary procedure, that 'the firm by their action were usurping the functions of the tribunals'.[2]

Tribunal prosecutions were, of course, at the very centre of the policy of the Ministry of Munitions to bring about a dramatic improvement in timekeeping in the factories and shipyards. Yet reliance was also placed on a variety of other techniques to persuade munitions workers to work their scheduled shifts. The approaches ranged, in fact, from 'responsible autonomy' at one end of the spectrum, to 'direct control'[3] at the other; and from crude repression to financial bribery.

Moreover, this diversity, with which not only the Ministry of Munitions, but also the Admiralty, employers, munitions tribunals, and even trade unions were forced to wrestle, pointed to the intractability of the authorities' problem of order. For a complete solution to 'bad timekeeping' was never found, despite the intensive enquiries into its causes which accompanied the deployment of the various corrective devices.

The authorities' campaign against bad timekeeping in the munitions factories and shipyards was, from the outset, premissed on tripartite involvement. The Ministry of Munitions were expected to be in the vanguard of the diffusely aimed assault upon working-class lawlessness, the employers were to provide, in the shape of information, the ammunition to sustain the assault, while the trade unions, watching from the sidelines, delivered exhortations to their members to be on their best behaviour. The assumption was that the 'problem' posed by recalcitrant individuals, flouting formalized and relatively uncontroversial rules, could be conquered by propaganda, by education, or by not-so-gentle persuasion.

As one Ministry of Munitions official argued, 'the most potent [cause of 'avoidable' lost time] is *indifference* which springs largely

---

[2] *Glasgow Herald*, 8 Feb. 1917. The distance from the works to the tribunal, entailing lengthy travelling time, was given as the reason by the firm for setting up their own procedure.

[3] Terms derived from A. L. Friedman, *Industry and Labour*, London, 1977.

from the natural independence of the British workman, from temperamental laziness and from the mental apathy so often found among the ill-educated and the illiterate.'[4] Character defects and the romanticized spirit of the free-born Englishman, it was suggested, conspired to hinder the output of munitions.[5]

As an antidote, the authorities could invoke the language of 'morality'. Thus *good* timekeeping, *good* order, and working diligently were all qualities likely to attract overwhelming social approval in the context of total war. And, of course, these qualities were consistent with the aims of trade unions intent on promoting continued membership, thrift, and friendly society benefits. Behaviour which challenged the norms of 'good' timekeeping might therefore be conceived as deviant or subversive. In consequence, the issues in respect to which the legal initiative was launched were likely to attract popular support and could even be invested with a moral quality. Though this may have rendered disciplinary prosecutions less controversial than proceedings under different provisions of the Munitions Act, it may also have distorted the effect of the Act by suggesting a greater degree of instrumental success for the Government than was actually gained. For within their own narrow sphere, and whether mediated through tribunal rulings or through their pervasive influence on the shop floor, the Ordering of Work rules struck only at the easiest and most visible of targets—a limited category of offenders—which policing was able to entrap. Whether wartime industrial relations could be 'controlled' in the manner in which individual workers could be disciplined was a different matter.

There was certainly no lack of imagination on the part of the Government in promoting a corrective, as distinct from a crudely punitive, approach towards bad timekeepers. A policy of shaming the alleged offenders into reforming their timekeeping habits seems to have been the first initiative, and was given expression, even before the Munitions Act had been passed, with the publication of a notorious government document of

---

[4] BEV v, 21, fos. 144–52, 'Memorandum on the causes of bad timekeeping of controlled establishments, June 8, 1916, by H. O. Quin'.

[5] The writer added that 'perhaps not more than 10 or 15% of the total number of workers' were allegedly thus affected. It probably did not occur to him that this would effectively undermine his own theory.

May 1915, the *Report and Statistics of Bad Time Kept in Shipbuilding, Munitions and Transport Areas.*[6] This document, compiled on the basis of partial evidence supplied by the shipbuilders and Government officials, purported to indict munitions workers for their unpatriotic conduct in maintaining poor timekeeping.[7] But though designed to expose the 'drink problem' among munitions workers, a careful reading showed that (as even a director of the large shipbuilding firm, Cammell Laird, admitted) 'On the whole, timekeeping was better than before the war, but not so good as it should be. Employers were asking too much and getting too little. Men could not work overtime and on Saturday afternoons and Sundays continuously.'[8]

Moreover, the position in the armament firms and in Government establishments similarly cast doubt on the widespread existence of a national scandal. Some avoidable losses of time were reported, but in the armament firms 'the great majority of the workmen were above reproach and their action was praiseworthy'. Indeed, Isaac Mitchell, an ex-trade unionist and now a Board of Trade official, categorically reported that irregular attendance did not exist.

But Lloyd George was not one to allow little matters of detail to intrude upon his grandiose schemes. A practised political campaigner, he was able to exploit scarcely substantiated accusations of bad timekeeping to generate a moral panic demanding the drastic remedy of legal compulsion. He told the Commons,

> The other point of the Bill is that we take power to establish discipline in the workshops. Here, again, we discussed this matter with the trade union representatives, and we are not going beyond the agreement we have entered into. They admit that where men who voluntarily go into this army [i.e. the War Munitions Volunteer scheme] habitually absent themselves and make bad time when they know that the work is very urgent for the country, there ought to be some means of enforcing

---

[6] PP 1914–16 (220), LV, 947.

[7] Wrigley, *David Lloyd George and the British Labour Movement*, Hassocks, 1916, p. 108; Wolfe, *Labour Supply and Regulation*, Oxford, 1923, p. 173. Part of the reason for bad timekeeping was said to be that the 'men preferred to work for double pay on Sundays and stay out some other day', or else just work till they had earned sufficient wages for the week. See *OHMM*, vol. I, pt. IV, p. 46. Disruption of work schedules might therefore have been contained by measures controlling the level of wages and labour mobility.

[8] Ibid., for this and following quotes.

better time. It is proposed that there should be a Munitions Court set up . . .[9]

It was a characteristically duplicitous argument. A grossly exaggerated picture of unsatisfactory behaviour affecting exclusively a restricted group of munitions 'Volunteers' (WMVs) is painted. It is then used as a justification for the more general application of draconian provisions to which trade unionists, through their co-operative leadership, are taken to have assented.

BAD TIMEKEEPING REMEDIES

From this specious premiss, the authorities attempted to monitor the record of timekeeping of major firms. The Ministry of Munitions reported in December 1915 that of 536 firms surveyed, 148 had complained of bad timekeeping. Of those 148, eighty complaints were directed against individuals and not against groups of workmen. Yet the ministry considered, somewhat surprisingly, that these results were gratifying. Perhaps they had been duped by their own rhetoric. Even the Admiralty, normally severe in its criticism of the performance of shipyard workers, pointed to marked improvements over earlier reports.[10] In a statistical survey of 1,500 firms in March 1916, over 500 responded to the invitation to offer general comments.[11] These showed that 319 establishments considered their timekeeping record to be 'excellent', or 'exceptionally good', or 'satisfactory on the whole'. Another sixty-one firms reported no complaints or no serious complaints or that timekeeping was 'fairly good'. Twenty-nine said the position was 'normal' or 'qualifiedly fair', while forty-two reported 'bad' or 'not very good' timekeeping. These results, the ministry thought, were 'remarkable'. Indeed, it may not be unreasonable to infer that bad timekeeping was not considered even problematic by the 1,000 companies which declined to offer

---

[9] HC Deb., 5th ser., vol. 72, cols. 1202–3, 23 June 1915.

[10] BEV II, 8, fos. 123–4, 'draft of Report of Labour Department . . . December 2, 1915'.

[11] BEV V, 19, fos. 139–42. Firms whose employees lost more than 5% of normal time were considered to be the problem cases.

general remarks on the matter. Table 7.1 shows the small scale of the 'problem' about which so much hot air had been ventilated by employers in the earlier part of the war but which did not abate in subsequent months and years.

Table 7.1 Timekeeping Returns to Questionnaire for Week Ending 17 March 1916

Loss expressed as % of total normal working hours	No. of firms responsible	% of total cases analysed
10% and over	26	1.73
7% and up to 10%	43	2.87
5% and up to 7%	72	4.80
Below 5% but over 20% of employees losing over 6 hours per week	11	0.73
Below 5%	1,348	89.87
Total cases analysed	1,500	100.00

Source: BEV v, 19, fo. 113.

The overwhelming majority of employees lost less than 5 per cent of their normal working hours which, if based on a 54-hour week, would amount to losses of less than 2.7 hours per week. In fact, a follow-up survey in May 1916 showed that the average loss per employee was 1.74 hours per week.[12] Thus the perceived 'improvement' in timekeeping during the previous twelve months was somewhat of an optical illusion in that the ministry, for propaganda purposes, had originally exaggerated the reports of poor timekeeping in order to secure compulsion. Once having achieved that object, the ministry's energies were pressed into bribing, coaxing, cajoling, threatening, and prosecuting workers to keep good time.[13]

AMBIVALENT EMPLOYERS

An initial difficulty for the ministry was to persuade employers to institute proceedings against employees suspected of bad

[12] Ibid.
[13] The threat of military call-up, the manipulation of good timekeeping bonuses, and the 'docking' of lost 'quarters' were among the less common techniques used. They are not discussed here.

timekeeping. For the employers sought to place the onus on the ministry to mount prosecutions, 'on the ground that the offence was rather against the State than the individual employer'.[14] Indeed, some unions even took it upon themselves to instil in their members the necessity for constancy and devotion to duty. What emerged was a combined, if disjointed, effort to eliminate the 'problem'. In fact, however, more and more responsibility gradually devolved on the State, culminating in the removal in 1917 of the discretion formerly available to employers to decide whether to undertake prosecutions. This revocation of the employers' authority to prosecute under ministry-approved factory rules or under the ministry's own detailed Ordering of Work regulations was symptomatic of two features. First, it reflected unease on the part of the Government that employers might abuse, or, what was worse, be considered by unions to be abusing, their right to prosecute. For such behaviour by employers might be seen to encourage yet more labour unrest. As one senior ministry official saw the issue,

It is no doubt necessary in the interests of the State to have the industrial discipline of the Munitions of War Act, but the difficulty of the present position is that the exceptional disciplinary powers are, or may appear at the present time, to be exercised by or on behalf of the employers, rather than by or on behalf of the State.[15]

It was therefore to counter suspicions that the employers' motives were not inspired by anything so noble as patriotism that the instituting of State prosecutions was encouraged. But the shift was, secondly, also a response to employers' *own* dissatisfaction at being asked to enforce the discipline of the State. This is not to say that employers objected to prosecutions. It was just that, apart from the time and trouble involved, they would prefer not to be exposed to adverse criticism, whether from their own work-force or even on occasions from tribunal chairmen, for having sought to enforce the law. The Clyde engineers and shipbuilders decided to inform the ministry in late September 1915 that it was 'objectionable to have complaints

---

[14] Wolfe, *Labour Supply and Regulation*, p. 177.
[15] MUN 5/20/221.1/40, 'Amending Bill—"Reciprocity" and Local Committees, December 1, 1915'. There is no indication as to which official drafted this document. It was, however, undoubtedly one of the senior men, probably Wolff or Beveridge.

against workmen at the instance of firms'.[16] Since the local ministry representative, James Paterson, confirmed to the employers that the ministry were now prepared to undertake prosecutions, the Clyde employers requested local firms to send the associations details of bad timekeeping. These would then be sifted, and selected complaints forwarded to Paterson with a request that the ministry institute a prosecution. In this way, it was reasoned, the relations between employers and workers, and especially those between foremen and workmen, would not be unduly strained, particularly where, as occurred in Glasgow during the second half of 1915, the tribunal hearing itself was disorderly and fines were ordered to be deducted from the men's wages by their employers.[17] Indeed, a year later the joint Clyde employers were telling C. F. Rey from the ministry that 'If the Ministry would apply the penal provisions of the Munitions of War Act and make the workmen work full-time, more especially in the shipyards, greatly increased production would be secured.'[18]

Such requests, it is submitted, are not to be construed as evidence of rampant lawlessness on the factory floor. There was,

[16] CSA, *Minute Book* No. 9, 28 Sept. 1915.

[17] MUN 5/353/349/1. According to Melling, 'The most direct consequence of the Munitions Act was to transform those foremen in controlled establishments into ambassadors of a servile state as well as the agents of unwelcome innovations.' In support, he cites generalized complaints of 'tactless and domineering methods of some foremen', instances of which we have already cited in ch. 3. See Joseph Melling, '"Non-Commissioned Officers": British Employers and their Supervisory Workers, 1880–1920', *Social History*, v (1980), 183–222, at 214–16. Burgess has recently argued that the labour controls vested in the Munitions Act deprived supervisors of their traditional 'discretionary authority' over the shop floor, while distancing supervisors from their employers. See Keith Burgess, 'Authority Relations and the Division of Labour in British Industry, with Special Reference to Clydeside, c. 1860–1930', ibid., xi (1986), 211–33, at 229. However, leaving aside the question of the appropriate theoretical perspective on the state to adopt, it is still debatable whether the relationship of foremen to their workmen was fundamentally transformed, and, if so, what impact this had on the pattern of workshop discipline. Melling (above) acknowledges that the evidence is ambiguous. There were, it is true, a few tribunal prosecutions in the district following assaults on foremen, but the offenders usually attributed their actions to drink rather than to provocation. See *Glasgow Herald*, 16 Jan. 1917. One suspects, therefore, that if tighter discipline was imposed by foremen, the level of resistance did not always match that in evidence at major confrontations or that implied by the Balfour–Macassey Commission. But it only needed a few spectacular incidents to provoke widespread working-class protest.

[18] CSA, *Minute Book* No. 9, 30 Aug. 1916. Cf. ibid., 3 July 1916, where Vice-Admiral Johnston-Stewart, the Admiralty representative, promised that prosecutions for bad timekeeping would be dealt with more expeditiously in the future.

as the ministry surveys revealed, a hard core of bad timekeeping which was officially attributed to 'indifference' or to 'laziness'. But for some employers, a ritual display of outrage seemed obligatory. None the less, in general, their bark was worse than their bite. Indeed, the fact that they continually turned to the ministry to take the matter in hand seems to point to this interpretation.

THE INTERVIEW TECHNIQUE

The ministry placed some reliance on interviewing alleged bad timekeepers, threatening them with a prosecution if their timekeeping did not improve. This scheme apparently originated in the recognition by the ministry that firms were reluctant to prosecute young workers or apprentices.[19] It therefore undertook to send standard warning letters to those singled out by the employers, and later extended the practice to all alleged defaulters.[20] The next step was to institute a formal system of interviewing workers identified by their firms as bad timekeepers. The ministry instructed its labour officers to monitor those munitions workers against whom complaints had been made by their employers. A complete card-index system was maintained for this purpose, backed up by visits to companies and by interviews with those against whom complaints had been lodged.[21] The culmination was a ministry prosecution in selected cases.[22] It was, however, stressed that the investigation officer 'must on no account act in such a way as to give grounds for complaint of undue interference in the affairs of

[19] BEV iv, 6. fo. 27, 'Model Ordering of Work Rules' (n.d., about early Sept. 1915).

[20] This caused some difficulty to employers towards the end of the war when they claimed that the letters sent by the ministry implied that the initiative had come from the employers, not the ministry. They pointed out that their employees, in a state of pique, simply left the firm on receipt of such letters. The wording was therefore altered to make it clear that the employers were absolved from any responsibility for instigating the complaints. Yet it is difficult to see from where else the prompting came. See NWETEA, *Minute Book* No. 9, 10 June, 30 July 1918.

[21] MUN 5/91/345/6, 'Memorandum on the Duties of the Timekeeping Branch of the Chief Investigations Officers' Office, February 6, 1918'.

[22] MUN 5/91/345/109, 'Instructions as to preparing prosecutions on behalf of the Ministry of Munitions for breach of a Works Regulation under s. 4(5) of the Munitions of War Act, March 1, 1917'.

the management,'[23] an indication, perhaps, of the particular blend of corporatism and *laissez-faire* which bureaucratic expediency demanded in regard to disciplinary matters.

This approach was 'adopted systematically'[24] on Clydeside with a view to determine whether a warning by the representative of the State would suffice, or whether a prosecution was necessary. James Paterson, for example, reported to the ministry in London in December 1915, that during the previous few weeks he and his colleagues, Cramond and Matson, had interviewed a large number of men.[25] Sixty had been summoned to his office the previous evening, and there they were told that if the employer did not report any improvement in their timekeeping then a prosecution would follow. Those within five miles of the office in Glasgow were called in at night, while those in Paisley, Greenock, and Dumbarton districts were 'taken in batches', though formerly Cramond and Matson themselves had travelled out of town for this purpose.[26]

Whether such warnings had a marked effect in curbing losses of time on Clydeside is not clear. It is the case that in October and November 1915, mass prosecutions were conducted almost fortnightly, with shipyard workers being the most prominent offenders.[27] From 1916, however, the pace of such ministry prosecutions slackened considerably,[28] though this was probably due less to the effectiveness of the warnings delivered than to the ineffectiveness of prosecutions as a deterrent to others. What is clear is that the 'scientific' search for explanations was undertaken at the same time as the trade unions were brought more directly into the disciplinary process.

THE INCORPORATION OF THE TRADE UNIONS

Potentially more rewarding to the ministry was the effort to enlist the men's trade unions in the struggle to reduce lost time.

[23] MUN 5/91/345/110, 'Instructions to Investigating Officers concerning timekeeping, Sunday Labour and overtime, December 7, 1916'.
[24] BEV II, 8, fos. 123–4; *OHMM*, vol. IV, pt. II, p. 33.
[25] BEV II, 8, fos. 126–7.
[26] Interviews were conducted in the town halls rather than in the Labour Exchanges so as not to damage the 'image' of the latter. See BEV II, 8, fo. 78.
[27] See *Glasgow Herald*, 15, 29 Oct., 17 Nov. 1915.
[28] Ibid., 9 Feb., 18 Oct., 15 Dec. 1916.

One senior ministry official considered that 'It will be quite possible, and indeed highly desirable, that [the ministry prosecutor] should act with the assistance of representatives of the workmen in the establishment.'[29] Every offender would therefore appear before a trio consisting of a ministry labour official, the workman's representative, and the company's manager, to ascertain whether more drastic steps were required. 'In effect,' continued the writer, 'we should substitute Shop Committees under the presidency of the Government official, for the Joint Local Committees of employers and workmen.' Similarly, local labour advisory boards could be asked to interview offenders, with the added sanction that, if repeated breaches of discipline which merited a prosecution occurred, the trade unionist would be unable to call upon his union to defend him.[30] An Admiralty scheme to incorporate the trade unions into the disciplinary process was even more ambitious. It was proposed that those shipyard workers habitually losing seven or more hours per week without adequate cause should in the first instance receive a warning letter from the Admiralty, followed by a personal warning delivered jointly by the Admiralty officer, by the offender's employer, *and* by his own union representative. More significantly, it was proposed '3. That the employers and Trade Unions should cooperate as fully as possible . . . in disciplinary action against offenders'.[31] Finally, those workers whose timekeeping records did not improve should be prosecuted 'forthwith', dismissed from employment, and be expelled from their unions.

This involvement by the trade unions in the task of enforcing disciplinary rules against their members conveyed the impression of casting them in a role diametrically opposite to their *raison d'être*. Yet the unions' albeit qualified adherence to the 'corporate spirit' did require them sometimes to assume unpalatable responsibilities. In any case, such involvement in disciplinary proceedings followed easily in the wake of incessant exhortations by union officials that their members should ensure

[29] MUN 5/20/221.1/40.
[30] *Glasgow Herald*, 22 Dec. 1916; BEV IV, 37, fo. 229, 'Dilution Sub-Committee, Intelligence Report for week October 26, 1915'.
[31] Amalgamated Society of Carpenters and Joiners (ASCJ), *Journal*, Dec. 1916, 778; USB, *Monthly Report*, Dec. 1916, 42.

that 'responsible' timekeeping was maintained. These officials included the ASE district delegate for the North-West, R. O. Jones, who in June 1915 had savagely attacked the forthcoming statute. Thus he announced that

The question of the hour is the Munitions of War Bill, with its far-reaching proposals. It is the neatest bit of class legislation ever devised. The Trade Union officials, one cannot term them leaders, have been hypnotised into bartering away the rights of the rank and file without so much as consulting them.[32]

Within a few months, however, he was complaining that 'Some of our members are not keeping as good time as they are capable of doing.'[33] Now he was enthusiastically exhorting his members to 'suppress the evil' and to be 'beyond reproach'.[34]

Meetings with employers on the introduction and working of clocking-in schemes also took place,[35] though some resistance to particular schemes did occur, for example, at Swan Hunter's yard on Tyneside.[36] At Vickers in London, the management produced evidence of men forgetting to clock in, action which the ASE district delegate A. B. Swales considered, 'cannot be justified by our society or any other'.[37] Indeed, a number of prosecutions for fraud were conducted in 1916 against men accused of falsifying their time cards or of slipping out of the yard and persuading other workers to lodge their cards in the time-box at the end of the shift. Trade unions kept their heads down on this issue, even when one Beardmore worker was imprisoned for thirty days following a trial at Govan Police Court.[38]

[32] ASE, *Monthly Journal and Report*, July 1915, 28.
[33] Ibid., Jan. 1916, 38.
[34] Ibid., Nov. 1915, 46.
[35] Ibid., Aug. 1916, 34.
[36] ABIS, *1st Quarterly Report*, Jan.–Mar. 1917.
[37] ASE, *Monthly Journal and Report*, Oct. 1915, 39. At least a conference was a less aggressive response than the ministry's initial proposal to the firm to prosecute a couple of workmen in early July 1915 under the Conspiracy and Protection of Property Act 1875. The ground of the proceedings was to be that the men's bad timekeeping (and, therefore, their breach of contract) was endangering the lives of the soldiers at the Front, by delaying the output of munitions. The advice was rapidly withdrawn once the Ordering of Work regulations were published. See MUN 4/13, 'Re Vickers Ltd. and loss of time. Note by Professor Geldart, July 8, 1915'.
[38] *Glasgow Herald*, 11 Nov. 1916, concerning cases in Dumbarton Sheriff Court (shipyard worker fined £25 or 60 days) and Govan Police Court (Beardmore employee imprisoned for 30 days; another employee fined £5 or 30 days). The 'double standard'

Within the Shipwrights' Association, similar pleas for an improvement in timekeeping were heard. The Ireland technical adviser (i.e. district officer) complained that 'whilst the majority of our members are doing splendidly, there is a minority who are not doing what might be done in this respect.'[39] Only where one firm prosecuted without first delivering a warning did the Shipwrights' North-West adviser see fit to criticize the employer for prosecuting a member.[40] But this apart, his views were quite explicit. As a union official, he candidly held 'no brief for men who persistently lost time', and considered that the 'full penalty' under the Act would be appropriate in the event of any repetition of bad timekeeping.

Within the Glasgow munitions tribunal, it was not uncommon for officials to express regret at the bad timekeeping of those members whom they were engaged in defending. Thus one official 'deprecated' his members' poor record at one ministry prosecution hearing.[41] On another occasion, William Mackie, an official of the Boilermakers' Society, promised the tribunal that he would that very night hold a meeting at the works gate to press on his members the 'gravity' of their conduct.[42] That such an attitude was often consciously designed to influence the tribunal in imposing a lenient penalty does not detract from the genuine commitment of such officials to assist employers in improving work discipline. The preference was, however, to achieve that aim without the necessity for a prosecution. Even Sheriff Fyfe, the tribunal chairman, recognized this point. For

---

was demonstrated by the failure to convict the Leith shipbuilding firm of John Cran & Co., charged at the High Court in Edinburgh with defrauding the Admiralty of nearly £3,000. A verdict of 'not guilty' of falsifying their accounts by falsely declaring the number of labour hours spent on Admiralty contracts was returned. As John Hill, general secretary of the Boilermakers Society, observed, 'There was a case of very bad timekeeping which ought to have rather more publicity, as this case does not seem to have been pressed upon the notice of newspapers in the way we have complained of.' The clear lesson was that 'It is always a more difficult thing to convict money and influence than labour and ignorance.' See USB, *Monthly Report*, May 1916, 11–12, 30. For Hill's outraged reaction to Cammell Laird's exploitation of tribunal prosecutions in Oct. 1915 in order to generate a moral panic against bad timekeepers (which resulted in one newspaper headline asking, 'Shall We Shoot Slackers?'), see ibid., Oct. 1915, 10–11.

[39] SSA, *Quarterly Reports*, July–Sept. 1915, 17.
[40] Ibid., 18. Cf. ibid, Jan.–Mar. 1916, 19.
[41] *Glasgow Herald*, 29 Oct. 1915.
[42] Ibid., 15 Dec. 1916.

when one official informed him that the union itself had machinery 'which dealt in bad timekeeping', the sheriff welcomed the news. He

expressed gratification to hear this and remarked that it was more effective for a man to be fined by his own union than by that tribunal. It brought home to him that the general sense of the community, including trade societies, was against all slacking of work. The union was to be commended for trying to help in the promotion of regular work.[43]

Indeed, the suggestion was sometimes made to confer total jurisdiction in such matters on trade union district committees, as an exercise both in voluntarism and in decentralization. For example, the Boilermakers' Belfast district committee reported that they

have been supplied periodically with the names of habitually bad timekeepers, and they decided—not from choice but in the interests of the local members and the Society generally—to deal with those men who wilfully neglect their work. Apart from the employers' complaints, which we could not ignore, the principal reason why the committee decided to deal with these men was to prevent them from being taken to another place, the Munitions Court, where the fines and punishment inflicted are fixed to meet the crime. None of our members have troubled the Munitions Court up to date. They prefer to be dealt with by their fellow members; and, while some may doubt it, it is quite evident that a noticeable improvement in the timekeeping has taken place.[44]

Similarly, James Ratcliffe, the ASE's Newcastle delegate, reported that

We receive from time to time complaints of serious bad timekeeping, mostly from small firms, who are pressed for men and who dislike appealing to munitions tribunals. It is somewhat difficult [to know] how to deal—apart from the courts—with habitually bad timekeepers. Publishing their names in the 'Monthly' may perhaps have some deterrent effect. Better still, however, would it be if they could be taken in hand by members whose influence as shopmates would be no doubt the best appreciated.[45]

Thus the unions' ready acceptance of the ideology of patriotism and of steadiness at work dovetailed neatly with their desire to immunize their members from the rigours of a tribunal prosecution. Yet the views expressed above did not solely emanate from the trade union movement. Even prominent employers recognized the 'salutary' effect which workshop committees composed of the men themselves might exert on the supposedly undisciplined few. In the midst of the Cammell Laird mass prosecutions in Liverpool in October 1915 (ch. 1), the company's manager suggested that the men might appoint a small workshop committee, 'to influence their mates . . . to do their utmost both for their country and for their union'.[46]

Indeed, during the Parliamentary debates on the Munitions Bill in June 1915, one speaker, Henry Duke (later appointed the High Court judge Lord Merrivale), argued against the original suggestion for a 'dignified' tribunal. For,

a tribunal that carried weight throughout the country does not inevitably carry weight in a particular factory. If you are going to dock the wages of a man in a particular factory, in a case where it is possible he will not be standing alone and where it is possible there will be little topics of controversy . . . would it not be very much better if you repaid the confidence which organized labour has put in the Government and Parliament by enabling the men who are concerned in the class of cases to which reference has been made, to themselves nominate a tribunal to deal with matters of this kind?[47]

Yet despite this forceful plea, a tripartite judicial body dominated by the 'neutral' lawyer-chairman, and entrusted with the enforcement of State discipline, was, of course, installed.

The suggestions for 'workers' control' of disciplinary questions were, therefore, stillborn. But it is important to recognize how far removed from revolutionary principles were such proposals. For, far from heralding a transformation in the ownership and control of industry, they would, if implemented,

---

[46] BEV IV, 37, fo. 283. For further details concerning the Cammell Laird prosecutions, see Rubin, 'The Enforcement of the Munitions of War Acts 1915–1917, with Particular Reference to Proceedings before the Munitions Tribunal in Glasgow, 1915–1921', Warwick Univ. Ph.D. thesis (1984), ch. 2.

[47] HC Deb., 5th ser., vol. 72, col. 1523, 28 June 1915.

have merely enlisted the unions as industrial policemen. District committees would have found themselves preoccupied with determining whether their members had broken Ordering of Work rules which they themselves had no part in framing (a national labour body, the National Advisory Committee on Labour Output, had originally scrutinized some details but not the principle). In other words, what had been proposed for the trade unions was self-regulation of worker misconduct, but within the context of rules of behaviour whose parameters were to correspond with what Government decreed to be in the 'national interest'.

A more radical approach within the labour movement was the attempt to relate local joint control of disciplinary questions to the joint control of industry in general. For example, the Glasgow Trades Council demanded that all disciplinary powers then currently exercised by the munitions tribunals should be transferred to local joint committees in all munitions areas. The object of the reforms was, *inter alia*, '(2) to guarantee fair treatment to the worker; . . . (5) to decentralise the control of the production of munitions; and (6) to give to the Trade Unions responsibility and a share in management.'[48]

The ASE chose, instead, to press for mutuality in the framing of disciplinary rules. Among its proposed amendments to the 1915 Act, it insisted that 'No workshop rules [should] be enforced other than those definitely agreed to by the workmen concerned, or those identical with the model rules issued by the Ministry of Munitions.'[49] But the fact was that there was absolutely no prospect of mutuality in such matters. As one senior ministry official wrote at the time,

the demand for 'reciprocity' is wrong in principle. In peace times, equality of treatment for employers and workpeople on the part of the State is important. In war times, it is irrelevant, because the only important object of the State is to win the war . . . In war times, the State is the substantial employer of everybody in the country and the nominal 'employer' is simply one of the State's agents for producing munitions . . . if we try to administer the production of munitions on

[48] See the four-page pamphlet on proposed amendments to the 1915 Act issued by the trades council in Nov. 1915. See also *Glasgow Herald*, 18 Nov. 1915.
[49] ASE, *Amending the Munitions of War Act 1915*, (1916), p. 19; cf., ASE, *Monthly Journal and Report*, December 1915, pp. 26–7.

the lines of 'reciprocity', we shall simply end by giving employers so little sense of responsibility for what they do that they will let their production of munitions drop. We must not do anything to weaken the employer's ordinary method of discipline in his establishment or his power of choosing and selecting his workmen or dismissing those whom he does not want.[50]

Here was clearly articulated the corporatist impulse towards bureaucratic centralism in policy making, accompanied by rigidly imposed local discipline in support of that policy by employers and by trade unions. For the latter were now fulfilling a more circumscribed role: as much an 'agent' of the State as the employer.

But it was clear that the attempt to harness union support for an essentially managerial function must work to the advantage of the employer. It is scarcely surprising therefore that Humbert Wolfe, the senior ministry official, concluded that joint shop committees dealing with bad timekeeping produced 'excellent results'. For, 'A prosecution following upon the warning of a Committee consisting as to half of workpeople, could not provide a grievance.'[51]

In pursuit of 'social control' of the workforce, wartime employers and the State could foster or support schemes of industrial discipline which sought to *include* trade unions, as an alternative to the development of schemes of industrial welfare which had, as one of their characteristic features, the determination to *exclude* trade unions.[52]

To a very limited extent, none the less, mutuality could exist in those firms which refused to prosecute under the Ordering of Work rules. But in these instances the firms in question found it to their own advantage to avoid the tribunals, on the grounds that the latter were simply a nuisance, or were time-consuming or ineffective, or that they generated further controversy. For example, the Whitehead Torpedo Works in Cleveland proposed a joint disciplinary committee to its employees (it is, indeed, significant that the initiative sprang from the employer's side).

---

[50] MUN 5/20/221.1/40.

[51] Wolfe, *Labour Supply and Regulation*, p. 178.

[52] Cf. Noelle Whiteside, 'Industrial Welfare and Labour Regulation in Britain at the Time of the First World War', *International Review of Social History*, xxv (1980), 307–31, at 309.

As the company explained,

There is a class of rules, offences against which are punishable by a fine of half-a-crown, dismissal or a prosecution under the Munitions Act. None of these penalties is a convenient one. Fines are as much disliked by the firm as by the men; dismissal entails the loss of services which may be badly needed; and the prosecutions entail great waste of time and may produce more evils than the original ones they are meant to cure.[53]

In so far as such employers were pragmatically exploring the most efficient means of eliminating labour disruption to munitions output, then the instituting of joint domestic disciplinary procedures could scarcely be construed as a vindication of the principle of the democratic control of industry.

The attraction to trade unionists of schemes of participation in employers' disciplinary procedures is understandable, in so far as they could hope to exert some influence on the outcome of domestic proceedings. On the other hand, it is possible that many shop committees refused to sit in judgment of their fellow workers where this might merely draw the fire which would otherwise be directed towards the employer himself. What is clear, however, is that despite vociferous complaints at tribunal injustice, trade unionists in general adhered to the values of 'good' timekeeping and 'good order'. In consequence, few of them thought fit to emulate the Amalgamated Weavers' leader, J. W. Ogden, at the 1916 TUC, by challenging the managerialist assumption on which disciplinary rules were based.

THE ROLE OF THE TRIBUNAL

Notwithstanding the variety of techniques adopted by the employers, by the State, and even by trade union district committees, there remained ultimately the prospect of a tribunal prosecution as a device aimed at tightening up workshop discipline. For example, Thomas Biggart, the secretary of the Clyde engineers and shipbuilders, reported favour-

---

[53] Quoted in Carter L. Goodrich, *The Frontier of Control*, London, 1920, p. 147.

ably to the ministry in December 1915 on the effects of recent prosecutions. He wrote,

With the exception of the 'incorrigibles' upon whom prosecution seems to have had little remedial effect, it would appear, on the whole, [that] the recent prosecutions have had a very steadying effect not only with respect to the men actually in fault but with respect to the shops generally. A very gratifying feature of these prosecutions is that, when they are undertaken at the instance of the Ministry, the men complained against seem to appreciate much more seriously the gravity of their fault. It is unfortunate that in some cases a heavier fine has not been inflicted by the Courts since, when men are making such good wages, a small fine is as a rule easily paid. At the same time, firms report numerous instances where the men have been thoroughly ashamed of their conduct.[54]

Thus Beardmore, for example, commented in October 1917 that

The general question of bad timekeeping is more or less kept within reasonable bounds by means of the local tribunal, the number of cases being dealt with showing a marked decrease . . . when fines are imposed on individuals, we have found them frequently to have a deterrent effect on the other workers.[55]

It is beyond doubt that employers were reporting significant improvements in timekeeping, as is clear from the findings of the questionnaire in March 1916 cited earlier. Indeed, in a later survey conducted in October 1917, only nine out of 351 employers expressing a general opinion on timekeeping commented critically on their employees' record.[56]

Yet the ministry historians concluded that there had been considerable criticism of the effectiveness of prosecutions in enforcing workshop discipline in the second year of the legislation.[57] The Birmingham tribunal in 1917, for example, reported that it was obliged to respond to offences in a manner calculated, 'not to drive men away from work altogether'.[58] Clearly, a punitive approach on the part of this tribunal was

    [54] BEV II, 8, fos. 126–7; *OHMM*, vol. IV, pt. II, p. 34.
    [55] MUN 5/91/345/3, 'Report on Timekeeping in Controlled Establishments in October 1917'.
    [56] Ibid.
    [57] *OHMM*, vol. V, pt. III, p. 143.
    [58] Ibid., p. 144.

viewed as dysfunctional. Moreover, alongside the optimistic remarks of Biggart and of Beardmore (above), one must place the numbers of timekeeping prosecutions actually conducted before different tribunals. The total monthly average for the six months from January to June 1917 was 2,122 timekeeping cases, while in January 1917, fines were imposed in 1,744 out of 2,681 timekeeping cases throughout the country, with the amounts varying from an average of 6s. 10½d. in Bradford, to the somewhat improbable figure of £3 at Huddersfield[59] (£3 was the statutory maximum).

Bad timekeeping represented by far the most numerous type of offence tried by the local tribunals, though other cases, concerning refusal to work reasonable amounts of overtime, absence from work without permission (often linked to visits to the pub), and gambling were also fairly common.[60] Such misconduct, whether manifested through bad timekeeping, drunkenness, gambling, swearing, smoking, sleeping, or fighting was necessarily viewed as an interference with the progress of munitions production. But some tribunal chairmen viewed such behaviour not only as unpatriotic, but also as a challenge to managerial authority. Moralizing sermons by tribunal chairmen therefore occasionally took the form of a round condemnation of the vices of slacking, drinking, and gambling, and might conclude with despairing regrets that the chairman possessed no power to send the recalcitrants to the Front.[61] Yet the more prosecutions for bad timekeeping which took place, and the more colourful were the excuses offered, the more it became clear to the ministry that not all explanations for loss of time advanced by offenders at the tribunals could be discounted as special pleading. Thus the authorities could safely ignore the excuse of the Glasgow workman caught climbing over the shipyard wall and who claimed to be seeking relief from cramp at the time.[62] But it was frequently submitted by accused workmen that excessive overtime and overwork in general, illness, and unhealthy working conditions had taken their toll. Among Glasgow cases, ironworkers explained that their absence

[59] Ibid., p. 143.
[60] See MUN 5/353/349/1, testimony of the Liverpool chairman, C. W. Surridge.
[61] Cf. *Glasgow Herald*, 9 Feb. 1916 for a typical lecture.
[62] Ibid., 27 Oct. 1916.

from work was due to ill health caused by being required to work in confined spaces aboard ship. As a result of being deprived of daylight, they complained, their general health was suffering. Another worker had worked 'day and night since the war commenced', and on the day in question had stood for six hours working in water. A further two pleaded that four-mile walks to and from work sapped their strength. When there was rain, they did not turn up, fully expecting to be turned away at the gate, since work was not usually undertaken in the wet.[63]

Yet, though the bulk of accused munitions workers were accorded scant sympathy by the tribunal, a number of those charged with offences were spoken of by their employers in otherwise favourable terms. Among those prosecuted for drunkenness, two furnace keepers at the Muirkirk Iron Works of William Baird & Co. in Ayrshire were described by their employer as 'capable men', against whom the company had 'no personal complaint'.[64] Similarly, a moulder and his helper, despite their drunkenness, were both said by their foreman to be 'good timekeepers'.[65]

There is little doubt as to the feeling of dejection on the part of Sheriff Fyfe when trying cases such as those where the characters of the accused were praised in spite of the prosecutions. On one occasion, indeed, he ventilated his exasperation by condemning the *employers* who had prosecuted a number of men who had taken a week's holiday in the summer. 'If you brought up weeds,' he protested,[66] 'we would know how to deal with them. But you seem to bring your best men here, putting them in the same position as the deliberate shirker.' It was therefore little wonder that, wearing the different hat of Scottish Industrial Unrest Commissioner in 1917, Sheriff Fyfe should recommend, with his two co-commissioners, that henceforth only the Ministry of Munitions should initiate Ordering of Work prosecutions. But that expression of opinion was no doubt also conditioned by the fact that the tribunal's impact as a deterrent

---

[63] Ibid., 22 July 1916; ibid., 15 Jan. 1917; ibid., 26 Oct. 1916.

[64] LAB2/63/MT167/6, J. Turner MacFarlane to Walter Payne, 6 Apr. 1916.

[65] *Glasgow Herald*, 10 May 1916. For further discussion of prosecutions for alleged drunkenness, see Rubin, 'The Enforcement of the Munitions of War Acts, 1915–1917', with Particular Reference to Proceedings before the Munitions Tribunal in Glasgow, 1915–1921', Warwick Univ. Ph.D. thesis (1984), pp. 415–23.

[66] *Glasgow Herald*, 11 Oct. 1916.

was on the wane, once the novelty of the proceedings had worn off and once war-weariness had become more pronounced. Moreover, through the surveys conducted by the government-sponsored Health of Munitions Workers' Committee, the ministry itself had already gathered large amounts of information on the causes of lost time.

From these enquiries it was apparent that, notwithstanding the views of Biggart and Beardmore (above), the tribunals could hope to make only a modest contribution to improved timekeeping. For the ministry survey of March 1916, referred to earlier, revealed the following different explanations for lost time. First, 109 firms stated that due to the shortage of housing, their employees had far to travel to work, 'and implied, if not necessarily stated, that this was a cause' of lost time.[67] Indeed, Beardmore itself, in the case of its Dalmuir site, considered the lack of housing to be an important factor,[68] prompting the firm to fund large housing schemes on Clydeside to counteract the shortage.[69] Barclay Curle shipyard, while stressing the distance between home and work, also pointed out the inadequacy of the tram and train services.[70] Bad weather was cited by sixty-three firms as a cause of lost time and clearly affected those employees with long journeys to work. Illness was mentioned by thirty-five firms, one firm even stating that its employees were 'run down'. Another twenty-five companies cited overtime as a cause of lost time, without clarifying whether workers were thought to be too tired or too well paid to attend regularly. Eighteen referred to 'moral defects' other than drink, that is, indifference and laziness; fifteen cited drink; thirteen mentioned high wages, and only two attributed bad timekeeping to the desire on the part of a few young workers to obtain leaving certificates allowing them to work elsewhere. The effect of air raids and shortage of materials were not included on the questionnaire. The latter could, of course, point to management incompetence, a common allegation made by trade unionists and officials in

[67] BEV v, 19, fos. 139–42.
[68] BEV v, 21, fos. 140–1.
[69] Joseph Melling, 'Employers, Industrial Housing and the Evolution of Company Welfare Policies in Britain's Heavy Industry: West Scotland, 1870–1920', *International Review of Social History*, xxvi (1981), 255–301.
[70] BEV v, 19, fos. 139–42.

repudiating charges against munitions workers.[71] From this survey, it was clear that what were termed avoidable causes, for which blame attached to workers, were dwarfed in significance by the unavoidable causes such as bad weather and inadequate local housing. As far as Glasgow was concerned, while there was a constant trickle of cases falling under the former category and which ended up at the tribunal, it may be charitable to say that the authorities' 'problem' was reduced to manageable proportions by the deterrent effect of a successful prosecution against those Glaswegians displaying the trait of independence.

Timekeeping did in fact appear to worsen nationally in the winter of 1917, by which time, of course, employers were no longer permitted to undertake prosecutions. However, this was also the time when munitions workers were sometimes driven to join the food queues at shops. Moreover, it is surely no accident that the subsequent improvement in timekeeping corresponded with the German spring offensive of 1918, an event which appears to have motivated factory workers to respond patriotically by attending punctually at work. In the event, concluded the ministry, its drive to conquer lax timekeeping standards seemed to have been well rewarded,[72] though whether prosecutions were primarily responsible is highly questionable.

CONCLUSION

In an important theoretical contribution, Panitch has recently written that

Corporatism must be seen as a system of state-structured class collaboration. As such, its extension poses not an opportunity, but a danger to working-class organizations. Based on communitarian premises and collaborative practices which articulate the interests of capital with the state, corporatist structures require of trade unions, as their contribution to the operation, *not that they cut their ties with their base,*

[71] Cf. BEV v, 21, fos. 144–52; Health of Munitions Workers' Committee, *Health of the Munition Workers* (1917), 42.

[72] Bernard Waites, 'The Effects of the First World War on the Economic and Social Structure of the English Working Class', *Scottish Labour History Society Journal*, No. 12, Feb. 1978, 3–33, at 17.

but rather that they use those ties to legitimate state policy and elaborate their control over their members.[73]

To a limited extent, the above analysis is applicable to the wartime experience in respect to factory discipline. Thus trade unions *did* collaborate with Governments and with the employing class in an effort to minimize the disruption to munitions output caused by bad timekeeping. In doing so, moreover, they must be taken to have acknowledged the legitimating effects of their activities on State policies. None the less, and in so far as the 'interests of capital' were thereby sheltered, so also, they reasoned, were working-class interests being protected from a worse fate in the shape of more draconian disciplinary controls over labour. Such trade unionists, indeed, would no doubt also have questioned the distinction drawn by Panitch between the 'unions' and their 'members'. Granted that union officials would in many respects be seen as standing apart from union members, especially when co-ordinating with employers in disciplinary proceedings against those members infringing the Ordering of Work rules, or their equivalent. But local trade union committees handling such matters were likely to be composed of elected lay members drawn from the rank and file. It is, surely, as fallacious to argue that such lay members were *inevitably* fired with a fiercer democratic-activist urge as compared to the rest of the rank and file, as it is to argue that trade union officials were *inevitably* more bureaucratic-centralist (and therefore less democratic) than the membership. Such a conceptual separation of the trade union on the one hand and the membership on the other, is, if advanced without qualification, a dangerous over-simplification. Thus, while trade union officers, in reporting to their membership, were fierce in their denunciations of management who indulged in 'petty tyrannies' by prosecuting for minor misdemeanours,[74] the managerial objectives of securing good timekeeping and good order seem to

---

[73] Leo Panitch, 'Trade Unions and the Capitalist State', *New Left Review*, No. 125, 1981, 21–43, at 42. Italics in original.

[74] For extensive documentation of such grievances, see Rubin 'The Enforcement of the Munitions of War Acts, 1915–1917', with Particular Reference to Proceedings before the Munitions Tribunal in Glasgow, 1915–1921', Warwick Univ. Ph.D. thesis (1984), ch. 2.

have been widely endorsed by both union officials and the rank and file in the munitions trades.

To sum up, therefore, it may be argued with some conviction that the enforcement of a statutorily prescribed system of factory discipline during the First World War was not a wholly negative experience for munitions workers. For it did offer trade union representatives an opportunity to extend their spheres of influence within management and the State. Of course one could point to the danger of such officials compromising their capacity to defend the class interests of their members. Yet, during the war, those distinctive class interests had been subordinated to the greater good, as even factory workers perceived it, of the nation at war. None the less, the weapon of prosecution by employers as a means of maintaining order in the workshop achieved only limited success. Principally aimed at bad timekeeping offences, it was directed mainly at symptoms rather than at causes, a finding which the Ministry of Munitions soon recognized. In addition, while they remained in the hands of employers rather than the State, prosecutions were seen by many workers as the exercise of a public power for private ends. Thus it was in the 'national interest' that anxious investigations were undertaken by the ministry into the social and economic causes of lost time. Moreover, it was in accordance with the 'corporate spirit' that trade unions were drawn formally into the disciplinary process with its plurality of techniques of persuasion. But it was, in a sense, the quid pro quo for this involvement that the right of prosecution was ultimately vested solely in the ministry. Thus the danger posed to union co-operation by petty and vindictive prosecutions by employers which had been a feature of the earlier period of the wartime legal regime,[75] was now quietly obviated.

The experiments with 'factory discipline' during the war were wide-ranging and ambitious. Perhaps 'corporate control' would be a more apt description.

[75] For extensive documentation of such grievances, see Rubin 'The Enforcement of the Munitions of War Acts, 1915–1917', with Particular Reference to Proceedings before the Munitions Tribunal in Glasgow, 1915–1921', Warwick Univ. Ph.D. thesis (1984), ch. 2.

CHAPTER 8

The Leaving Certificate Scheme

INTRODUCTION

No provision of the Munitions Act generated more hostility among munitions workers than did the leaving certificate scheme contained in Section 7 of the 1915 Act. As the embodiment of the 'badge of slavery', it bound reluctant munitions workers to their employer, whose refusal to issue a certificate of release compelled them to resort to munitions tribunals. Yet even here, the prospects for changing employers were not high, as on average the tribunals granted certificates in only 26 per cent of hearings.[1] However, while the array of abuses of the leaving certificate scheme by employers can scarcely be brushed aside—even if such examples do not necessarily point to unremitting, as distinct from episodic harshness—none the less, we will also indicate that this most restrictive of labour controls contained more than a hint of an ambiguous, double-edged quality. For the apparently inhospitable context of leaving certificate hearings offered munitions workers the opportunity, on occasion, to embarrass employers in court, by enabling them to point to alleged managerial malpractices designed to benefit the firm, rather than the 'national interest'. And though, on the merits of the individual complaints of workers addressed to him, the response of Sheriff Fyfe in Glasgow was lukewarm (and on occasion indignant), he none the less expressed himself ready to act against employers on any substantiated charges levelled by leaving certificate applicants. In effect, therefore, the 'corporate spirit' impelled him to scrutinize, and, if necessary, to impugn managerial policies which might offend his notion of the national interest.

For a small number of munitions workers, therefore, the experience of leaving certificate hearings was of educative value in prompting them to question the employer's unfettered right

[1] See Rubin, 'The Enforcement of the Munitions of War Acts 1915–1917, with Particular Reference to Proceedings before the Munitions Tribunal in Glasgow, 1915–1921', Warwick Univ. Ph.D. thesis (1984) p. 450, Tables 9.1 and 9.2.

to manage under wartime collectivist controls. Indeed, when the manipulation by employers of the leaving certificate scheme was compounded by their misuse of the military service scheme, some labour voices expressed the demand for what they considered to be *genuine* national service. Thus they called for *comprehensive* industrial conscription, which would enrol private employers into the ranks of public servants of the State. It is, indeed, arguable that this specifically wartime proposal contributed to the process of socialist reappraisal in 1918 of the role of Labour (and of the State itself) in the post-war world. Of course, it would be claiming too much for munitions workers' experiences of leaving certificate hearings to point to the latter as a formative influence in the generation of post-war Labour Party doctrine. There was a contemporary tendency, also reflected in historians' treatment, to compartmentalize, and thus keep separate as conceptual entities, the leaving certificate scheme and the military service scheme. Yet in respect to the employer's power over the fate of his employees, they were of a similar genre. Thus it is suggested that a radical analysis of the military service scheme, which pointed in the direction of a *higher* national service as the appropriate response by Labour, is likewise applicable to a critique of the leaving certificate scheme. In other words, its defect, it will be suggested, was not that it was a corporatist device in a traditionally pluralist industrial environment, but that, inasmuch as it failed adequately to rein in the discretion of employers, it was not corporatist enough.

The argument of this chapter, then, is that much (though not all) of the extensive criticism of the leaving certificate scheme, in so far as expressed in the name, effectively, of freedom of contract, was misdirected and confused. For the demand for restoration of the pre-war status quo, when workers could change their employment with few restraints, was not an accurate reflection of the aims of these critics. The real objective, hints of which emerged during some of the tribunal hearings in 1916–17, was in fact the imposition of reciprocal controls on employers to counterbalance the discretionary powers which the latter enjoyed under the leaving certificate scheme. With the advent of military service, the synthesis which emerged from this analysis was 'national service', or what one might describe as 'neo-corporatism'.

HOSTILITY TO THE SCHEME, 1915–1916

According to the *Official History of the Ministry of Munitions*, the leaving certificate scheme constituted

the most drastic restriction of normal liberties contained in the Act, and, while Section 7 has been described as the most powerful instrument of industrial efficiency which the War has produced, in practice it gave rise to discontent which could only be finally allayed by its repeal.[2]

The scheme's first task was to control wages. Thus employers were entitled to refuse leaving certificates to employees desirous of moving elsewhere,

as a means of checking the constant drifting of labour in the direction of higher wages—a tendency which not only interfered with regular work, but was likely to cause a general rise of wages. Cases occurred where men left skilled to go to unskilled work on higher wages; where men were drawn from permanent work of national value to temporary employment at higher rates; and where men were finally lost to some industries by drifting into temporary employment at the end of which they were taken for the Army.[3]

In the absence of direct wage regulation imposing uniformity of rates and earnings, employers were vulnerable to the enhanced market power possessed by skilled labour, for whom 'the instinct to sell in the dearest market was not restrained by the general belief that Capital was exploiting to the full the needs of the country'.[4] With employers desperate to attract and complete munitions contracts, a widespread bidding-up of wage rates and bonuses took place, resulting in a chaotic free-for-all to the detriment of the supply departments. To add to the employers' miseries, it was suggested that, since

any competent engineer found no difficulty in getting work, he was ready on the least cause, or perhaps through mere restlessness, to throw up his job and go elsewhere. Thus, at a time when direction was above all things necessary, the movement of labour was in a peculiar degree at the mercy of caprice.[5]

---

[2] *OHMM*, vol. I, pt. IV, p.3. Cf., Roger Davidson, 'Sir Hubert Llewellyn Smith and Labour Policy, 1886–1916', Cambridge Univ. Ph.D. thesis (1971) p. 358.

[3] *OHMM,* vol. I, pt. IV, p. 38.

[4] Ibid., vol. IV, pt. II, p. 14.

[5] Ibid., p. 15.

The second task of the scheme, therefore, was to discourage mobility of labour on the merest whim or fancy of the employee. But not only was freedom of movement to be circumscribed dramatically; there was a further and related task conferred on the leaving certificate scheme. As Lloyd George explained in the Commons,

It is absolutely impossible to obtain any discipline or control over men, if a man who may be either slack or disobedient to a reasonable order is able to walk out at the moment, go to the works which are only five or ten minutes off, and be welcomed with open arms without any questions being asked. That must be stopped.[6]

Thus the trinity of labour immobility, wage deflation and factory discipline was emblazoned on the leaving certificate.

In the first few months of the scheme's existence, the Labour press regularly denounced Section 7 in all its manifestations. For example, by preventing workers from moving freely from one firm to another, it rendered them 'little better than slaves', complained the *Woman's Dreadnought*.[7] The *Cotton Factory Times*,[8] emphasizing a different feature of the scheme, noted that employers were withholding certificates on the ground that they 'never gave testimonials', the object being in some cases to 'coerce men into working at scab rates', that is, below the district rate.

But there were more fundamental objections which challenged the scheme's lack of reciprocity. The most obvious, pointed out by John Hodge for the Labour Party in the Commons debate on the Bill, was that while the worker could not leave his employment without a certificate, the employer was left free to dismiss him.[9] Moreover, there was nothing in the 1915 Act to compel an employer to issue a certificate even if he dismissed an employee or suspended him for a lengthy period without pay.[10]

One would naturally suppose that a man who had been dismissed, kicked out, sacked, had left so entirely with the consent of his employer,

---

[6] Ibid., vol. I, pt. IV, p. 40; ibid., vol. V, pt. I, p. 34; HC Deb., 5th ser., vol. 72, col. 1199, 23 June 1915.

[7] *Woman's Dreadnought*, 7 Aug. 1915. Cf., ibid. 11, 18 Sept. 1915.

[8] *Cotton Factory Times*, 10 Sept. 1915.

[9] *OHMM*, vol. I, pt. IV, p. 41; HC Deb., 5th ser., vol. 72, col. 1519, 23 June 1915.

[10] Wolfe, *Labour Supply and Regulation*, Oxford, 1923, p. 221; *Forward*, 11, 25 Sept. 1915.

that, fined or unfined, he would, at any rate, be entitled to his 'consent certificate'.
But no! Neither under this Act, nor under any other, nor by common law, is the employer bound to give a certificate. He cannot be compelled to put into writing a statement of fact that he cannot deny. So this is what happens: A man is dismissed; the employer refuses the certificate—'A bad workman! Let him rot!'—and for six weeks the man is unemployable, starving perhaps, degenerating certainly—and this at a time when every workman is needed, even the indifferent.[11]

Of course, the employee could apply to the tribunal for the certificate, but as we shall see later, even the tribunal could refuse a certificate in the above circumstances. If it *did* grant one, moreover, the employer incurred no penalty, no matter how unreasonable or vindictive his refusal had been, and even though the employee had undoubtedly suffered loss of wages during the period without a certificate.[12] 'The total effect', concluded the *Official History*, 'was to arm employers, managers and foremen with arbitrary powers that were certain to be abused in unscrupulous hands.'[13]

Indeed, criticism of employers was even endorsed by one of the ministry architects of the scheme, Humbert Wolfe, who later agreed that many employers and foremen had used the power conferred on them in an oppressive manner.

They enforced changes in the methods of working, they penalized men by delay in issuing certificates, and they refused certificates to men thrown out of work by a strike or breakdown of machinery; they would not allow men who had come from a distance to return home, and they would not grant certificates to workmen leaving to take up better work elsewhere.[14]

The local ministry official in Glasgow, James Paterson, had in fact warned his department heads of trouble afoot as early as 4 August 1915. Already, he pointed out, a number of skilled men were walking the streets unemployed because of their inability to satisfy prospective employers that their previous employers had consented to their leaving. He wrote

---

[11] *Nation*, 9 Oct. 1915, 53.
[12] *OHMM*, vol. I, pt. IV, p. 41.
[13] Ibid., p. 42.
[14] Wolfe, *Labour Supply and Regulation*, p. 223.

It is only now that employers are beginning to understand the operation of Section 7(1), but even those who had thought of it appear to be considering only one part of its application, i.e. the right that it confers on them to retain their men in their employment and the fact that any other firm which engages the workman without a certificate is guilty of a contravention of the Act. I have not yet heard of an employer, large or small, who is adopting the practice of issuing certificates of consent under Section 7(1).[15]

The Ministry of Munitions attempted to remedy the situation by distributing a circular to the engineering and shipbuilding employers' federations which declared that 'The Minister regards it of great importance that when a certificate is refused, the workman should, if he so desires, be retained in the employer's service, and that certificates should never be withheld when a workman is dismissed.'[16]

Yet not only did suspensions or discharges without certificates continue unabated; employers also attempted to convert their certificates into character notes, stating that the reason for dismissal was breach of discipline or poor timekeeping. This practice, though not widespread, effectively prevented the recipients of such certificates from obtaining alternative employment until the Fairfield shipwrights' case (ch. 3) brought such matters to a head. Thereafter, new regulations stipulated that no endorsements to the standard form of certificate prescribed in the regulations were to be permitted, and scarcely any further trade union complaints on this score were recorded.[17]

A number of mass meetings and conferences provided trade unionists with the opportunity to vent their anger at the restrictions on their freedom and to demand drastic changes in the law. As early as mid-August 1915, a meeting of all Clyde trade unions affiliated to the Federation of Engineering and Shipbuilding Trades (FEST) had taken place in the Christian Institute in Glasgow.[18] Yet despite the fact that it was held

---

[15] *OHMM*, vol. IV, pt. II, pp. 17–18.
[16] Ibid., p. 18.
[17] For an isolated example of a prosecution of an employer for wrongly endorsing a certificate after the Fairfield shipwrights' episode, see ASE, *Monthly Journal and Report*, Apr. 1916, 55; *The Times*, 14 Mar. 1916. The employer, a Dumbarton foundry, was fined £2 by Professor Gloag.
[18] *Glasgow Herald*, 14 Aug. 1915.

within a few days of the Fairfield coppersmiths' and Lobnitz holders-on prosecutions (ch. 3), the principal complaints were, significantly, directed against the operation of the leaving certificate scheme.[19] A month later, a mass meeting of 300 ASE shop stewards, chaired by David Kirkwood of the CWC, was held in Diamond's Hall in Gorbals. A resolution was carried demanding that the district committee communicate with the London executive for 'effective steps' to abolish the 'slavery clauses'. As the ILP-inclined *Forward* commented,

The feeling among the rank-and-file is gathering in bitterness and the declarations at the shop stewards' meeting that free Britons were better than slave Britons for shell or any other kind of manufacture were received with an applause that any politician—Mr Lloyd George or any other— would do well to understand before making fresh compulsory regulations.[20]

Two weeks later, J. T. Brownlie, the chairman of the ASE, came up to Glasgow to address a local aggregate meeting in the City Hall. The meeting, described by Paterson in his report to London as a 'bear garden',[21] effectively rejected Brownlie's plea for co-operation with the Munitions Act and passed a number of hostile resolutions, including one condemning the system of leaving certificates.[22] Indeed, William Brodie, the local district delegate, simultaneously reported in the ASE *Journal* that 'We are still having trouble through the application of the Munitions

---

[19] In fact teething troubles at the outset compounded the difficulties in administering the scheme since the actual certificates only became available 2 weeks after the regulations were issued. Particular individuals—an ASE member at Burmeister & Wain and a woodcutting machinist at John Brown's shipyard—were immediately affected when they desired to leave their employment at the end of July, at a point in time when no certificates were available. At the Balfour–Macassey enquiry, the employer's representative expressed his regret at the 'unfortunate experience' suffered, but pleaded that the employers 'had really no more control than the workmen themselves'. See MUN 5/80/341/3, pp. 268–9, 345–9, 369–70; also MUN 5/73/324/15/1, 'Memorandum by Lynden Macassey: Causes of Unrest among Munitions Workers on Clyde and Tyneside . . ., 18 Dec. 1915'. The point in this example is not that the men's original employers refused to release them, but that no employer would hire them without a certificate.

[20] *Forward*, 18 Sept. 1915.
[21] *OHMM*, vol. IV, pt. II, p. 55.
[22] *Glasgow Herald*, 1 Oct. 1915.

Act, many of our members being almost in revolt at being bound over to one employer.'[23]

Lynden Macassey, one of the ministry's trouble-shooters on the Clyde, did at the time express the view that the local union officials, under pressure from their rank and file, were 'forced to inflate and paint as crowning tyrannies of the Munitions Act, every pettifogging complaint that in peacetime would not have secured a report by a shop steward to his union's local branch'.[24] For he could point to the relatively trivial origins of some of the more celebrated confrontations, including the Fairfield shipwrights' and Lobnitz holders-on disputes. On the other hand, the manipulation of the leaving certificate by the shipyard employers in particular, whereby it was being fashioned into a new and powerful instrument of factory discipline, matched the deployment of the recently instituted Ordering of Work rules elsewhere. Moreover, the seemingly endless list of apparently indefensible refusals of certificates, readily accessible from sources such as the ILP Member of Parliament W. C. Anderson's series on 'The Munitions Act at Work', which appeared in the *Forward*,[25] provided ample chapter and verse for a damning critique of the scheme.

While it remains true, none the less, as Macassey did point out, that the scale of unrest among Clyde and Tyneside workers was not equalled elsewhere, the expression of dissatisfaction with tribunal rulings on leaving certificate applications was country-wide. Indeed, whereas criticisms of leaving certificate decisions delivered by the Glasgow tribunal perhaps failed to match the anger vented at the outcome of strike prosecutions, elsewhere hostility was specifically directed to the tribunal's handling of leaving certificate applications. For example, the *Yorkshire Factory Times* considered that 'investigations into cases before such tribunals will surely open the eyes of the working-class public to the devilish contrivance that means their semi-enslavement.'[26]

Thus it was reported in the *Nation*[27] that, even where an

[23] ASE, *Monthly Journal and Report*, Oct. 1915, 27.
[24] MUN 5/73/324/15/1.
[25] The series ran for a number of weeks in the *Forward* during Sept. and Oct. 1915. The leaving certificate item was published on 25 Sept. 1915.
[26] *Yorkshire Factory Times*, 11 Nov. 1915. Cf. ibid., 7 Oct. 1915.
[27] *Nation*, 9 Oct. 1915, 53.

employer had effectively dispensed with the services of an unsatisfactory employee but had vindictively refused him a certificate, the munitions tribunal itself could not be relied upon to issue the certificate. For, 'the astonishing thing is that (in Yorkshire, at any rate) the Munitions Tribunals are taking the same line as the employers, and deliberately preventing men who have misbehaved from obtaining employment . . .'.[28] The regular reports from trade union officials reinforced the nature of these complaints. For example, from Middlesex, it was stated that

Munitions tribunals are still giving palpably unfair decisions, and in order to square their consciences, many members are being compelled to take their six weeks' holiday, in compliance with the Munitions Act, 1915, in order to enable them to transfer their productive ability to centres where employers are apparently less given to pre-war commercialism in the present national crisis.[29]

At the Edinburgh tribunal, it was complained that the evidence of a works manager was preferred to that of three ASE members giving testimony, with the result that the leaving certificate application in question was refused,[30] while the Cardiff district delegate of the ASE denounced the institution of 'courts of three where one decides'.[31] Though an official might occasionally report that the local tribunal was making little impact in his particular district,[32] two national conferences of engineering

---

[28] Ibid. Tribunals could act in this way, because even if they believed that an employer had acted 'unreasonably' in refusing a certificate to a worker no longer employed, the wording of Section 7 none the less declared that tribunals 'may', rather than 'shall', issue a certificate unreasonably withheld. A convoluted and inadequate amendment was made in Section 5 of the 1916 Amendment Act, while a further proposed change, ostensibly aimed at reducing the employers' and tribunal's discretion to refuse a certificate to a worker no longer with the employer, was drafted in May 1917. As the leaving certificate scheme was soon to be abolished, the 1917 provision never became law. The problem was to discourage employers from vindictively refusing certificates to employees whom they no longer wanted, for one reason or another, while discouraging workmen from leaving firms which still wanted to retain their services. The paradox within the leaving certificate scheme, that it could, for a period, *prevent* workers dismissed for misconduct from undertaking necessary munitions work elsewhere, was never resolved during its lifetime. For details of the statutory amendments, see *OHMM*, vol. IV, pt. II, pp. 75–7; ibid., vol. VI, pts. II–III, p. 2.
[29] ASE, *Monthly Journal and Report*, Nov. 1915, 55.
[30] Ibid., Oct. 1915, 27.
[31] Ibid., Feb. 1916, 45. Cf. ibid., Oct. 1915, 42 (also Cardiff).
[32] SSA, *Quarterly Reports*, Jan.–Mar. 1916, 19 (East and South-East district).

and shipbuilding trade unions, convened specifically to review 'glaring cases of arbitrary decisions' by tribunals,[33] were held in October.[34] Once again, the principal focus of complaint was the administration of the leaving certificate scheme by the tribunals, though the recent imprisonment of the Fairfield shipwrights (ch. 3) inevitably prompted the demand that the tribunals' powers of imprisonment be abolished.

Finally, a national conference of fifty-five trade unions in November and a separate meeting with the ASE in December 1915 left Lloyd George in no doubt where the official trade union representatives stood on the matter. As the press reported,

He noticed that most of the amendments were in the direction of what might be called reciprocity. There was a feeling that if a workman could not discharge his employer without a certificate from the tribunal, the employer ought not to be able to discharge the workman without a similar certificate.[35]

It is clear that from such conferences emanated the thoroughgoing programme of replacing the tribunals by local joint committees. These would have had the authority to determine not the leaving certificate application by a worker where the employer objected, but the request of the *employer* to retain the worker if the latter submitted his notice to leave.[36] But, as with the proposal for joint disciplinary committees (ch. 7), the principle of 'reciprocity' was indigestible to the Government.

The overall picture portrayed by the critics of the scheme during its first few months, is, therefore, one of enduring repression on the part of employers. Furthermore, it was alleged, employers were sustained in their endeavours by the refusal of the tribunals to intercede on the workmen's behalf. Moreover, the Balfour–Macassey Report,[37] set up in the wake of the imprisonment of the Fairfield shipwrights, seemed to endorse the complaints following its close investigation of the local

---

[33] ASE, *Monthly Journal and Report*, Nov. 1915, 36.

[34] *Glasgow Herald*, 23 Oct. 1915; *Engineer*, 15 Oct. 1915; SSA, *Quarterly Reports*, July–Sept. 1915, 25.

[35] *Glasgow Herald*, 1 Dec. 1915; *OHMM*, vol. IV, pt. II, p. 69.

[36] See, for example, Glasgow Trades Council, *Munitions of War Act 1915* (1915) para. 7. Cf. n. 9, above.

[37] *Clyde Munition Workers*, Report of the Rt. Hon. Lord Balfour of Burleigh and Mr Lynden Macassey, KC, Cd. 8136, 1915.

operation of the scheme on Clydeside. Though it deliberately diverted its gaze from the decisions of the local munitions tribunal, the report clearly deemed it urgent that, in the cause of social peace, adequate curbs be placed on the Clydeside employers' exploitation of the leaving certificate primarily as an instrument of discipline or retribution.

Perhaps the example which left the deepest impression on the Government-nominated investigators concerned David Fleming, one of the Fairfield shipwrights previously prosecuted for striking in early September 1915. As recounted before the Balfour–Macassey Commission, it appeared that shortly after the trial of the shipwrights, Fleming had been ordered to work with another foreman in a different part of the yard, but had refused because of previous disagreements with him. Instead, he asked for his insurance books and a leaving certificate. Though told that his books would be delivered to the Labour Exchange, which would indicate that Fairfield no longer had need of his services, his books were not in fact sent on. As a result, Fleming,

walked about the streets from 12 September to 6 October pleading between the Fairfield firm and the Labour Exchange in Govan for his books and clearance line, and he was refused from the fact that the Fairfield firm reserve to themselves the right to refuse a man his clearance line on application . . .[38]

Eventually he applied to the munitions tribunal for a certificate where Cmdr. Gibson lambasted the shipyard for having shamelessly abused its power. 'The Chairman', reported the *Glasgow Herald*, 'said the conduct of the company was most reprehensible in those circumstances. It was grossly unfair to the workmen that they should be made to walk the streets practically unless there was some reasonable ground that could be adduced for the action of the firm in withholding the certificate.'[39]

Of course, as presented to the Balfour–Macassey Commission, the episode was not seen as an isolated incident, but was symptomatic of the manner in which 'unregulated power'[40] was conferred on management by virtue of their hold over

---

[38] MUN 5/80/341/3, pp. 406–7, 539–52, at p. 407.
[39] *Glasgow Herald*, 5 Oct. 1915. Cf. AIMS, *Monthly Report*, Jan. 1916, 250.
[40] *OHMM*, vol. IV, pt. II, p. 61.

workmen's freedom of movement. Thus workers who wished to take up promoted posts as foremen or inspectors were prevented from so doing by their employers, as were skilled men temporarily on labouring work who wished to return to their trades. Medical certificates were frequently not accepted by employers as justifications for the grant of clearance lines, while young journeymen who had just completed their apprenticeships were deprived of certificates which would have enabled them to obtain elsewhere the standard, and not just the improvers', rate.[41] As the *Official History*, summarizing the evidence to the commission, added,

Men dismissed for words with a foreman or refusal to do what they were told, were penalised by delay in issuing certificates, and kept idle for a week or more. Men thrown out of work by a breakdown or a strike were retained without compensation by the refusal of clearance lines. Men attracted from other districts by the prospect of working overtime and earning good money were not allowed to leave, although the loss of overtime made it very difficult to keep up two homes.[42]

Indeed, we have already seen in previous chapters the complaints of, *inter alia*, Beardmore caulkers put on to less agreeable water testing, the hoarding of skilled labour, the grievances of Fairfield coppersmiths at the threat posed by rival plumbers, and the insistence of Barclay Curle shipyard on transferring men between separate sites, a demand which struck at the prevailing custom which prevented the management from deploying rivetting squads as it pleased. In all these cases, the presence of the leaving certificate scheme served to exacerbate the existing conflicts over managerial prerogative claims.[43]

[41] Ibid., pp. 62–3.

[42] Ibid., p. 61; see also Reid, 'The Division of Labour in the British Shipbuilding Industry, 1880–1920', Cambridge Univ. Ph.D. thesis (1980), pp. 342–9, for account of the Balfour–Macassey proceedings.

[43] For details of the changes to the leaving certificate scheme eventually incorporated in the 1916 Munitions Amendment Act, see *OHMM*, vol. IV, pt. II, pp. 64–5. Among the most important recommendations of the commission which became law were: 1, that the employer be forbidden to enter reasons for dismissal on the certificate (in order to prevent a repeat of the Fairfield shipwrights' incident); 2, that on a *dismissal* occurring, a workman should immediately receive a certificate; and 3, that a tribunal might award a workman compensation if a certificate had been unreasonably withheld. None the less, as an exception to (2) above, the punishment of 6 weeks unemployment was still retained as a deterrent against employee misconduct which resulted in a sacking, in spite of the dire need for manpower. Workers who were merely surplus to requirements were protected, however, under (2). Cf. n. 28, above.

THE ABANDONMENT OF THE SCHEME, 1917

The year 1917 was one of enduring domestic crisis for the Government. For as Wrigley has written,

Long hours, changing workshop conditions, restricted industrial relations under the Munitions of War Act, high prices, food scarcity, growing war weariness, scepticism as to war aims, the widening influence of conscription, the popular democratic feelings released by the revolutions in Russia, all combined to make Labour uneasy in this year.[44]

It is against this background that one must place the Government's decision to abolish the leaving certificate scheme, even before confirmation of its continuing unpopularity with munitions workers had been obtained from the reports, in mid-1917, of the regional Commissions on Industrial Unrest. For, although the scheme had survived the barrage of labour protests during its first six months of existence, none the less extensive negotiations between the Government and trade union leaders over the terms of the 1917 Munitions Bill had reaffirmed that, 'the principal grievance, apart from the central question of the extension of dilution, was the restriction which the leaving certificate system imposed on the workers' freedom of movement.'[45] Of course, the tribunal might be persuaded to render a favourable decision to an applicant whose employer had refused to grant his release. Indeed, there is statistical evidence which suggests a gradual shift among a number of tribunals, including Birmingham, Coventry, London, and Sheffield, towards a more generous treatment of applicants. In the period from July 1916 to October 1917, there was both a rising grant rate *and* a falling refusal rate in the case of leaving certificate applications to the above tribunals[46] (the statistics also give the numbers of withdrawn and 'unnecessary' applications, the latter pertaining to those submitted by workers

[44] Wrigley, *David Lloyd George and the British Labour Movement*, Hassocks, 1976, p. 182. Cf. *New Statesman*, 9 June 1917, 221. See also n. 50, below.
[45] *OHMM*, vol. VI, pts. II–III, p. 2.
[46] Rubin, 'Enforcement of the Munitions of War Acts', Tables 9.9 to 9.16, pp. 456–9. For Glasgow, the *rate* of refusals fell significantly for a year after July 1916, but there was also a reduction in the *number* of certificates granted during this period. However, in the last 4 months of the scheme, there was a significant rise in the number of refusals and a modest increase in the number of certificates granted in Glasgow. See ibid., p. 454, Tables 9.5 and 9.6.

deemed not to be covered by the Munitions Act (see appendix)). Perhaps the grip of statutory labour restrictions was beginning to loosen as the war dragged on through a fourth year. Yet, more favourable statistical results might have been little consolation to those workmen caught by the controls. For, as the Radical Liberal Member of Parliament, William Pringle, observed,

The very fact that men need to go all through this machinery and all this legal process for the simple purpose of attaining a change of employment is felt by them in itself to be a grievance and a hardship, and matters of grievance with their existing employers which ordinarily would be regarded by them as negligible, very often swell in importance largely owing to the fact that they know they cannot change their employment.[47]

There were, in fact, more immediate explanations for the abolition of the scheme, such as a negotiating blunder by Christopher Addison, the Minister of Munitions at the time, who pledged its repeal without receiving in return from the trade unions a watertight commitment to dilution on private work. Moreover, the employers' resigned acceptance of abolition in preference to further tinkering with the scheme no doubt hastened its demise.[48]

Thus, despite a strong rearguard action by civil servants intent on retention of the scheme, the Parliamentary Secretary to the Minister of Munitions, James Kellaway, insisted that objections to repeal were 'far outweighed by the advantages derived from the disappearance of a restriction which had irritated labour more than anything else'.[49] Indeed, were he still in two minds on the matter, the regional reports of the Commission on Industrial Unrest published shortly thereafter would give further emphasis to the aggravating role of the leaving certificate scheme.[50] Its repeal was therefore effected in October 1917.[51]

---

[47] HC Deb., 5th ser., vol. 92, col. 2764, 27 Apr. 1917. Cf., Wolfe's remark that 'It was not . . . that workers wished to move: they wished to be able to move, which was quite a different thing'. See Wolfe, *Labour Supply and Regulation*, pp. 228–9.

[48] For these features, see *OHMM*, vol. VI, pts. II–III, pp. 2–4; Wrigley, *David Lloyd George and the British Labour Movement*, p. 203.

[49] *OHMM*, vol. V, pt. I, p. 53.

[50] Ibid., p. 47; ibid., vol. VI, pts. II–III, p. 5; W. C. Heron, 'The Commission of Enquiry into Industrial Unrest of 1917', Warwick Univ. MA thesis (1975), pp. 108–9.

[51] For the details of repeal, see n. 91, below.

But the tribunal decisions between the upheavals of 1915 and the abolition of the scheme in 1917 are not without interest. For, as suggested in the introduction to this chapter, leaving certificate hearings afforded munitions workers and trade union officials a limited opportunity within the interstices of the legal reticulation to demonstrate the potential ambiguities within the scheme, and, in some instances, to subject the actions of employers to the close scrutiny of whether the conduct of the *latter* was in the national interest.

Thus the feeling among munitions workers that the scheme was still being exploited by Clydeside employers for their own private gains long after the traumas of 1915 had led to the 1916 Amendment Act continued to express itself before the Glasgow tribunal. For example, a shipyard riveter who had been engaged in Government work for two years was transferred to work on a merchant vessel at less favourable piece-rates,[52] and when his request to return to munitions work was refused, he applied for a leaving certificate. The fact was, his trade union representative told the tribunal, that as long as there was urgent government work available elsewhere on the Clyde, 'the men were not prepared to give their services to help the profits of the 500 per cent patriots'.

More damaging assertions were levelled by three engineers who alleged that their employer was using munitions workers, 'for the purpose of manufacturing stock to store and preserve for the coming of peace and then, [Sheriff Fyfe] presumed the suggestion to be, used for the private emolument of the firm'.[53] Fyfe perhaps had visions that, if substantiated, such revelations might have serious effects on morale in the factories and shipyards, already in some danger of flagging after the Somme massacres and as the war dragged on remorselessly. The seriousness of the allegations, insisted Fyfe, therefore merited stronger evidence than was otherwise acceptable before a tribunal, and hearsay evidence, especially when contradicted by

---

[52] *Glasgow Herald*, 18 July 1916.
[53] Ibid., 2 Aug. 1916.

the management, was clearly inadequate.[54] Indeed, as he declared in another case, where it was alleged that the employer was hoarding labour unnecessarily,

the majority of these statements were the irresponsible expressions of workmen who had no idea as to the actual contracts upon which their employers were engaged. The statement that controlled firms were not fully engaged was likely to create a wrong impression. . . . As matters stood, however, many of the workmen seemed inclined to take upon themselves the responsibility of saying what was and what was not important work.[55]

Therefore, one scarcely noticed result of the experience of munitions workers in resorting to the tribunal was that some of them were prepared to question the proper limits of managerial decision-making in a wartime 'collectivist' economy. And though Sheriff Fyfe's initial response was to register his indignation at what he no doubt considered were preposterous suggestions from the applicant workers, he was none the less prepared to announce that 'If any applicant was in a position to bring forward proof to establish his assertion that he was not being sufficiently employed and was being forced to stay with his firm, the Court would deal with the employer in an effective manner.'[56]

The scheme could be conceptualized, then, not simply as a crude instrument of *labour* control. For a further dimension to the leaving certificate case-load was that it permitted munitions workers to pose modest challenges to the scope of managerial autonomy and to seek its harnessing to the broader corporatist interest. It was, surely, one fragment of the wartime development noted by the *New Statesman*, whereby

The changing status of the wage-earner necessarily involves a further retirement, very gradually, and possibly even slowly, from the position of autocracy in the factory which the employer has inherited; and a further taking into council and even into partnership, of all the wage earners, so far as concerns the conditions of their working life.[57]

---

[54] Lord Dewar had declared in another case that 'It is clearly intended that the facts, in ordinary cases, should be ascertained informally, and the cases decided expeditiously.' Sheriff Fyfe obviously chose to ignore this guideline. See *Scottish Tube Co. Ltd.* v. *McGillivray*, 1916 SMAR 16–19, at p. 18, 26 July 1916.

[55] *Glasgow Herald*, 15 Nov. 1916.

[56] Ibid.

[57] *New Statesman*, 23 June 1917, 270.

Some historians have suggested[58] that the lessons of war collectivism were prompting elements within the labour movement towards more profound analysis; that is, to question not only the role of labour within the State apparatus, but also to challenge the role of the State itself within the social and political order. Thus the expression of workmen's complaints at tribunal hearings against a cosy relationship between the State and the manufacturers, where only the latter were privy to State secrets, and where the labour interest was purposefully excluded from such deliberations, might lead trade unionists to draw broader conclusions as to the purpose for which they were making sacrifices.

Perhaps this radical potential accompanying the leaving certificate scheme's restrictive quality was in fact perceived by Sheriff Fyfe himself, and duly alarmed him. For he reminded applicants who presumed to 'take upon themselves the responsibility of saying what was and what was not important work' (above), that 'If employers could not find work for their men, it was obvious that many workmen who were at present engaged in starred occupations should be in the Army.'[59] As a barely concealed attempt to deter applicants from pursuing their challenges to managerial indifference to the claims of labour, Fyfe's remark may well have been heeded locally. Yet, paradoxically, the hint of military service as an adjunct to the leaving certificate scheme offered further ammunition for those exploring a radical critique of the wartime corporate economy.

LEAVING CERTIFICATES AND MILITARY SERVICE

The trenches were, indeed, the awful nemesis awaiting those munitions workers falling into the category of 'unbadged' labour, who were not exempt from military service. For the various categories of protected employees, that is, 'starred' workers, 'trade card' holders, or those designated in a Government schedule of protected occupations, the withdrawal

---

[58] See, for example, Harrison, 'The War Emergency Workers' National Committee', in A. Briggs and J. Saville (eds.), *Essays in Labour History*, vol. II, 1886–1923, London, 1971, and Winter, *Socialism and the Challenge of War*, London, 1974.

[59] *Glasgow Herald*, 15 Nov. 1916.

of immunity from recruitment was the ultimate deterrent. It may be observed that the relationship between military service and the Munitions Act had been made plain to bad timekeepers threatened with military call-up if they persistently lost time.[60] Moreover, the stories of harassment of exempted workers by the military, in particular one controversial case in Sheffield involving an engineer, Leonard Hargreaves,[61] were far from being isolated occurrences. However, the interaction of the leaving certificate scheme with the provisions for military conscription seems not to have been clearly perceived at the time by contemporaries, nor subsequently, by historians.[62]

Munitions workers had very quickly learned how their employers could turn the statutory provisions for military conscription introduced in January 1916 to their advantage. As the ILP politician, Philip Snowden, pointed out,

From the first day of the operation of that measure [the Military Service Act] it became an instrument for industrial compulsion. Tribunals all over the country have used the Act for that purpose. Workmen who have been prominent in Trade Union matters have been debadged and sent into the Army. Employers of labour have used

---

[60] Rubin, 'Enforcement of the Munitions of War Acts,' pp. 375–8. For the practice of the Sheffield munitions tribunal chairman, Sir William Clegg, who not only fined workmen who lost time, but reported them to the military authorities, see ibid., p. 479.

[61] The Hargreaves case concerned a skilled Sheffield engineer who, despite being in a 'starred' occupation which should have exempted him from military call-up, was enlisted by the Army in Nov. 1916. A strike broke out immediately and was only called off 2 days later, when Hargreaves was released by the military and made his appearance at a strike meeting. A month later, the government agreed to a new exemption scheme, the trade card scheme, which more securely entrenched the immunity from call-up of skilled munitions workers. See ASE, *Monthly Journal and Report*, Sept. 1916, 22; ibid., Oct. 1916, 16; ibid., Nov. 1916, 40; Hinton, *The First Shop Stewards' Movement*, London, 1973, pp. 174–6; Wrigley, *David Lloyd George and the British Labour Movement*, pp. 171–4.

[62] There are scattered references which link the two, but which do not explore the connections. See Wolfe, *Labour Supply and Regulation*, p. 227; *Report of the (McCardie) Committee on Labour Embargoes* (Dec. 1918), sec. 26. Rodney Lowe has stated that the powers of the Ministry of Munitions 'bordered on industrial conscription because no man could change jobs unless he had a leaving certificate stating the reasons for his leaving his previous employment; should a man leave without such a certificate, or be dismissed, he became immediately liable for military conscription.' Both statements are inaccurate, as is Lowe's further footnote comment that, 'The Ministry itself was not directly responsible for the issue of these certificates until the autumn of 1917.' For these statements, see Lowe, 'The Demand for a Ministry of Labour, its Establishment and Initial Role, 1916–1924', London Univ. Ph.D. thesis (1975), p. 37. For a possible explicit connection, reflected in provisions of the Military Service legislation of 1916, see Rubin, 'Enforcement of the Munitions of War Act,' app. 3.

the Act to discriminate between workmen in regard to military service. Cases of this character might be quoted in large numbers. A notorious case of this sort happened in Dundee where workmen came out on strike and a number of them were seized by the military authorities and passed into the Army. Military Service Tribunals have imposed the condition that an exempted man, while following his usual civil employment, should only receive army pay and allowances. Men who have been given exemption on the condition that they engage in work of 'national importance' are employed under penal conditions at sweated wages.[63]

Yet the denial of leaving certificates, though undoubtedly less dramatic than strike-breaking, was similarly facilitated by the advent of military service. It was alleged in one case by a Clydeside official of the Shipwrights' Association, William Westwood, that the general manager of Beardmore at Dalmuir, Archibald Campbell, had withheld a leaving certificate from a shipwright who had refused to attest,[64] that is, register with the army authorities and await call-up in due course. In another case,[65] a young engineer was called up but was able to present his exemption certificate to the recruiting officer who promptly sent him back to his work. His employer, however, refused either to restart him or to grant him a leaving certificate. Instead, he informed him, 'You are for the Army'. As William Brodie, the ASE official, complained to the munitions tribunal, not only was this a case of an employer keeping a skilled man idle for three weeks, but it was also the 'case of a manager forcing a young man into the Army'. Indeed the ASE, jealous of preserving its members' favourable exemption status, informed Lord Hunter in the Appeal Tribunal, in a case involving an Edinburgh apprentice alleged to have been slacking, that, 'It was becoming very common for employers to threaten men and apprentices with the Army as a spur, and the society took a serious view of these threats to skilled engineers.'[66] Moreover, apart from employers' objectives of punishing employees or of

---

[63] Philip Snowden, *Labour in Chains: The Peril of Industrial Conscription*, Manchester and London, (Jan. 1917), p. 10. Fears that such developments would occur had been expressed in the debates on the first Military Service Bill of Jan. 1916. See *OHMM*, vol. IV, pt. III, pp. 58–9.

[64] *Glasgow Herald*, 24 Mar. 1916.

[65] Ibid., 2 Apr. 1917.

[66] Ibid., 26 July 1917.

compelling them to modify their behaviour, there were also examples of employers' relying on the threat of military service to grind down the level of wages. In one case heard in Glasgow, a machinist in a paper mill applied for a leaving certificate on the ground that his wages had been reduced by seven shillings. As the applicant's representative, Owen Coyle of the Amalgamated Society of Steel and Iron Workers, pointed out, immediately after the firm had obtained conditional exemption from military service on the applicant's behalf from the Lanarkshire military tribunal, it transferred him to another department where his wages fell from £2. 1s. 6d. per week to £1. 14s. 6d. Indeed, when he objected, he was told that the firm could now make him work for £1 a week. Rejecting the possible objection to the grant of a leaving certificate that evasion of military service was the applicant's intention, 'He (Mr Coyle) had come to the conclusion that the firm had used the conditional exemption they obtained for these men to try to keep then under fear of military service, and to make them work for less wages.'[67]

There was in fact very little prospect of using the leaving certificate scheme in order to evade military service. Take, for instance, the case of a plumber of military age employed by Glasgow Corporation Tramways Department, and who had now been offered employment in a shipyard. He explained to Sheriff Fyfe that he had been in the department for a lengthy period and had previously refused to undertake munitions work out of loyalty to the department. He was shortly due to appear before the military tribunal. Therefore, if the department desired to retain him, they ought to obtain exemption from military service for him. If, however, he was not indispensable enough to merit military exemption, then he ought to receive a leaving certificate to join the shipyard (which no doubt would be happy to apply to the military tribunal on his behalf). His ingenious suggestion, however, received short shrift from the chairman. 'We cannot', Sheriff Fyfe announced, 'give anybody an opportunity to get a badge for his coat to use at the tribunal. We are not going to interfere with the military tribunal. They are evidently dealing with you. The application is refused.'[68]

[67] *Glasgow Herald*, 6 Sept. 1916.
[68] Ibid., 18 Oct. 1916.

Thus, for leaving certificate applicants desirous of avoiding military service (and some who were exempt in their existing employment were prepared to take their chances of losing their exemption by obtaining employment elsewhere[69]), there was a bleak future in prospect where the munitions tribunal refused to be drawn on the matter. For if the employer refused a certificate on the ground that his employee was an essential part of his work-force, then it might have been expected that the former would appeal to the military tribunal on behalf of the employee for at least conditional exemption. But in fact there were a number of instances where the employer not only refused leaving certificates, but also refused to apply to the military tribunal to exempt their employees from call-up.[70] In the case of the North-Eastern Railway, the Yorkshire delegate of the ASE reported that 'The company has definitely declined to release these men to get work elsewhere but were quite prepared to let them go into the Army in spite of all the cry there is for munitions and suspensions of holidays to make the same.'[71] In another case, the West Country delegate of the union reported that '200 stars were removed by one employer at the same time he was refusing leaving certificates to some of the same men.'[72] Even Sheriff MacDiarmid, chairing the Dunbartonshire East military tribunal, felt sympathy with employees debadged under the Military Service Act passed in May 1916 and who

---

[69] Ibid., 27 Oct. 1916. As Sheriff Fyfe told the applicant, 'Don't you think you will be between the devil and the deep sea?' Indeed, there were even more bizarre outcomes. The Midlands ASE organizer reported in May 1916 that over the previous 12 months, a number of young ASE members, anxious to enlist in units where their skills could be of assistance, had been thwarted by their employers. 'In one particular case,' he wrote, 'an uncontrolled firm applied for exemption for several of our members—without their knowledge—to a local military service tribunal, which contrary to the instructions officially issued, refused exemption. The firm are on work which they state is munition work, but in view of the above decision, I applied for certificates from the local munitions tribunal. This body refused the certificates on the grounds that the men were engaged on important munition work. The position thus is that mechanics are refused exemption from military service because it is no longer necessary in the national interests that they shall continue in their usual occupation and are refused certificates of release because they are engaged on munition work of urgent national importance. This is only one of the silly results of the shifting policy of the authorities with which I am coming in contact in one capacity or another every day, and which tends to make one tired of trying to understand.' See ASE, *Monthly Journal and Report*, May 1916, 37.

[70] Ibid., July 1916, 34.

[71] Ibid., June 1916, 30.

[72] Ibid., Feb. 1916, 42.

were in consequence apparently abandoned by particular employers to the horrors of the trenches. During one exemption hearing, he remarked, 'I think it is very bad luck that this man should have to go in those circumstances. I cannot understand those debadged men at all. Singer's people never seem to make any enquiry into personal cases. I think the applicant should go to Beardmore's and try to get munition work.'[73] It was therefore clear that not only could employers manipulate the leaving certificate scheme to their advantage in respect to employment matters pertaining to discipline or to earnings; they also possessed, albeit indirectly, the power of life or death over their work-force where they (and indeed the munitions tribunal) chose silence.

Thus, whereas the munitions tribunals continued to adjudicate on leaving certificate applications on such regular grounds as failure to pay standard rates; the time-workers' grievance; ill-health; the maintenance of two homes; changes in working arrangements; and promotion or transfer to 'more important' work, the added ingredient of military service, in the words of an ASE official, 'appears to have undermined the small amount of mobility left to Labour under the Munitions Act 1915 and 1916'.[74]

It was not difficult for Labour critics to view this additional and, indeed, more deadly compulsion on munitions workers to resign themselves to their existing employments, as the embodiment of industrial conscription. Hitherto, the Munitions Act, with its provisions for workshop regulations and its' irritating'[75] scheme of leaving certificates, was only dimly perceived in this light and then only as a glint in the eye of the Minister of Munitions.[76] Now, however, the interaction of the two coercive measures appeared to transform nightmare into reality.

If we are searching for the causal factors which explain the demise of the leaving certificate scheme, it is not enough to

[73] *Glasgow Herald*, 26 June 1916. Singer of Clydebank was the famous sewing machine company.

[74] ASE, *Monthly Journal and Report*, June 1916, 34.

[75] The relatively mild description 'irritating' was frequently used to depict the limited effect of the scheme.

[76] Most notably in a widely publicized speech in Manchester in June 1915. See Lloyd George, *War Memoirs*, vol. I, London, 1933, pp. 258–61; Wrigley, *David Lloyd George and the British Labour Movement*, pp. 116–7.

reiterate trade unionists' complaints of 1915 relating to discipline, restrictions on freedom of movement, wage restraint, and the absence of reciprocity which enabled the employer to dismiss at will, whereas the employee could leave only under six weeks' penalty; nor enough to accept that the scheme had perhaps reached the end of its useful life; nor sufficient, even, that the Government's drastic offer of repeal was the trade unions' indispensable price for agreement to dilution on private work. The further dimension was simply that, as the Labour MP Stephen Walsh explained to Lloyd George in another context, 'a man must either be a civilian or a soldier'.[77] By dovetailing the one scheme with the other, the Government had fudged the distinction and was believed by some observers, more sharply that at any time since July 1915 when the first Munitions Act was passed, to have inaugurated a regime of industrial conscription. This was the *political* lesson which some critics drew from the administration of the leaving certificate scheme after 1916. It is a perspective which cannot be neglected despite the apparent primacy of *economic* grievances which the scheme fostered and perpetuated.

The *New Statesman* observed in July 1917 that, in respect to military service, labour unrest was due not so much to the

manifold unfairness and inequalities incident to the successive changes of policy of the Army Council, the inconsiderate and even brutal arrangements for medical re-examination and the occasional failure of the recruiting officers to carry out their instructions, as the belief which the Government has created that the military authorities, either wilfully or negligently, play into the hands of the employer who wishes to get rid of the more 'troublesome' workers, and to choose as 'indispensable', those who are 'docile'.[78]

Favouritism was rife while

men who have 'stood up for their rights' (and those of their class) have been 'sent to the trenches' or even overtly threatened by the foreman that if they were not docile, they would be so sent. This is what the workmen call Industrial Compulsion, against which they threaten a universal strike.[79]

---

[77] *Glasgow Herald*, 28 Aug. 1916.
[78] *New Statesman*, 28 July 1917, 389.
[79] Ibid.

As the reports of the Commission on Industrial Unrest in 1917 confirmed, the fear of industrial conscription continually haunted workers who otherwise were protesting their loyalty and patriotism.[80] But the current powers enjoyed by employers, armed with the right to withhold leaving certificates, underlined the

> uncertainty of men of military age as to their position when an employer, on account of a difference that has arisen, or from any cause—imaginary or otherwise—threatened to discharge a workman and report him to the Military authorities, when he is left in doubt whether he will be called up before he is enabled to start elsewhere.[81]

The Government could, of course, issue a further 'definite pledge against the introduction of industrial compulsion',[82] as did Neville Chamberlain, the Minister of National Service, after the publication of the Commission on Industrial Unrest reports. But the Government was simply no longer trusted; its 'solemn pledges', in the words of the summary report of the Commission's findings compiled by George Barnes, the former ASE general secretary and Minister Without Portfolio in 1917, had been broken time and again; and its lack of good faith in appearing to allow employers to manipulate the military service scheme to their own advantage, as had been alleged with the leaving certificate scheme, was difficult to shrug off or to challenge.

In any case, who was likely to believe Chamberlain when three weeks earlier Robert Young, the general secretary of the ASE, had argued that 'industrial conscription in agreed form [had been] permitted' by the trade unions?[83] Here was yet another 'scrap of paper' emanating from a Government reluctant to conscript riches. Thus, as the *New Statesman* argued in 1918,

> If industrial conscription has to come, they [British workmen] will serve, as they do in the Army and Navy, no-one but the State. They

[80] Heron, 'The Commission of Enquiry into Industrial Unrest of 1917', pp. 109–11, citing West Midlands report, p. 5; London and South-East, p. 3; Yorkshire and East Midlands, p. 4; North-East, p. 6; North-West, p. 24; Wales, pp. 36–7; Scotland, p. 9.

[81] AIMS, *Monthly Report*, July 1917, 128, publishing the Ironmoulders' evidence to the Scottish Commission on Industrial Unrest.

[82] *Labour Gazette*, Oct. 1917, 355; *Glasgow Herald*, 15 Oct. 1917.

[83] Ibid., 24 Sept. 1917.

resolutely refuse to be, as they say, enslaved, so long as the private employer is not also conscribed, put to work like an Army officer at a fixed salary, and compelled to cease making profits for his own benefit.[84]

To the extent that the leaving certificate scheme, especially when intertwined with military service, had prevented the attainment of national service all round, in a pure and unadulterated form, and had prevented labour from taking part 'in the affairs of the community as partners rather than as servants',[85] then a further justification for its removal had been provided, even if that dimension had only been dimly perceived at the time.[86]

CONCLUSION

In analysing the experience of the leaving certificate scheme, there remains a tantalizing paradox. For if, as the *New Statesman* (above) implied, working-class opposition was rooted in hostility not to industrial conscription *per se*, but to the latter's perceived exploitation by private profiteers (which also, significantly, was at the base of the negotiating problems over the lifting of trade union restrictive practices), then might it not be the case that *more*, rather than less, corporatist direction in manpower allocation, perhaps akin to Essential Works Orders during the Second World War, would have been more acceptable to labour? The evidence is, however, confused. On the one hand, as the Industrial Unrest commissioners indicated, some animosity was directed against vague and unspecified 'Government interference'.[87] But on the other hand, criticism by unions was also directed against the arrangements which permitted profiteering to flourish, implying, it is suggested, support for a system of State regulation whose controls worked effectively. Moreover, it must be recognized that the opposition to military service and to military victory (and, indeed, to the

---

[84] *New Statesman*, 27 July 1918, 325.

[85] *Summary Report of Commission on Industrial Unrest*, recommendation 4.

[86] For further discussion of the issue of 'industrial conscription', see Rubin, 'Enforcement of the Munitions of War Acts', app. 3.

[87] Cf. Edwin Cannan, 'Industrial Unrest', *Economic Journal*, xxvii (Dec. 1917), 459.

'servile state') was confined to a minority who cherished higher values than nationalism or xenophobia. In this light, therefore, the observations of the *New Statesman* may not have been as outlandish as the history of opposition to industrial conscription might have implied. In the case of the leaving certificate scheme itself, perhaps the flaw was that it lacked sufficient corporatist discipline by conferring too much autonomy on employers who could initially withhold leaving certificates, while at the same time it enabled tribunal chairmen to exercise discretion as they saw fit. In the case of tribunal chairmen such as Sir William Clegg at Sheffield,[88] perhaps their conscious awareness of order and nationalism was not always consistently matched by an appreciation of the reciprocal nature of 'unity'. For this required State institutions, including the munitions tribunal, to take seriously the triangular composition of the 'nation at war' and to demonstrate that subjection to corporate discipline was to be trilateral, not unilateral. The failure on the part of the Government and of tribunal chairmen to drive home this message in the case of the leaving certificate scheme was perhaps the most critical factor leading to its demise.

The initial autonomy conferred on employers whether to grant or to withhold leaving certificates, a freedom fiercely resented by labour, could have been constrained by requiring *employers* to seek the permission of the tribunal where they wished to *retain* staff desirous of moving. Yet this proposal, advanced in June 1915 by John Hodge, Labour MP for Manchester, Gorton, was decisively rejected in April 1917 by John Hodge, Minister of Labour.[89] Thus the opportunity was lost of reducing the status of the employer, *vis-à-vis* his own employees, to that of a supplicant of the State, while the proposal of the *New Statesman* to transform the employing classes into non-profit-making, salaried public officials, a vision containing hints of Fabian bureaucracy, was not put to the test.

In the end, therefore, the employers' autonomy remained relatively undisturbed until the demise of the scheme, while the activities of a minority of tribunal chairmen, lacking the intelligence and vision to appreciate the effects of even a single

---

[88] For details of Clegg's tribunal record, see Rubin, 'Enforcement of the Munitions of War Acts', pp. 460–1, 464–5, 470–1; Tables 9.15, 9.16, 9.21, at pp. 459 and 471.
[89] *OHMM*, vol. VI, pt. I, p. 58.

inflammatory tribunal decision on a truculent and distrustful labour force,[90] ensured that hostility to the scheme would not flag.[91]

[90] For example, the Sheffield ILP politician, W. C. Anderson, had referred in Parliament to a particularly poignant bad timekeeping conviction at Birmingham. The accused woman in the case had lost time at work as a result of having looked after her sick baby which subsequently died. As the *Official History of the Ministry of Munitions* commented, 'unless a policy of coercion, however mild, can reduce the misuse of coercive powers to negligible proportions, it risks losing all its gains and far more in a single upheaval.' See *OHMM*, vol. VI, pt. I, p. 59, n. 2.

[91] For the lengthy negotiations over repeal involving the Government, trade unions, and employers, together with the relevant parliamentary debates, see ibid., vol. V, pt. I, pp. 33–5, 45–6, 51–7; ibid., vol. VI, pt. I, pp. 57–62; ibid., pts. II–III (combined), pp. 1–9; also Wrigley, *David Lloyd George and the British Labour Movement*, pp. 202–4. As well as extending the WMV scheme in preparation for abolition, the Government also inserted a number of statutory safeguards in the 1917 Act to prevent the expected widespread migration of workers. For example, Section 1 of the Act dealt with a skilled time-workers' wage grievance, thereby removing one possible incentive for skilled labour mobility; Section 3 required a week's notice before leaving employment; and Section 2 prohibited employers from recruiting workers for private work without the consent of the minister. A new Defence Regulation, 41AA, enabled the military to call up any man unemployed for more than 14 days without reasonable cause, and Regulation 8A(b) was dusted down in preparation for the imposition of embargoes on employers hiring a larger quota of skilled workers than the Ministry of Munitions considered justified, a prelude to embargo troubles in the Midlands in July 1918. For these matters, see *OHMM*, vol. VI, pts. II–III, pp. 12–14, 61–71; Hinton, *The First Shop Stewards' Movement*, pp. 229–34; Wrigley, *David Lloyd George and the British Labour Movement*, pp. 228–30; *Report of the (McCardie) Committee on Embargoes, passim;* Fabian Research Department (FRD), *Monthly Circular,* III (1 Aug. 1918), 15; *Glasgow Herald,* 25 July 1918; ASE, *Monthly Journal and Report,* Aug. 1918, 27; Wolfe, *Labour Supply and Regulation,* pp. 229–34; USB, *Monthly Report,* Nov. 1917, pp. 7–9. The Government also sought to rely on exhortatory appeals from its Trade Union Advisory Committee, that workers should respond to abolition of the certificates with restraint and not engage in a 'free-for-all'. See USB, *Monthly Report,* Oct. 1917, 13; ASE, *Monthly Journal and Report,* Oct. 1917, 56; Amalgamated Society of Coremakers (ASCM), *61st Quarterly Report,* 8 Dec. 1917, 60, supplement; *Labour Gazette,* Oct. 1917, 356; MUN 5/79/340.1/4; *Glasgow Herald,* 26 Sept. 1917. For a similar appeal from the Admiralty Transfer Committee, see ibid., 1 Oct. 1917, and AIMS, *Monthly Report,* Dec. 1917, 243 in connection with the Clyde district. The immediate effect of repeal and the wider lessons to be drawn therefrom will be discussed briefly in the final chapter.

CHAPTER 9

Dilution and Legal Proceedings

INTRODUCTION

'The second thing', declared Lloyd George in announcing the provisions of the Munitions of War Bill 1915, 'is the removal of all regulations and practices, or rather, I would not say removal but suspension, during the War . . . of all these restrictions and practices which interfere with the increase of the output of war materials'.[1] Thus the Government had boldly trumpeted its reliance on the law to ensure that no restrictive practices were imposed by unions or work groups which might prevent the maximization of munitions output. However, there was a different view of the Government's real motive. For as two post-war observers noted, 'The radicals claim that the [Munitions] bill was passed primarily not so much to give legal sanction to "dilution", as to prohibit strikes and to minimise the leaving of munitions work by individuals.'[2] The alternative and, we would claim, more persuasive interpretation of the Government's intentions is, then, that the lifting of trade union restrictive practices in general and the imposition of dilution of skilled labour in particular were secondary, perhaps even incidental, concerns of the munitions code. Indeed it may be argued that Lloyd George's invocation of these 'justifications' for legislating enabled him to exploit a moral panic for the more realistic objectives of restricting labour mobility and imposing tighter factory discipline.[3] For, like the dog which failed to bark, there

---

[1] HC Deb., 5th ser. vol. 72, col. 1199, 23 June 1915.

[2] I. O. Andrews and M. Hobbs, *The Economic Effects of the Great War on Women and Children*, New York, 1921, p. 55.

[3] Indeed, Lloyd George seems implicitly to have acknowledged the limits of law as early as the first month of the Act's existence, that is, in July 1915. For even if we leave aside the débâcle that month involving the South Wales miners (ch. 3, n. 14), he noted, in a parliamentary debate on the work of his ministry, that 'We arrived at an agreement with the engineering societies of this country that there should be a complete relaxation of trade union rules and practices in respect of the establishments which are controlled. I regret that up to the present, I cannot make a very satisfactory report, *and I should like to appeal to the trade union leaders to bring pressure to bear—such pressure as they can legitimately bring*

was throughout the war a virtual absence of legal proceedings in the munitions tribunals, in order to underpin the Government's widely proclaimed policy of dilution of labour. Indeed, the terminological inapplicability of the Munitions Act for this task points to the statute as being more accurately interpreted as a simple tool of labour discipline, as a deflationary measure, and as a symbolic gesture of determination by the Government that it be seen, like so many other Governments, to be 'doing something positive' about strikes and restrictive practices. If not actually irrelevant to the removal of the latter, the erroneously perceived threat which dilution allegedly posed to skilled workmen none the less provided a focal point for opposition which only careful and protracted voluntarist negotiations could dispel.[4]

Yet this structural weakness did not fail to dampen the Government's expression of determination to exploit to the full the rigours of the Munitions Act in pressing home their dilution policy. Lloyd George told the Commons in December 1915 that

the law must be put into operation by some body, and unless the employer begins by putting on unskilled men and women to the lathes, we cannot enforce that Act of Parliament. The first step, therefore, is that the employer must challenge a decision upon the matter and he is not doing so because of the trouble which a few firms have had. But let us do it.[5]

Similarly, Lynden Macassey, the Clyde dilution commissioner, told the Clyde shipbuilders in March 1916 that the Govern-

---

to bear—*upon the men in their societies to work the arrangement made with the Government in a more liberal and in a more favourable and satisfactory sense*'. See HC Deb., 5th ser. vol. 72, col. 2362, 28 July 1915 (italics added). Not only is there absent from this statement any threat to deploy the Munitions Act to force through the lifting of trade practices; there is not even the appeal to the *moral* force of law to inspire the patriotic British workman to abandon his selfish restrictions on output.

4 Indeed the use of draconian regulations under DORA to deport the Clyde shop stewards (ch. 3) did not in fact address the obstacles to dilution negotiations, since those deported were previously prepared to engage in such negotiations. The fundamental disagreement between the Government and engineers was in relation to safeguards against exploitation by private employers; and these safeguards, not dissimilar to those in a CWC proposal to Lloyd George in Dec. 1915, were obtained after the deportations. For the shop stewards' proposals, see Hinton, *The First Shop Stewards' Movement*, London, 1973, pp. 129–38.

5 Cited in Wrigley, *David Lloyd George and the British Labour Movement*, Hassocks, 1976, p. 153.

ment's emergency powers were in readiness to underpin the dilution campaign. Thus, 'all customs opposed to the introduction of unskilled and female labour, and therefore restrictive of output, would be abrogated, their maintenance being contrary to the law.'[6] But it was just a case of empty rhetoric on the part of the Government.

THE STATUTORY PROVISIONS

What exactly did the Munitions Act provide in respect to dilution? The legislative authority, inasmuch as it could be so interpreted, was contained in Section 4(3) of the 1915 Act and provided that

> Any rule, practice or custom not having the force of law which tends to restrict production or employment shall be suspended in the establishment, and if any person induces or attempts to induce any other person (whether any particular person or generally) to comply, or continue to comply, with such a rule, practice or custom, that person shall be guilty of an offence under this Act.

The word 'dilution' is conspicuous by its absence from the statute. What does appear is the broader demand for the removal of a restrictive workshop 'rule, practice or custom' whose suspension would permit dilution of labour. But the lifting of trade practices had potentially more far-reaching consequences than the replacement of skilled by other workers, as we shall observe shortly.

To Section 4(3) had to be added Schedule II to the Act, which embodied the Treasury Agreement commitment made by the Government in March 1915 to the large number of unions in the munitions trades who were signatory to the agreement. By Section 4(4) of the Act, employers were now deemed to have undertaken to comply with the provisions of Schedule II. Thus was laid down that any departures from pre-war practices, in respect to which 'due notice where reasonably practicable' had to be given to the work-force, were to be only for the duration of

---

[6] Cited in Reid, 'Dilution, trade unionism, and the state in Britain during the First World War', in Steven Tolliday and Jonathan Zeitlin (eds.), *Shop Floor Bargaining and the State*, Cambridge, 1985, p. 50.

the war and that the post-war position of workers and trade unions was not to be prejudiced by such wartime changes. Wage guarantees in the case of displacement of skilled labour were also given. Thus, paragraph 5 of Schedule II declared that

The relaxation of existing demarcation restrictions or admission of semi-skilled or female labour shall not affect adversely the rates customarily paid for the job. In cases where men who ordinarily do the work are adversely affected thereby, the necessary readjustments shall be made so that they can maintain their previous earnings.[7]

Though a succession of wage regulation orders issued throughout the war sought to apply these exceedingly prolix and tortuous guidelines, originally set out in ministry Circulars 'L2' and 'L3', to munitions workers employed in different trades,[8] the promotion of statutory wage regulation was predominantly conducted by negotiating or arbitration bodies other than the munitions tribunal. Indeed, the volume of such business settled without resort to legal adjudication was staggering.[9] Perhaps the wages guarantee question arising from dilution was not perceived by trade unionists or employers as justiciable by the tribunal, or perhaps practical difficulties over the application of the guarantee did not in fact materialize frequently.

Moreover, the obstacles to the legal enforcement of dilution were not only the product of the idiosyncratic drafting of the statute. They were also a consequence of the protracted procedures to be followed in ascertaining whether, under Section 4(3), a 'rule, practice or custom' did in fact 'tend . . . to

---

[7] There was some fudging at the margins, particularly in the cases of unskilled workers who were not mentioned in the schedule, and also in the case of female workers on time rates whose work did not include the more complex operations which skilled men continued to perform (most notably, the 'setting-up' of machinery). None the less, the clause purported to guarantee no loss of earnings for skilled men. It also sought to ensure the customary rate for semi-skilled males on skilled work; though whether, in the case of diluted labour, the skilled rate applied to *all* the tasks customarily undertaken by skilled craftsmen, even when the latter, prior to dilution, had been performing work of a lesser standard, was hotly debated. Finally, the customary rate was guaranteed for female piece-workers, as well as for female time-workers in the uncommon event that they were undertaking all the work which a skilled man would have performed prior to, or during, the war.

[8] For details, see *OHMM*, vol. v, pts. ii and iii, *passim*.

[9] The comprehensive list of arbitration proceedings is published in the *12th Report of Proceedings Under the Conciliation Act 1896 etc.*, pp. 1919, xiii (391), 1.

restrict production or employment'. Thus, in the first instance, the question was one for the Board of Trade to settle or for the Board to refer to arbitration. Second, if a restrictive rule were thereby identified, then it became necessary to accuse a particular person, whether employer, trade union official, employers' association representative, or indeed anybody else, such as a journalist or political activist, of having 'induced' another to comply with the rule, practice, or custom. But as Lynden Macassey pointed out in April 1917,[10] Section 4(3) was largely inoperative, since an arbiter might conclude that a practice was restrictive without being able to suggest what should replace it. Moreover, if both employer and employees failed to refer the matter to the Board of Trade, then there was no machinery to enable a Government department, such as the Ministry of Munitions, to do so. Macassey did suggest amendments to remedy the situation. But they were floated at the wrong time, in the midst of the delicate negotiations in 1917 over the extension of dilution to private work, and were therefore not taken up.

In the event, there is surely no little irony in the fact that on the few occasions when Section 4(3) was cited before the tribunal, the complainants were frequently trade unionists and the defendants were employers.[11] We examined in Chapter 1 the case of *Guillet* v. *E. H. Bentall & Co Ltd.* in 1916, in which the *employer's* pre-war practice of refusing to employ trade unionists was held to be an unlawful restrictive practice in wartime.[12] Indeed, this method of proceeding was originally canvassed by J. C. Miles, a legal adviser at the Ministry of Munitions, when Messrs Tweedales & Smalley, a Rochdale textile engineering firm, triggered off the widespread industrial unrest in 1917 known as the 'May Strikes', following the company's attempts to extend dilution to private work.[13] Similarly, in another case, the employer's practice of suspending men for trivial offences

---

[10] *OHMM*, vol. v, pt. 1, p. 59.

[11] For an abortive attempt to use Section 4(3) against its supposed, intended targets, that is, against obstructive workers, see MUN 5/98/349/100, 'Prosecution of Workmen Before General Munitions Tribunals, December 6, 1915' (charge against 3 Newcastle workers dismissed, though they were found guilty of Ordering of Work offences).

[12] Cf. the case of the Loughborough employer, also discussed in ch. 1.

[13] *OHMM*, vol. vi, pt. 1, p. 104. See also n. 27. The approach suggested by Miles was in fact dropped, and a different section of the Act used against the firm.

was condemned as a restriction on output. The fly in the ointment, however, was that the employer in question was the Royal Small Arms Factory at Enfield, which, to the regret of the Metropolitan tribunal chairman Sir Robert Wallace, was immune from prosecution on the ground that 'the King can do no wrong'.[14] Finally, the only Scottish case under Section 4(3) which we have been able to discover arose in Motherwell, in the wake of the abolition of the leaving certificate scheme. In this episode, the ASE lodged a complaint that the managers of two firms, the Lanarkshire Steel Company and Messrs Marshall, Fleming & Co., had agreed among themselves, and without the knowledge of their foremen, to refrain from hiring each others' staff once the men became free to move.[15] The matter had in fact become academic by the time of the hearing, for the Ministry of Munitions had intervened to ensure that the two engineers in question could take up the new posts offered by the foreman of one of the companies. The ministry was no doubt already nervous at the prospect of unrest being stirred up by the behaviour of a number of employers' federations in England which continued, once leaving certificates had been abolished, to advise members to refuse to hire labour without the previous consent of their employers.[16] Therefore, the Ministry of Munitions added the prosecution of the above employers to the forceful guidance it swiftly issued to all employers, to the effect that such practices were contrary to Government policy and instructions.[17] Yet apparently they were not contrary to the law; at least, as far as the case of the Lanarkshire steel firms was concerned. For Sheriff Fyfe could not find sufficient evidence to establish that an infringement of Section 4(3) had occurred.[18] Thus yet another illustration of the substantive impotence of the provision was added to its sorry history.

Indeed, when G. D. H. Cole had commented in November 1915 on the progress of the Munitions Act, he had been scarcely premature when he had noted that

[14] ASE, *Monthly Journal and Report*, Nov. 1917, 38.
[15] *Glasgow Herald*, 14 Nov. 1917.
[16] ASE, *Monthly Journal and Report*, Nov. 1917, 32 (Yorkshire); ibid., 33 (Manchester); *Glasgow Herald*, 5 and 8 Nov. 1917; cf. ASCM, *6oth Quarterly Report*, 1 Sept. 1917, 2.
[17] ASE, *Monthly Journal and Report*, Nov. 1917, 20; AIMS, *Monthly Report*, Dec. 1917, 242.
[18] *Glasgow Herald*, 28 Nov. 1917.

It will be remembered that the Act was passed and secured assent mainly for two reasons. It was urged that strikes on war-work must be prevented, and that trade union rules limiting production must be abrogated for the period of the war. It is, to say the least of it, significant that neither of these points bulks at all large in the cases that have arisen under the Act. There have been hardly any strikes, and, in a careful survey of the available cases, I have only found a single case which turns on the refusal to abrogate trade union rules, and this is identical with one of the very few strike cases. *In short, while the Act is in daily use in every town where munitions are made, it is being used almost entirely for purposes other than those which were used as arguments for its passage.* [19]

Though Section 4(3) was, therefore, effectively a dead letter, we have, none the less, to record that the dilution question, as well as the more broadly defined issue of the removal of restrictive practices, did arise from time to time in tribunal hearings in Glasgow. Yet the most significant feature was the infrequency with which the matter was considered in legal proceedings. Prosecutions were rarely used as a means of removing opposition to compulsory overtime or of overcoming resistance to the employment of non-unionists, while the dilution scheme was advanced scarcely at all by applicants as a justification for the grant of leaving certificates. Moreover, even the principled opposition to the employment of women in place of men, which could be taken to the extent of a point-blank refusal to work alongside female workers, was reflected on Clydeside, so far as can be gathered, in the prosecution of a single workman at a steel works, rather than at an engineering shop where male trade unionists were thought to be more sensitive to the introduction of female dilutees. It is not, however, clear from the newspaper report that the introduction of women into the steel firm, Stewart & Lloyds, entailed *any* dilution of labour as narrowly conceived. Nor can it be confirmed from the report that the prosecuted workman was himself a time-served craftsman whose job skills were rendered vulnerable to female encroachment. [20]

It may, indeed, be suggested that the determined campaign by the craft unions for wage guarantees for skilled workers,

[19] *Nation*, 20 Nov. 1915. Italics in original. The case to which he referred was probably the boilermakers' strike at Thorneycroft of Southampton. See ch. 1.

[20] *Glasgow Herald*, 8 July 1916.

culminating in the issue by the Ministry of Munitions both of Circulars L2 and L3 (above) and a constant stream of statutory successors designed to reassure the skilled trade unions, only served to distort the scale of the threat facing such workers in the Clyde district. For the magnitude of their 'problem' is underlined by the ironic discovery that the only wage regulation hearing before the Glasgow tribunal directly relevant to the dilution question exposed the difficulties which confronted *semi-skilled* workers, rather than those facing the skilled workers themselves.

The case, in fact, touches the very core of dilution in that the complainant, John Cairney, was a semi-skilled workman transferred to skilled work, but denied the craftsman's wage.[21] He had joined Beardmore at Dalmuir as a labourer in February 1916, and after about five months was put on to a lathe, turning base plugs for shells. Subsequently, he was transferred to the gun-mounting shop where he was undertaking a class of work which prior to the war would have been performed by a time-served turner. As a dilutee, Cairney would therefore have been entitled to rely upon Article 2 of Circular L3, which, as embodied in subsequent statutory orders, enabled semi-skilled or unskilled male workers employed on work identical to that customarily undertaken by skilled labour to obtain the rates to which skilled workers were entitled. As Sheriff Fyfe realized during the tribunal hearing, the logical conclusion was that once put on to work hitherto performed by a skilled workman, a dilutee 'automatically becomes entitled to the skilled trades-man's time rate of pay, whatever may be the dilutant's [sic] own skill, or want of skill, in doing the work'.[22] While Sheriff Fyfe, not altogether surprisingly, took this to be, 'a result too absurd to be entertained for a moment,'[23] it did, none the less, reflect the fact that most (though not all) of a skilled craftsman's work was graded as less skilled. Craft rates were, in effect, being paid because the *residual* skilled tasks could only be performed by time-served workmen.[24] Cairney himself lacked the all-round

---

[21] Ibid., 14, 25 May 1917; *Cairney* v. *William Beardmore & Co. Ltd.*, 1917 SMAR 102–8, 30 June 1917.

[22] Ibid., 103.

[23] Ibid.

[24] See Charles More, *Skill and the English Working Class, 1870–1914*, London, 1980, ch. 2; discussed below.

competence of the skilled craftsman. He was undertaking only roughing work which, prior to the war, either second or third year apprentices could perform. He had not in fact progressed to the finishing work which only the skilled turner was able to undertake in the gun-mounting shop at Dalmuir. For under the Dalmuir dilution agreement, he had still to demonstrate to a skilled overseer that he could work without supervision. Therefore, Sheriff Fyfe had no difficulty in holding that he was not employed on work 'identical to that customarily undertaken by skilled labour . . .'.

No doubt the employer was pleased at the outcome of the hearing inasmuch as a class of dilutees was denied access to the skilled rate so long as the *employer* (and this point was emphasized in the judgment) was of the opinion that the work of the dilutee was not 'identical' to that performed by the craftsman. The ASE, of course, saw the decision as a blow to its policy of demanding the full, skilled rate for dilutees performing any portion of work formerly undertaken by skilled workers.[25] In this respect, whereas most decisions by the Glasgow tribunal in the sphere of wartime wage regulation might be said to have been tactical, the *Cairney* decision was surely more profound. It was, in fact, strategic.[26]

There is, moreover, little evidence that legal disputes over restrictive practices took place before munitions tribunals elsewhere. Thus, whether mediated through the vehicles of Ordering of Work prosecutions, wage complaints, leaving certificate applications, or even Section 4(3) itself, the conspi-

[25] Thus cf. ASE, *Monthly Journal and Report*, June 1918, 31-2 where, to the Middlesex district delegate's 'unbounded disgust', *Cairney* was successfully cited against the union's claim. None the less, the *Cairney* decision did emphasize once again those indispensable qualities displayed by craftsmen, which wilder and more speculative journalistic exposés, foretelling the demise of the skilled all-rounder, chose to ignore. Whether this indirect vindication of the prized status of time-served engineers offered any consolation to the ASE is, however, doubtful.

[26] Cf. the case of the labourer in a Clyde engine shop who found that he had to work harder to keep pace with his craftsmen who had been transferred from skilled time rates to the premium bonus system. As mates could not be accommodated within the new payments scheme, the labourer's extra exertions went unrewarded: another example of workshop changes hurting workers other than the skilled craftsmen. See *Glasgow Herald*, 16 Aug. 1917.

cuous lack of legal proceedings over dilution which obtained for Glasgow broadly mirrored the picture nation-wide.[27]

THE SUBSTANCE OF DILUTION

Apart from the difficulties presented by the phrasing of the legislation, there is another straightforward explanation as to why the express statutory prohibition on restrictive practices was, as Sir George Askwith admitted, 'soon found to be of small value'.[28] The simple fact is that dilution, as narrowly conceived, was not itself an issue of substance during the war, though its symbolic significance to Government, employers, and trade unionists cannot be over-exaggerated.

For example, Reid has recently argued that in shipbuilding the threat posed to craftsmen by 'extensive mechanisation and dilution'[29] did not materialize. Only 1,000 women were in fact introduced into the yards, scarcely at all replacing men,[30] prompting the conclusion that the Government's 'publicity about extensive dilution in the shipbuilding industry was little more than morale-boosting propaganda'.[31] It is possible that the

[27] For minor exceptions, see ASE, *Monthly Journal and Report*, May 1916, 36, concerning the subsequently withdrawn prosecution of a Sheffield engineer for having refused to perform work on certain lathes; ibid., June 1916, 36, *re* the prosecution of 5 Welsh engineers for having refused to take on work abandoned by ship's engineers. The ASE complained both of failure to consult before changes in working practices were implemented and also that the tribunal had no jurisdiction until Board of Trade arbitration had been decided. The prosecution was therefore adjourned, presumably *sine die*. Finally, the exceptional tribunal prosecution of Messrs Tweedales & Smalley in fact took place under Section 4(4) and Schedule II, para. 7 to the Act. This concerned the employer's duty to give due notice of changes, wherever practicable, and also opportunity for local consultation with his workmen. The dispute arose when craftsmen were ordered by the firm to instruct women previously on shell work how to operate grinding machines on ring spindles, so as to enable commercial work to be undertaken. The firm were fined a total of £35, plus £21 costs. The fullest account of the tribunal proceedings is in *OHMM*, vol. VI, pt. I, 102–6. See also n. 13.

[28] Askwith, *Industrial Problems and Disputes*, London, 1920, p. 391. He went on to argue that, 'In practice, employers tried to make use of this section . . .'; ibid. This may, of course, have been true in respect to 'pre-trial' procedure. The tribunals, however, as we have shown, had little part to play in this activity.

[29] Reid, 'Dilution, trade unionism and the state', p. 53.

[30] Cf., Scott and Cunnison, *Industries of the Clyde Valley during the War*, Oxford, 1924, pp. 86–7, who pointed to the limited, but none the less wide-ranging, penetration of women into the Clyde shipyards.

[31] Reid, 'Dilution, trade unionism and the state', p. 51.

impact of dilution in the engineering trades was no more significant in substantive terms, despite the hostility engendered, though there had been technological innovations during the war in branches of production engineering (for example, in screw gauge manufacture) which suggested that not all engineering craftsmen were indispensable. None the less, it is arguable that in engineering also the demand for dilution was little more than the symbolic rallying cry of a Government continuously pressed by the military to multiply munitions output.

Indeed, the brief but careful account of wartime dilution presented by Charles More emphasizes that on the Clyde the 'complete substitution of women for skilled men was only rarely effected'.[32] Indeed, the Ministry of Munitions itself considered in 1916 that there had been 'no clear cases where a woman was doing all the work customarily done by a fully skilled tradesman'.[33] In the exceptional case, it was, as an example from Beardmore illustrated, technically possible for semi-skilled and unskilled workers, male and female, to undertake the entire repertoire of tasks customarily performed by skilled craftsmen. But in this example, eighty-eight fitters, turners and machinemen had been replaced by 600 other workers. In other words, not only had extreme subdivision of labour taken place, which required many times the numbers of staff previously employed in order that the entire work be performed; but, were it not for the exigencies of war, such manpower deployment would have involved financially crippling outlays for the employers, a point which they readily acknowledged in justifying the continued employment of the craftsman after the war and the maintenance of his rate during it. Whenever women and lesser skilled males replaced an equal number of skilled fitters or turners, they were invariably, as at the engineering firm of Weir's of Cathcart, put on to scraping, rough turning, and boring, that is, on to the less precise areas of the craftsman's all-round duties:[34] indeed, precisely the nature of the work undertaken at Beardmore's Dalmuir yard by John Cairney, whose unsuccessful claim to the craftsman's rate we examined earlier.

[32] More, *Skill and the English Working Class*, p. 30.
[33] Ibid.
[34] Ibid.

Thus, as More has concluded,[35] not only did women scarcely ever perform all the work customarily undertaken by skilled men; but even the up-grading of semi-skilled men to skilled status seems to have amounted to only 4 per cent of all changes in working practices registered with the Ministry of Munitions.[36]

CONCLUSION

The wartime legislation concerning dilution was no more than a smokescreen behind which the Government could advance its campaign to tighten up factory discipline. Dilution could not be imposed through legal proceedings because dilution was not a practical problem of substance on Clydeside. Indeed, even if it had been, the legislative provisions were too unwieldy to permit of a smooth application of Section 4(3). In the light of both these reasons, the virtual absence of cases on dilution before the munitions tribunal is explained. Dilution, however, remained of enormous symbolic importance to the participants; and it is in this respect that the relevant provision of the Munitions Act could be perceived as a weapon of considerable potency.

[35] Ibid., pp. 30–1.

[36] Yet the picture presented above does, of course, dwell on the most visible manifestation conjured up by a campaign of dilution, that is, upon the rapid and expansive deployment of women in the metals section of industry, hitherto lightly penetrated by female labour. But dilution, as more broadly conceived, entailed not just the replacement of skilled craftsmen by women and less-skilled men. It also embraced the inter-changeability of classes of workers across craft lines as well as the suspension of internal lines of demarcation; the deployment of technological innovation, including the introduction of pneumatic, hydraulic, and electric tools; and a wide variety of other changes in working practices. Thus the 'Transformation of Industry', as Sidney Webb described the process, extended not only to the 'relationship of the operatives to the machines and of the various grades and classes of operatives to each other; and, above all, as regards the grades, classes, ages, trades and sex of the operatives employed'. It extended also to the speeding up of production, and to the abandonment of traditional notions of what constituted 'a fair day's work', or of customarily agreed times for different jobs. Thus, extending far beyond the machine question, which was the conventional understanding of dilution, the tidal wave of changes ultimately swept into its path 'the hours of labour, mealtimes, overtime and holidays; the methods and rates of remuneration; the conditions of engagement, suspension and dismissal; [and] the disciplinary code with its fines and other penalties'. Many of the latter issues did, of course, form the subject-matter of tribunal proceedings. For the quotations, see Sidney Webb, *The Restoration of Trade Union Conditions*, London, 1917, p. 27; cf. review in the *Shipbuilder*, xvii (Sept. 1917), 81–4.

CHAPTER 10

Conclusions

INTRODUCTION

When Sheriff Fyfe came to deliver his valedictory message on the closure of the Glasgow munitions tribunal on 11 April 1921,[1] he found himself sucked into an orgy of mutual back-slapping and tributes on the part of the assembled audience of regular advocates and tribunal assessors. The engineering union official William Brodie, for example, made an impassioned speech regretting the passing of the tribunal, and called for the establishment of similar machinery in the future. One of the employers' assessors, Sam Mavor of Mavor & Coulson Ltd., together with Archibald Gilchrist of Barclay Curle shipyard, echoed these sentiments, and spoke of the 'calamity' in prospect if the experience of Fyfe's tribunal were to be cast aside.[2] But it was the joint representative of the Clyde shipbuilders' and engineers' association who neatly (if perhaps unintentionally) pinpointed the fatal weakness in those optimistic sentiments which seemed in keeping with the clubbable atmosphere of the County Buildings where the tribunal hearings had been conducted. For while regretful that industry would become bereft of the services of Sheriff Fyfe's tribunal in the future, the association's spokesman, David Higgins, none the less felt bound to say that 'They were glad that the cessation of the Ministry of Munitions and the consequent termination of the Tribunals had come about, because it was the severing of the last tentacle of the octopus of Government control which gripped industry and employers and employed alike during the past six years.'[3] Yet the absence of support from the Clyde shipbuilding and

[1] *Glasgow Herald*, 12 Apr. 1921.

[2] As James Gavin, the chief conciliation officer at the ministry in Glasgow (and a former Iron and Steel Workers' Union official) informed the ministry in London, 'The speakers do not appear to have any real constructive policy to submit on this point but there was clear unanimity on the general theory.' See LAB 2/676/34, 'Restoration of Pre-War Practices Act 1919 etc. . . .', Gavin to T. S. Owen, 12 Apr. 1921.

[3] *Glasgow Herald*, 12 Apr. 1921.

engineering employers' association for the retention of the munitions tribunals perhaps signified something more than this. For as Cronin observes of the experience of war controls,

intervention often meant an increase in the leverage of workers at the same time as it involved the co-option of businessmen and labour officials in the daily tasks of administration . . . [with employers] complaining vociferously over state intervention in general and the government's conciliatory attitude towards labour in particular.[4]

Employers' objections to legal controls, it is suggested, were therefore not simply a ritual genuflection to a theoretical postulate. Their objections were also to the fact that, paradoxically, labour controls frequently had the nasty habit of boomeranging on *employers,* who might find themselves, rather than their workmen, condemned at the bar of the munitions tribunal and compelled to mend their ways. Indeed there could not, perhaps, have been a clearer affirmation that the boot was on the other foot than the fact that the winding-up of the Glasgow tribunal left a number of *workers'* complaints under statute high and dry without means to pursue them.[5] Thus, as we turn to the broad question of the evaluation of the Munitions Acts as an exercise in wartime employment legislation, this double-edged quality, hidden under the surface of an ostensibly labour-restrictive code, will become more clearly apparent.

A SUCCESSFUL MEASURE?

At a superficial level, the 'success' of the Munitions Act is attested by military victory; by the achievement of the British State in driving its labour force to continue the manufacture of munitions of war in sufficient quantity that the enemy's fighting capacity and morale at last collapsed. It seems probable, for example, that munitions workers were responsive to ministry initiatives, backed by legal sanctions, to eliminate the worst excesses of slack timekeeping; and that the nomadic propensity

---

[4] James E. Cronin, 'Coping with Labour, 1918–1926', in James E. Cronin and Jonathan Schneer (eds.), *Social Conflict and the Political Order in Modern Britain*, London, 1982, pp. 118, 139 n.

[5] LAB 2/435/25, 'EEF Correspondence etc. . . .', Gavin to Ministry of Labour, 5 Apr. 1921.

of skilled craftsmen to flit from factory to factory in search of higher rewards, with its consequent effects on wage drift, was significantly hindered by the introduction of the leaving certificate scheme.[6] But to measure the contribution of the Munitions Act to the achievement of the 'great munition feat' is surely a quantitative impossibility,[7] given the variety of further factors such as manpower allocations, productivity, technological innovation, capital investment, managerial skills, and morale of the labour force, which would require to be evaluated. Indeed, as early as November 1915, the *New Statesman* had caustically remarked that 'It is doubtful whether the net effect of the Act itself has been to increase our resources by a single shell.'[8] Moreover, the embarrassed tone of the *Official History's* *post mortem* on the Clyde troubles in 1915–16 might justifiably lead one to infer that munitions production had been increased in spite, rather than because, of the existence of labour controls. Thus it concluded that

In a chronicle of the relations between the Ministry of Munitions and Labour it is inevitable that administrative difficulties, disappointed expectations, mistakes, strikes, grievances and failings should occupy a large space and dominate the argument. The uneventful steady work alike of the Department and of employers and workpeople afford little

[6] No turnover figures for factories in the post-July 1915 period can be located to compare with those cited by Henry Clay for 3 armament firms between Apr. and May 1915. This showed that for every 100 workers employed, 50 left the establishment. See Clay, *The Problem of Industrial Relations*, London, 1929, p. 61. In fact, no sudden dislocation of the labour market, through widespread shifts of employment, occurred immediately on repeal of the leaving certificate scheme. For the Clyde district, see USB, *Monthly Report*, Nov. 1917, 21. For elsewhere, see ASE, *Monthly Journal and Report*, Nov. 1917, 39 (West of England); ibid., Dec. 1917, 26 (Sheffield). Where movement *did* occur, it was construed by trade union officials as a protest against unsatisfactory employers. See ibid., Nov. 1917, 32 (Yorkshire); ibid., Dec. 1917, 29 (West of England). Abolition was claimed to have had an impact on wages in that the Ministry of Munitions thereby lost some of its power to resist wage demands as a result of which, declared Clay, an 'avalanche of claims' was submitted, eventually leading to the 'administrative confusion' of the $12\frac{1}{2}\%$ wage award extended to ever-increasing categories of munitions workers. See Clay, *The Problem of Industrial Relations*, p. 66. For the $12\frac{1}{2}\%$ award, see ch. 6.

[7] As a team of researchers, examining the effects of the Employment Act 1980, have recently remarked, 'The use and impact of law cannot be determined in a mathematical fashion.' See Kahn *et al.*, *Picketing: Industrial Disputes, Tactics and the Law*, London, 1983, p. 194.

[8] *New Statesman*, 13 Nov. 1915. Cf. ibid., 19 Aug. 1916, 460–1 for similar views at a later date.

material for the imagination, and can only be recorded in statistical tables of output, from which individuality, human nature, and life itself have been eliminated. But a false impression of the achievement of the country can only be avoided by bearing constantly in mind the fact that the troubles and failures set forth in this narrative were only eddies in the great stream of national effort. It is the fashion in some circles to deride voluntary action and exalt coercion. But such coercive measures as the Government adopted were only rendered practicable by the free will and forbearance of the great majority of the people. The voluntary spirit was not superseded. It was at most disguised from the public view.[9]

Indeed, it should not be forgotten that the presence of a legal code did not automatically result in the abandonment of voluntarist methods of settling disputes. In the first instance, not every prosecution was pursued to the bitter end. Many tribunal complaints were settled without a formal hearing having taken place, wherever the chairman thought it preferable to rely on informal channels to correct perceived failings. An anonymous tribunal chairman recorded that

A telephone message has remedied many a grievance and secured observance of the principles of the Act. Just as a personal note to a workman has often improved his timekeeping, so a timely hint to an employer that a foreman's methods had become too arbitrary has prevented shop friction which might well have led to serious trouble. The general policy has been the open door to all parties and the prevailing spirit conciliation.[10]

While much of the stress in the above remarks was laid on what were evidently considered as examples of individual delinquency, the management of collective conflict (as we shall also see shortly) characterized the 'voluntarist' initiatives of the tribunal. Thus, in one case, eighteen workers from a Glasgow shipyard had been prosecuted by their employer for having refused to comply with management instructions.[11] In retaliation, they themselves submitted leaving certificate applications. Sheriff Craigie, however, successfully arranged a settlement satisfactory to each side, thereby earning the gratitude both of

---

[9] *OHMM*, vol. IV, pt. II, p. 34.

[10] Anon., 'Munitions Tribunals', *Juridical Review*, XXXI (1919), at 159.

[11] *Glasgow Herald*, 18 Apr. 1916.

William Mackie, the Boilermakers' Society official, and of A. S. Biggart representing the employer.

Apart from this expedient, more calculated steps were taken to avoid becoming entangled in the legal reticulation. The experiment at Whitehead Torpedo Works, to which reference has been made in Chapter 7, is perhaps the most notable example of the deliberate refusal by a company to rely on the Munitions Act for the enforcement of factory discipline. But other instances of a less formal and institutionalized nature can be cited, where union officials sought to persuade employers to bypass the tribunal machinery. The Sheffield ASE delegate reported in November 1915 that

> We are having a few cases at the Munitions Tribunals, but mostly by reason of the arbitrary manner of one or two foremen or managers who expect impossibilities from the workmen. I have suggested to one or two large firms that it would be much better if they would make their complaints to our D. C., and give us an opportunity of investigating their complaints before bringing [them] before the Tribunal, which only creates a feeling of resentment which is not at all desirable.[12]

Indeed, as we saw in Chapter 7, the tentative moves to involve local trade union committees in the administration of management disciplinary processes sought to combine in one effort a genuine venture into law-avoidance, an ideological initiative to foster the corporate spirit, and a pragmatic attempt at damage limitation.

Moreover, the number of strikes eventually settled without recourse to legal proceedings may well have exceeded 2,000 (on the footing that the total number of strikes between August 1914 and March 1918 in all industries was 2,504).[13] In particular, the effective immunity from prosecution of many significant strikes, such as one which occurred in February 1916 at Lang of Johnstone[14] over attempts by the ministry to bring about dilution of labour without engineering union agreement, is symptomatic of a broader trend. For even a host of minor strikes were settled voluntarily without the slightest whiff of impending

---

[12] ASE, *Monthly Journal and Report*, Nov, 1915, 52.

[13] Moses, 'Compulsory Arbitration in Great Britain during the War', *Journal of Political Economy*, XXVI (1918), 889.

[14] Hinton, *The First Shop Stewards' Movement*, London, 1973, pp. 68, 146; McLean, *Legend of Red Clydeside*, Edinburgh, 1983 p. 68.

tribunal proceedings to jog the parties into urgent remedial action. Typical is this report from an ASE delegate:

> At Aylesbury, our men, disgusted with the dilatoriness of the firm in applying national awards, left work and remained out for six days. At an interview held whilst the men were out, we secured the offer of the firm to settle our claims by immediately paying up to the full the national awards, including the December 5*s*. plus $2\frac{1}{2}\%$ on piecework prices. The members commenced work on 12th November, and we are now requesting retrospective payment of those overdue awards by application to the Ministry of Labour.[15]

Few could have remained unaware that the Munitions Act, in the words of the *Official History*,[16] 'did not prevent strikes from happening [nor] even reduce them to negligible proportions'. Moreover, even before the war had ended and when the legal prohibition on strikes was still in existence, the Government-sponsored Whitley Committee on the relations between unions and management did not attempt to disguise the obvious. The Fourth Report of the Committee concluded that 'The experience of compulsory arbitration during the war has shown that it is not a successful method of avoiding strikes, and in normal times it would undoubtedly prove even less successful.'[17]

Indeed, the minimal deterrent effect of a prosecution track record which revealed that the number of workers convicted of illegal striking up till July 1916 was just over one-fifth of 1 per cent of those actually participating in such strikes,[18] and that the amounts paid in fines amounted to less than one-sixteenth of 1 per cent of the statutory maximum of £5 for each day or part-day on strike,[19] no doubt encouraged the atmosphere of disregard for the law.

But perhaps the most savage indictment of the efficacy of the Act may be located in the analysis of its relationship to the

[15] ASE, *Monthly Journal and Report*, Dec. 1917, 28. Other sample illustrations include a week-long strike at Barr & Stroud in Glasgow over an arbitration award of bonus payments. See ibid., Mar. 1918, 20. Also a one-day stoppage of blacksmiths at Hawthorn Leslie at Hebburn, on Tyneside, arising out of complaints over physical working conditions at the yard. See ABIS, *1st Quarterly Report*, Jan.–Mar. 1917, 2244.

[16] *OHMM*, vol. IV, pt. II, p. 9.

[17] PP 1918, Cd. 9099, VII, 763 (1918); *Labour Gazette*, July 1918, 262.

[18] Moses, 'Compulsory Arbitration in Great Britain during the War', pp. 896–7.

[19] I. G. Sharp, *Industrial Conciliation and Arbitration in Great Britain*, London, 1950, p. 318.

Government's dilution campaign. As we saw in the previous chapter, the 'relevant' penal provisions were, on this criterion, mere excess baggage.

With such a variable track record covering disparate aspects of labour control, it has to be admitted that any assessment of the Act from the perspective of wartime Government policy-makers is likely to be inconclusive. Like the proverbial curate's egg, the Act could be said to have been good in parts. Such an analysis will, however, not suffice for our purposes, though it does hint at the ambiguities and paradoxes which inform our own summation of the Act and of the experiences of munitions workers at the hands of the Glasgow tribunal.

Broadly speaking, at the level of structure, the Act sought to induce the statization of trade unions, endeavouring to shift essentially voluntarist organizations whose rationale had been premissed on the maximization of sectional interests, towards objectives which conflicted with those narrow terms of reference. As Beatrice Webb had predicted in June 1915, 'If the Government persists [with the Munitions Bill] there will be considerable and perhaps dangerous reaction against the patriotism of some of the [union] leaders.'[20] In the event, the pleas for co-operation by national trade union leaders such as J. T. Brownlie of the Engineers, were repudiated, and the local officials, such as Sharp, Bunton, and Brodie, whom the CWC had despised for their sell-out over the Munitions Act, were themselves swept up in the mass mobilization on Clydeside to demand the repeal of the more obnoxious provisions of the Act.[21] The reaction of rank-and-file trade unionists was in part directed against the national leadership's policy of collaboration, which appeared to sanction employers' efforts to continue promoting their class interests while denying to trade unionists the opportunity to defend theirs.

For, at the same time as the State was attempting to alter, albeit temporarily, the character of trade unionism, rank-and-file trade unionists were being assailed, through the Munitions Act, from another quarter. As Beveridge, writing shortly after

[20] M. I. Cole (ed.), *Beatrice Webb's Diary 1912–1924*, London, 1952, pp. 41–2.

[21] For these points, see Rubin, 'The Enforcement of the Munitions of War Acts, 1915–1917, with Particular Reference to Proceedings before the Munitions Tribunal in Glasgow, 1915–1921', Warwick Univ. Ph.D. thesis (1984), ch. 2.

the war, disclosed,[22] 'I have no doubt that the real difficulty about the Munitions Act is that the statutory powers of compulsion were given to the employers—i.e. the workman's natural enemies.'[23] In fact, what emerged was a tension between two distinct conceptualizations of law, that is, between what Donald Black[24] has described as social-welfare law on the one hand, and entrepreneurial law on the other. The first-named model, which promotes a 'proactive' legal system, assumes that the good of citizens is defined by Government with the help of interest groups. Governments therefore *impose* the law, rather than merely make it available. The latter entrepreneurial model, which stimulates a 'reactive' legal system, assumes, on the other hand, that each citizen voluntarily and rationally pursues his or her own interests on a utilitarian basis, with the greatest good deriving from selfish, atomized enterprise. As Black observes, it is the legal analogue of the market economy.

Yet, by enabling individual employers such as Cammell Laird to institute proceedings, and by enabling firms to withhold leaving certificates, the Munitions Act, an avowedly proactive corporatist measure, was in fact relentlessly permitting, and being *seen* to permit, the pursuit of an individualist entrepreneurial initiative. *This* was Beveridge's 'real difficulty', and one consequence was the sense of outrage when trade unionists inveighed against the 'Prussian' tendencies of employers who sought to drag them through the tribunal on a vindictive charge. As with those landlords threatening to evict soldiers' wives who could not afford rent increases, such proceedings under the Munitions Act not only constituted a violation of the moral economy of the district,[25] but could be construed by munitions workers as being in direct conflict with Government efforts to promote unity. Thus, the Act could be understood as

---

[22] MUN 5/328/160/R.2.

[23] Beveridge's idea was that a labour officer be attached to each factory with sole authority to grant or to withhold leaving certificates, as well as to institute prosecutions against workmen. Though Llewellyn Smith was sceptical that a sufficient number of 'discreet' officers could be recruited, the latter step was, of course, eventually taken in the 1917 Act, while the initiative in respect to leaving certificates till their abolition remained firmly with the employers. See ibid. Cf. *OHMM*, vol. IV, pt. II, p. 33n.

[24] Donald Black, *The Behavior of Law*, New York, 1976.

[25] Cf. Joseph Melling, 'Scottish Industrialists and the Changing Character of Class Relations in the Clyde Region, c. 1880–1918', in Tony Dickson (ed.), *Capital and Class in Scotland*, Edinburgh, 1982, esp. at p. 126; see also ch. 3, n. 46.

an instrument in the separate armouries both of private employers and also of the State, in a context where the distinction between the two tended to be maintained by all but the 'advanced' minority of trade unionists closely associated with the shop stewards' movement.[26] Perhaps this duality, which could, on occasion, paint the Government in a benign light and the employers in a divisive one, was one pointer to the non-revolutionary stance adopted by the reconstructed Labour Party in 1918.[27]

CONFLICT 'MANAGEMENT'

It has long been recognized that, at the institutional level, one of the more sensitive points within the British system of industrial relations is the level of the workplace itself. While significant innovations in the development of substantive and procedural norms, such as industry-wide bargaining and wider trade union recognition, emerged during the war, none the less there tended to be lacking any institutional mechanism at the shop-floor level (where the Munitions Act had its most direct impact) which could handle the multitude of problems arising daily in the factories and shipyards. In the absence of any satisfactory local machinery for resolving rapidly and efficiently those differences which the extraordinary demands of war production generated (an engineering industry shop stewards' agreement in late 1917 did offer a potential though belated remedy), resort to direct action, entailing breaches of the Munitions Act, became commonplace. As Phelps Brown has remarked,

In the typical British situation, [the factory worker's] union will have negotiated no agreement that regulates his relations with management in detail, showing what rights and obligations he has in the issues that arise in the course of his daily work and his service with the firm; nor will he always or often have ready access to a grievance procedure on which he can rely as definite and expeditious. Bargaining on matters that affect his interests goes on at his workplace, but in a rough and

---

[26] Many employers, of course, consistently viewed strikes as being directed against the Government rather than against themselves. It suited them to do so.

[27] Cf. J. M. Winter, 'A Note on the Reconstruction of the Labour Party in 1918', *Scottish Labour History Society Journal*, No. 12, 1978, 63–9.

ready way which, because it does not recognize a procedure, cannot stigmatize departures from it. So situated, the worker cannot be blamed for fighting his own battle. So long as these conditions persist, legal sanctions are unlikely to deter him.[28]

As an explanation for continued industrial unrest, such a conclusion is unexceptionable. But it is also unexceptional and unsurprising. What is of deeper interest, however, is that the institutional mechanism *was* improvised. For if wartime industrial relations, like Nature, abhorred a vacuum, then the munitions tribunal itself rushed in where others feared, or were unwilling, to tread. Thus the tribunal, as we have seen, became the focus for campaigns waged by trade unionists to activate a further outlet through which collective bargaining might be conducted, given the tight reins on wage negotiations imposed through centralized direction and through the operation of the leaving certificate scheme. At first resistant, then reluctant, and finally indulgent, the tribunal was transmogrified over time, becoming yet another legal institution in which form and content were divided one from the other. Indeed, so much so that Fyfe himself proposed the legitimization of this subtle transformation through the inauguration of local arbitration tribunals.[29] Collective bargaining by litigation might certainly appeal to those 'sympathetic to the pragmatic behaviour characteristic of trade union officials (including most socialist ones) [who] see only sectionalism and a readiness to settle for modest gains'.[30] And no doubt it could be said that those trade unionists who engaged in such intricate proceedings had much to be modest about. For many of those trade union officials pushed into the tribunal crucible to indulge in sharp verbal exchanges with the employers' representatives and with the tribunal chairmen, conflict management was, more often than not, the name of the game being enacted. And, indeed, it was a game in which the tribunal chairmen, conscious that there was

---

[28] E. H. Phelps Brown, 'Unofficial Strikes and the Law', *Three Banks Review*, No. 83, 1969, 3–19, at 12.

[29] See ch. 5. Also Rubin, 'Labour Courts and the Proposals of 1917–19', *Industrial Law Journal*, XIV (1985).

[30] James Hinton, 'The Rise of a Mass Labour Movement: Growth and Limits', in C. J. Wrigley (ed.), *A History of British Industrial Relations, 1875–1914*, Brighton, 1982, ch. 2, at p. 21.

more than one way to coax munitions workers to expedite production, found it necessary to co-operate, once the earlier dismal failures of legal coercion had become apparent. For the fact is that the Munitions Act, despite popular endorsement of the nationalistic aims which it, however imperfectly, embodied, was virtually in a no-win situation in respect to the 'rank and file', whether militant or moderate, radical or liberal, once it began to operate with bite, as the campaign to reform the Act clearly demonstrated.[31] Those radicals who criticized voluntarism for its inability or lack of will to transform capitalist economic relations into socialism were hardly likely to be appeased by corporatism, which, to them, appeared to supplement the domination of the capitalist employer with the coercive apparatus of state controls; while voluntarist-inclined trade unionists, for their part, would be fiercely critical of a corporatist law which, as they saw it, punished those who sought to pursue conduct which voluntarism considered legitimate, such as striking over wages, or over union recognition, or even over the employment of a non-unionist in a union shop. Given the existence of such oppositional forces to the Act, we would argue, therefore, that an important feature of its enforcement, certainly in Glasgow, was the slow emergence of an unspoken and somewhat inchoate collusion of the central figures in the tribunal machinery, the chairmen and workmen's representatives. Where they colluded was in the gradual, though not wholly complete, transition from set-piece conflict over rigorous law enforcement against major strikes (ch. 3), to the more discreet, subtle, and sensitive task of 'managing' industrial strife, shown particularly in the tribunal's handling of wage-related and Ordering of Work cases (ch. 5 and ch. 7). Moreover, without fatally harming the broad, consensus-based corporate goals which had been under stress in the first few months of the Act's existence, the 'reconstructed' tribunal's approach proved, in our view, ultimately successful as a technique of labour 'control'. There were, it is true, daunting impediments in the path of success. The Government had to obviate the hostility of a resentful and irritated labour force, while trade unionists had to divert their gazes, as best they could, from the punitive aspects of the tribunal. But in spite of the obstacles, both Government and

---

[31] Ch. 8, and Rubin, 'Enforcement of the Munitions of War Acts, 1915–1917', ch. 2.

trade unionists, albeit the more 'deserving' or more strategically important for the war effort, could derive *some* limited advantage from an otherwise rigid system. Thus, under the broader influence of the military effort and shifts in working-class morale, 'conflict management' appropriately describes the delicate task of teasing out the potential gains and losses for the participants.

Indeed, some years after the war, Henry Clay concluded that the 'control exercised over wages during the war . . . was rather a policy of interpreting than of superseding the play of supply and demand.'[32] In matching this description, the Glasgow munitions tribunal stumbled uncertainly towards becoming a kind of barometer of the social and political temperature, with judicial decision-making in the tribunal tending, with occasional exceptions, to respond to criteria such as the level of militancy or the relative importance of the class of work involved in the case. In wage-related hearings, Fyfe's local application encompassed both dogmatic refusals to budge in some cases, and tactical concessions to strategic groups of munitions workers in others, a tendency which became more noticeable from 1917.[33] In this respect, his wage regulation 'policy' bore comparison with shifting wage policy set nationally, which was also sensitive to the emerging atmosphere of war-weariness throughout the country.

THE CHARACTER OF GLASGOW TRADES UNIONISM

In respect to the tactics of trade union representatives at the tribunal, the delicate juridical cut and thrust, involving the

[32] Clay, *The Problem of Industrial Relations*, p. 72.
[33] There are indications from wage-related cases from 1916 onwards that Fyfe was less susceptible to granting leaving certificates to single applicants, airing grievances over their rates of pay, than to groups of applicants from the same firm. But he was not always consistent in this respect. There is also some evidence from the same period that engineering and shipbuilding claimants were more favourably treated than those from other trades. But again, the evidence should be treated cautiously in the light of exceptions to this tendency. In so far as one can claim to have detected the outlines of a pattern, however, it served both to pacify the more important groups of munitions workers (even if individual engineers or shipbuilding workers might sometimes experience a rebuff) and to discourage optimism amongst munitions workers from other sectors, such as iron and steel. Thus was conflict management exercised. For details, see Rubin, 'Enforcement of the Munitions of War Acts, 1915–1917', pp. 315–9.

lodging of complaints against employers, the submission of leaving certificate applications, and the vigorous approaches to defending prosecutions, were often promoted by union officials as much to contain their membership as to provoke them to more demonstrative and destructive conduct. Yet the paradox is that such robust though none the less inherently constitutional (and frequently successful) methods of proceeding could only be mounted by means of an assault on established levels of authority. The 'erosion of legitimacy' and the 'fundamental advances in consciousness' which Melling has detected for Glasgow prior to the war[34] seemed to blossom even among the bowler-hatted brigade of hitherto cautious and uninspiring local trade union officialdom. Certainly the pragmatic and resourceful exploitation of the munitions tribunal by trade unionists was principally directed to short-term gains; but the drive and determination, indeed bravado, which inspired their actions surely broke new ground in penetrating and rupturing the bonds of deference and relations of authority which had hitherto guaranteed the dignity of legal proceedings against insidious attacks on the law's ideological pretensions. Such an assault on the symbols of Government may not, of course, have pointed to the vista of possibilities for working people to wrest their entitlement in peacetime from State institutions. But no doubt the non-revolutionary, moderate, socialist Labour Party of 1918 was a congenial home for the likes of those veterans of the munitions tribunal who had successfully traded controlled aggression for wage concessions and modified punishments.

It has, of course, to be acknowledged that by mobilizing the Munitions Act, by counselling moderation, or by entreating their members to observe factory disciplinary rules, the local trade union officials, set apart from the rank-and-file, were liable to 'become "incorporated" into the collective bargaining machinery, and to occupy an "equivocal position" as "mediators of conflict" between employers and employed'.[35] Yet, as Lovell has pointed out, it is too simplistic to conclude that 'In

---

[34] Melling, 'Scottish Industrialists', p. 105.
[35] John Lovell, paraphrasing the argument of Keith Burgess, *The Origins of British Industrial Relations* (1975), in *British Journal of Industrial Relations*, XIV (1976), 112 (book review).

this situation, collective bargaining developed on the employers' terms.'[36] For it was the self-same local trade union leadership on Clydeside, the targets of CWC vilification, who frequently adopted an aggressive stance on behalf of their members during the tribunal hearings, by denouncing the Act following its exploitation by local employers.[37] Constitutionalism was to be stretched to its limit, the normal courtesies dispensed with, the restraints on moderate, 'civilized' and dignified proceedings deliberately cast aside. *Épater les bourgeois* may not have been their motto; but such boldness of denunciation must have been shocking to their respectable middle-class listeners. Indeed, as V. L. Allen has warned,

The distinction between unions [or officialdom] and rank-and-file is analytically unsound and empirically absent. It arises from an uncritical acceptance of conventional analyses of bureaucratization and an acceptance of appearances as reality [and] obscures a real understanding of trade unionism . . .[38]

In similar fashion, Van Gore has recently reminded us that the term 'rank and file' 'designates a dialectical relationship between leaders and led; it focuses attention on the ambiguities and problems of popular participation and control.'[39] Thus the relationship between the Glasgow 'rank and file' and local trade union officialdom, in respect to the Munitions Act, was much more complex and ambiguous than can be subsumed in any simple proposition which postulates a sharp and unbridgeable schism between the two. For the relationship between decentralized autonomy and local trade union officialdom on Clydeside was not inherently antithetical and hostile, with the latter straining to stifle the spontaneity of the former. The absorption of the local officials into the corporatist organs of the State did not mean abject capitulation to the domination of employers. For, paradoxically, it was in support of the aims of the wartime

[36] Ibid.

[37] That accusations of 'incorporation' were not wholly misplaced is none the less apparent from the assumption of office as tribunal assessors by some of the local trade union officials. They may well have concluded that that was a proper step to take in order to protect their members' interests under the Act.

[38] V. L. Allen, reviewing Tom Clarke and Laurie Clements (eds.), *Trade Unions under Capitalism* (1977), in *Industrial Relations Journal*, IX (1978), 80.

[39] Van Gore, 'Rank-and-File Dissent', in Wrigley (ed.), *A History of British Industrial Relations*, ch. 3, at p. 47.

industrial State that the officials were often roused to the vigorous condemnation of employers abusing their powers under the Munitions Act. The defence of class interests, in pursuit of which the officials could embark before the tribunal, could not only overlap with the 'national interest', but was, in such instances, indispensable to it. The full-time officials were no monolithic entity, intent on unconditional cooperation with employers and the Government. The Fairfield coppersmiths were, after all, following official union instructions.[40] Even the 'tuppence an hour' strike in February 1915 (ch. 3, n. 1) which led to the formation of the CWC, was acknowledged by William Gallacher to have enjoyed the stamp of limited official approval.

The strike was, and still is, wrongly referred to as an 'unofficial' strike. Such a term is entirely misleading. Branch officials, district officials and in some cases, executive officials (like myself) were involved. The more correct term for such a strike is 'spontaneous strike'. Such strikes have played an important part in the development of the trade union movement and are often recognized and supported by the national officials. Such a strike is necessary when something occurs, leaving only the option of submitting or fighting. It may be the introduction of a non-unionist, where trade union membership is insisted on by the union as a condition of employment. It may be a cut in a recognized rate or, as was the case at Weir's, the introduction of privileged workers from outside at the expense of Weir's own employees.[41]

This frank recognition by Gallacher that trade union officialdom was *not* invariably the enemy of devolved authority is the more surprising given his consistent vilification of the local full-time officials in Glasgow. He identified Bunton, Brodie, Sharp, John Thomson, and Lorimer as the embodiment of collaboration and class harmony with the employers and with the State.[42] Yet, as we have seen, such fulsome advocates of the national interest were not averse to casting aside noble sentiments when sectional wage claims were being pursued or when their constituents' workshop interests were seriously threatened by the iniquitous application of the Munitions Act.

---

[40] Gallacher, *Revolt on the Clyde*, London, 1936, p. 63, even claims that the imprisoned Fairfield shipwrights were acting under official union instructions.

[41] Ibid., p. 42. Cf. McLean, *Legend of Red Clydeside*, p. 12.

[42] Gallacher, *Revolt on the Clyde*, pp. 35, 37, 64, 81–3, 87–9. For Lorimer, see Tuckett, *The Blacksmiths' History*, London, 1975.

Perhaps part of the explanation for this dual perspective lay, first, in a need by the officials for some ritual genuflection toward populist sentiment within the ranks of local trade unionists. Second, the fact that the Munitions Act could be mobilized by an individual employer against their members meant that it was understandable for such officials to conceptualize the Act, not as a measure necessary in the national interest (an interest of which they approved), but as the private instrument of the employer. The capacity of law to individualize otherwise collective-political conflict thus ironically made it easier for trade union officials inveigled into the machinery of the corporatist munitions sector to view the legal assaults of the employers as the actions of those intent on maximizing *private* advantages, rather than as necessary steps in the restoration of order and unity to industrial relations, which the 'national interest' plainly demanded.

Indeed, the transformation of attitudes is well captured in the conversion of trade union leaders from enthusiastic support for the Munitions Act on its enactment, to insistent demands for its amendment, though not, significantly, its repeal.[43] Thus, within Glasgow, the views of W. G. Sharp of the Boilermakers, a member of both the local and general tribunals, a resolute defender of his members prosecuted before the tribunal, and object of savage criticism by the revolutionary shop stewards— 'Bill Sharp had ratted on the movement during the war—he was a boilermakers' official and had taken a job with the employers'[44]—adequately convey the transition. In replying to a presentation made to him by members of the Boilermakers' Society, he remarked that

At a time like this he supposed he would be expected to make some reference to the war. He felt strongly the many malicious statements which were being made against the working classes. The working men had never worked harder in their lives than they were doing now.

[43] For full details, see Rubin, 'Enforcement of the Munitions of War Acts, 1915–1917', ch. 2.

[44] McShane and Smith, *Harry McShane: No Mean Fighter*, London, 1978, p. 131. Cf. Gallacher, *Revolt on the Clyde*, p. 89, where it is claimed that Sharp became a technical adviser with the employers. In early 1917, Sharp's name was submitted by his union to the Ministry of Munitions as a temporary technical adviser. See USB, *Monthly Report*, Mar. 1917, 20. On his appointment to the 'Shipbuilding and Engineering Employers' Federation' [sic], see the *Shipbuilder*, xvi (June 1917), 324.

There had been a few slackers, there was no question about it, and they all knew what he would do with them. But he thought that every man in that room realised how necessary it was that everyone would have to do his utmost in order to bring the war to a successful conclusion. That led him on to make some reference to the Munitions Act. Although he had not been against it at the first, he never for a moment thought that it would be interpreted in the narrow, miserable one-sided manner in which it had been by certain employers. (Loud applause.)[45]

Thus while politically advanced rank-and-file movements conceived of the employers (together with union leaders) as part of the apparatus of the capitalist State, individuals like Sharp, who probably represented the dominant strand within the trade union movement, quickly became disillusioned, not only by the employers' contempt for the Government's assumedly corporate objectives, but also, to some extent, by the tribunal's apparent affirmation of this partisan behaviour. The typical response by local trade union officials was therefore not to repudiate the Munitions Act outright, as an implacable adversary beyond redemption. Instead, the reaction was to condemn its abuse and to endeavour to manipulate and re-orient the measure in order to expose the selfishness and inadequacies of the employers. Not only was a campaign of law reform, 'in the national interest', conducted at both the official and unofficial levels;[46] but the Glasgow tribunal proceedings themselves witnessed the hitherto patriotic and moderate local union officials conducting a vigorous and aggressive defence of those trade union members subjected to legal intimidation by their employers. In principle favouring a policy of industrial peace, compromise, and collaboration, the local officials such as Sharp, Brodie, and Bunton were, none the less, frequently resolute in defending their members before the tribunal.

One important qualification must, however, be made. Given the antipathy existing between the local officials and leading members of the CWC, it is no surprise to learn that prominent members of the latter, when prosecuted before the tribunals, were on occasion defended by persons other than their trade union representatives. For example, the shop stewards prosecuted after the deportation strikes in 1916 were defended by the

[45] USB, *Monthly Report*, Nov. 1915, 76; *Govan Press*, 22 Oct. 1915.
[46] Ch. 8, and Rubin, 'Enforcement of the Munitions of War Acts, 1915–1917', ch. 2.

politically sympathetic lawyer Rosslyn Mitchell,[47] while the
strikers prosecuted after the Dalmuir gun-mounting dispute in
December 1915 were also defended by a local solicitor. On the
other hand, it was Sam Bunton, the reviled ASE official, who
represented James Bridges, the Weir's shop steward who was
later deported, in an abortive prosecution in October 1915.
There was admittedly a greater tendency, in the case of
collective industrial action, for trade union officials to defend
members engaging in official disputes, and to abandon them
where the industrial action was unofficial, as in the case of the
Fairfield shipwrights. Yet this principle was not always
consistently followed, and unofficial strikers were able in some
cases, for example, that involving the Lobnitz shipyard holders-
on in September 1915, to avail themselves of the services of their
union representatives.[48]

Not only is the 'iron law of oligarchy' (whereby bureaucracies
come to serve the interests of the administration at the expense of
constituents or members) seriously deficient as an analytical tool
in exploring the behaviour of trade union organization;[49] but in
addition, there existed on Clydeside no single homogeneous
rank and file, but different groupings which sometimes merged,
but which often remained separate over time. Some trade
unionists, including, obviously, those involved in the shop
stewards' movement, undoubtedly conceived of the Act in
politically hostile terms, and viewed it as the instrument of a
class conspiracy, mounted by the Government and the
employers. Others may have welcomed the measure as the
embodiment of the spirit of patriotism and of sacrifice. For most
rank-and-file trade unionists, however, the Act was surely seen
mainly as a drastic economic and spatial restriction on their own
individual market freedoms, with which they were obliged to
come to terms, or which they sought to evade or manipulate
wherever practicable. If there *was* a political lesson to be derived

[47] His fees were 'extremely moderate'. See *Clyde Workers' Committee, Defence and Maintenance Fund: Financial Statement*, 15 Sept. 1917; copy in Highton Collection on Munitions, Dept. of Economic History, University of Glasgow.
[48] For all these cases except the Bridges hearing, see ch. 3. For the Bridges case, see ch. 4.
[49] Cf. Richard Hyman, *Marxism and the Sociology of Trade Unionism*, London, 1971, pp. 28–33. The 'iron law of oligarchy' is a theory associated with Robert Michels, a sociologist writing at the time of the First World War.

by less politically active trade unionists in the light of their experience with the Munitions Act, then it was more likely to be applicable to the future, once the war had ended. For it could be reasoned that if the legislative obstacles of State institutions could be scaled; and if the legal snares could not only be neutralized but also exploited by unionists for their own advantage during the war; then the prospects of capturing, through vigorous and aggressive though none the less 'democratic' means, the apparatuses of the State in peacetime might not be such a remote possibility.

In the light of the foregoing analysis, it should be clear that, *pace* the recent view expressed by Alastair Reid,[50] it is possible to advance a corporatist analysis of wartime labour developments without concentrating exclusively on the engineering industry, without identifying dilution as the central labour 'problem' of the war, and without adhering to the existence of an unambiguous schism between the rank and file and trade union officialdom. Moreover, the corporatist position as advanced here does *not* portray the State 'as an impartial arbiter striving to defuse conflict', but, in the shape of the Ministry of Munitions, as a bureaucratic élite intent on advancing *its* conception of the national interest and on disciplining both capital and labour to achieve *its* goals. If it was forced into retreat or into crisis management from time to time, that did not lessen its determination to pursue an overall, coherent strategy. Of course, as Reid correctly points out, the internal structure of Government was complex, and external forces exerted an influence on the fine details of policy. But the overall strategy of subordination of both capital and labour to a 'national interest' was the leitmotif running through munitions policy from mid-1915. We would readily concede Reid's point that the corporatist 'school' (as well as the 'revolutionary', 'muddling through', and 'administrative' schools of interpretation of wartime events which he identifies) saw an 'opposition between the state and shop floor bargaining'. But such a summation over-simplifies complex relations. For, wherever inflation was far outstripping the wage increases permitted by the Committee

---

[50] Reid, 'Dilution, trade unionism and the state in Britain during the First World War', in Steven Tolliday and Jonathan Zeitlin (eds.), *Shop Floor Bargaining and the State*, Cambridge, 1985, at pp. 48–9, for following quotations.

on Production, hostility to Government wage controls was bound to exist, even where conflict was not inspired by revolutionary aims. There is, surely, nothing surprising in this, and indeed we have frequently stressed throughout this work that wage disputes were *the* principal source of industrial conflict during the war. Moreover, there is no incompatibility between the existence of widespread trade union dissatisfaction with the level of wage settlements or with, say, aspects of the leaving certificate scheme, and, on the other hand, popular approval among munitions workers for the Government's production aims. In the final analysis, German militarism remained the common enemy among all but a handful of Clyde munitions workers inspired by the revolutionary pacifism of campaigners such as John Maclean. It should not be forgotten that, apart from the falling value of real wages, what animated trade unionists' discontent under the Munitions Act was the perceived inequity in its operation rather than the corporatist assumptions on which it was premissed. Opposition between the State and trade unionists was not on the basis of wholly divergent aims, but was because trade unionists believed that the State was not pursuing their *common* aim with sufficient vigour when treating with employers. In short, a corporatist analysis can yet withstand the criticisms recently levelled against it.

CONCLUSION

At the close of Chapter 1 we referred to the 'two faces' of corporatist labour controls, that is, to the display of blunt restrictiveness on the one hand, and to the presence of flexibility and opportunism for trade unions on the other. One face depicted a battery of legal restraints which sought to prohibit munitions workers from disrupting production schedules and from capitalizing on the scarcity value conferred on them by abnormal wartime circumstances. It would therefore be futile, as well as a gross distortion of the evidence, to deny the substantive impact of the munitions code on the freedom of action of countless factory and shipyard workers. For those subjected to tighter discipline at the hands of a number of foremen and under-managers; for those frustrated in their desires to advance their careers elsewhere; for those suffering the indignity of petty fines for various misdemeanours; and for those dragged to the tribunal for presuming to flaunt their right to withdraw labour as free men, the Munitions Act was, indeed, a tool of repressive intent, even if it might only touch the tip of the iceberg of lawlessness.[51]

But the alternative perspective on bureaucratically structured legal restrictions which this study reveals is the flexibility of their enforcement and the opportunism with which the Act's manifold provisions could be manipulated to the advantage, admittedly not always unqualified, of those munitions workers against whom it was primarily targeted. It was therefore the ambiguous and double-edged quality of wartime legal controls which justified our analysis in terms of the two faces of corporatist law. The 'national interest' cut both ways by requiring *employers* to conform to State directives which appeared to confer certain benefits on employees at the expense of their employers. The examples in Chapter 1 of the illegality of suspensions as a disciplinary tool of employers and the prohibition on the 'yellow dog' contract of employment which forbade trade union membership, are illustrations of the policy of subordinating the employing class to corporatist standards.[52] Indeed, the amendment of the 1915 Act only became politically feasible once the 'national interest' had been invoked as the justification for reform. As G. D. H. Cole had written in October 1915, 'Those who desire to save the situation must not merely censure Mr Lloyd George for refusing rights and responsibilities to the unions: they must also show how the rights and responsibilities they claim for Labour could be exercised in the national interest.'[53]

Though flexibility and opportunism are probably best exemplified in the case of 'collective bargaining by litigation' to which we have already referred in these conclusions, even the

[51] The rank-and-file reaction to the selectively vigorous and particularly repressive implementation of the Act in the Fairfield case also, of course, illustrated the capacity of restrictive labour legislation to amplify, rather than to stifle, industrial unrest (perhaps thereby displaying yet a 'third face' of corporatist law).

[52] For Sir George Askwith's view of the distinctive 'public interest' in the settlement of industrial disputes, see Rodney Lowe, 'Review Article', in *British Journal of Industrial Relations*, XIII (1975), 115–20, at 118–19.

[53] *Nation*, 16 Oct. 1915.

sphere of Ordering of Work prosecutions enabled trade unionists, both full-time officials and lay officers, to expand their orbits of influence with employers by sitting on joint disciplinary committees where their presence could only have ameliorated the chances of acquittal or minor reprimand of errant trade union members who fell foul of factory disciplinary rules. Moreover, it was not unknown for *employers* to be discomfited by the results of a munitions tribunal prosecution, under the Ordering of Work rules, where foremen and *not* the accused munitions workers might end up shamefully exposed and discredited.[54] The 'national interest' demanded that the autonomy of employers be no longer immune from interloping outsiders. Moreover, the leaving certificate scheme, otherwise an unmitigated disaster for munitions workers, even managed to attract the criticism of the Clyde engineering and shipbuilding *employers*, who objected to tribunal decisions granting certificates to applicants seeking higher wages elsewhere.[55] The employers, it seemed, were now showing *their* impatience at the spectacle of restrictive labour legislation being appropriated by the very workers whose freedoms it was designed to curb.

Indeed, the scheme even offered munitions workers a limited opportunity to expose some employers' unpatriotic habits of hoarding under-utilized labour. Although such claims by workers were commonly cast aside by the tribunal, the symbolic gesture had been made. The leaving certificate applicants' moral superiority had thus been publicly displayed before both the tribunal and their employer, and had also been vindicated to themselves and to their fellow workers.

Thus not only might the paradoxical position be reached whereby a measure, severely criticized by trade unionists at the local level, could none the less be invoked by them in an attempt to hold back, or overturn, those workshop changes (apart from dilution) which the Act itself authorized; but resort to the law by *employers*, as distinct from their reliance on its mere brooding presence, sometimes led to unpredictable and, for employers,

54 The tribunal's insistence on 'conformativist' conduct on the part of employers was also especially noticeable where women were indicted before the tribunal. See Rubin, 'Enforcement of the Munitions of War Acts, 1915–1917', ch. 10.

55 CSA, *Minute Book*, No. 9, 28 Sept. 1915; NWETEA, *Minute Book*, No. 7, 24 Sept. 1915. In the view of the employers, these were wages questions which ought to have been dealt with by Board of Trade arbitration.

unwelcome results. An act perceived by both workers and management alike (not wholly accurately) as embodying managerial prerogatives did not consistently work in accordance with their expectations. And this was because they misunderstood the Act's wider purpose, which was to uphold such prerogatives, but only if their endorsement corresponded to the tribunal chairman's conception of what furthered the national interest. And that national interest, as we have stressed time and again, was one built on the corporate spirit of 'unity' which repudiated a selfish, competitive ethos, if this threatened bureaucratic objectives.

The most powerful and enduring image emerging from this study, however, is one in which industrial militancy by trade unionists and law enforcement by the Glasgow munitions tribunal frequently engaged in a subtle duel with one another. Within this struggle, the enforcement side of the equation, as often as not (especially during the first nine months of the tribunal's turbulent existence) was forced to yield, not to outright lawlessness, but to the force of a rational resistance to penal imposts and to a deeply-rooted tradition of hard bargaining and collective negotiation. Indeed, it was a resistance buttressed by what Melling has recently described more broadly for Glasgow as 'an alternative perspective on civil society challenging the dominant role of established institutions and authority relations'.[56] Trade union officials, as well as rank-and-file unionists, refused to be cowed by legal straitjackets or by legal paraphernalia. Tribunal chairmen, representatives of law and order, were frequently unable to resist the transformation of their roles from judge to, at most, arbiters. Indeed, there was, on occasion, little hesitation by the legal officials in divesting themselves of judicial functions which even *they* found constricting, inappropriate, and dysfunctional. No doubt the level of militancy displayed during hearings influenced the exercise of judicial discretion towards leniency in many cases. Indeed, in respect to strikes and other forms of industrial action, it seems apparent that, with few exceptions, the tribunal chairmen thought better of implementing the full rigours of the law available to them. For, given the heightened

---

[56] Melling, 'Scottish Industrialists', p. 116.

tension on Clydeside, the road to co-operation in production was not paved with summonses and amercements.

An American anthropologist, Sally Falk Moore, has described the life of the Chagga people in Tanzania, or of the garment trade in New York, in terms of

semi-autonomous social fields which can generate rules and customs and symbols internally, possessing rule-making capacities and the means to induce or coerce compliance [but which remain] also vulnerable to rules and decisions and other forces emanating from the larger world by which they are surrounded.[57]

Glasgow munitions workers during the First World War fell far short of constituting such a sufficiently coherent and unified social field set within the wider social matrix of the national endeavour. What we do assert, however, is that by both vilifying *and* grasping the Munitions Act, by teasing and taunting those who sought to deploy it against them, by scanning its ubiquitous provisions, and by exploring its positive potential, they were able to recreate their relationship to it. In this respect, they reconstructed a 'social field' which, if not quite semi-autonomous, none the less embodied a distinctive and perhaps radicalizing experience of legal authority far removed from that intended by its draftsmen.

In 1917, Sheriff Fyfe, who was a noted authority on Charles Dickens,[58] became president of the Glasgow Dickens Society. In his presidential speech, he observed that if Dickens was hostile to the law, that was probably due to the novelist's personal experience, 'for experience coloured the views of most people in regard to the law'.[59] Such enigmatic remarks, we venture to think, would have met with nods and murmurs of approval from those trade union officials who had assembled with Fyfe to bid farewell to the munitions tribunal in April 1921.[60]

---

[57] S. F. Moore, *Law as Process: An Anthropological Approach*, London, 1978, pp. 55–6.

[58] One of his works, *Charles Dickens and the Law* (1910), is still listed in a popular student textbook today. See Glanville Williams, *Learning the Law*, 11th edn., London, 1982, p. 228 n.

[59] *Glasgow Herald*, 23 Oct. 1917.

[60] Ibid., 12 Apr. 1921.

A Munitions Tribunal Transcript of Proceedings

MUNITIONS COURT[1]

11.28 A.M.

Enter CHAIRMAN, *two* ASSESSORS, CLERK, *and* REPORTS OFFICER, *who take their respective seats.*

CLERK. Pincher and the Royal Arsenal. [*Hands complaint form and pad of paper to* CHAIRMAN]

CHAIRMAN (*to* CLERK). This pencil has no point. [CLERK *produces another*] Now we can get on. [*Carbon paper flutters off dais, and is restored by* REPORTS OFFICER] Thank you. I wish the Ministry would devise a better system for taking notes. Please convey this expression of opinion to Dr. Addison.

REPORTS OFFICER. Yes, sir. I have already drafted three minutes on this subject; we propose to call a conference of Chairmen at the Albert Hall to settle the matter. I understand Mr. Rusher has consented to take the chair, so that no time may be lost over unnecessary trifles.

CHAIRMAN. Thank God. Now let us get on. In this case A. Pincher is asking for a certificate, and his grounds are [*reads*] (1) There is never no work to be done; we are kep' idling for weeks. (2) The foreman and chief superintendent make use of foul language. (3) My health is breaking down through the strain of continuous labour.

[*To* APPLICANT] Is your name Pincher?

APPLICANT. Yes, my lord.

CHAIRMAN. Christian?

APPLICANT. No, Jew by conversion.

CHAIRMAN. What I want to know is your first name. Albert? Alfonso? Augustus?

APPLICANT. Alf.

WORKMAN'S ASSESSOR. There's a good, honest ring about the name.

EMPLOYER'S ASSESSOR. I don't agree. Pincher sticks in my gizzard.

CHAIRMAN. Let's get on. How long have you been at the Arsenal?

---

[1] ASE, *Monthly Journal and Report*, July 1917, 51–2.

APPLICANT. Twenty-five years, man and boy, and I'm about fed up.

CHAIRMAN. What do you mean?

APPLICANT. I want a sustificate.

CHAIRMAN. I know that; hence your presence here to-day.

APPLICANT. Beg pardon, sir; I'm a bit deaf.

CHAIRMAN. I said, hence your presence here to-day.

APPLICANT. No, sir; I can't 'ear to-day; nor I don't expect to tomorrow.

CLERK [*shouting*]. The Chairman said 'Hence your presence here today.'

APPLICANT. Yes, sir; I knew that hymn as a boy. I think I can recall the next line.

CHAIRMAN. This Tribunal is not a Sunday school. Let's get on.

REPORTS OFFICER (*handing up pink pamphlet*). Have you seen this appeal case, sir? The Scotch judge has held that hymns may be given in evidence, except in cases where the oath has been administered.

CHAIRMAN. I am not bound by any Scotch decisions—especially in matters of religion. [*To* APPLICANT] What are you?

APPLICANT. Consumptive.

CHAIRMAN. We'll soon see about that. What's your work?

APPLICANT. Boot cleaner in the chief superintendent's 'ouse.

CHAIRMAN [*to* CLERK]. I question if this is munition work. Do you think it is?

CLERK. Yes and no. Yes, if the boots are used when inspecting shells; no, if used for dances, cinema visits, and night clubs.

CHAIRMAN (*to* ASSESSORS). A very clear-headed man, the Clerk. This is a difficult point. [*To* REPORTS OFFICER] Do you know of any case governing this?

REPORTS OFFICER. There are two cases, approximate to, but not quite on all fours with this. We are having certain boots examined by the Public Analyst at this moment.

CHAIRMAN. There is the further point, whether he was working in the controlled establishment. [*To the* ARSENAL REPRESENTATIVE] Is the Chief Superintendent's house controlled?

ARSENAL REPRESENTATIVE. We maintain that it is. It is within the compound, and only sixteen miles from the main entrance.

CHAIRMAN. I will hold the legal issue in abeyance for the moment.

WORKMAN'S ASSESSOR. I hold Pincher's a boot black, and can go where 'e chooses when 'e chooses. [CLERK *has a slight seizure, but recovers on hearing*]

EMPLOYER'S ASSESSOR. The country is at war; let the matter be thrashed out.

APPLICANT. Thrashed out? I'd like to see 'im try it on with me.

CHAIRMAN. Let's get on. I understand you have no work to do.

APPLICANT. That's right.

CHAIRMAN. Piecework or day rate?

APPLICANT. You've 'it it. It is piecework, I don't think. His feet's so tender 'e can't get 'is boots off. I can't keep two 'omes on the day rate.

CHAIRMAN. Now as to language, what has the foreman said?

APPLICANT. — — — —.

CHAIRMAN. Clearly this is munition work, and the establishment is within the order.

Certificate refused.

Index